I07505337

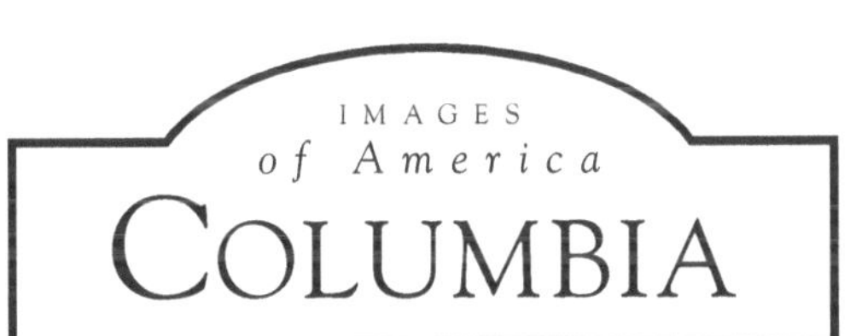
IMAGES
of America
COLUMBIA

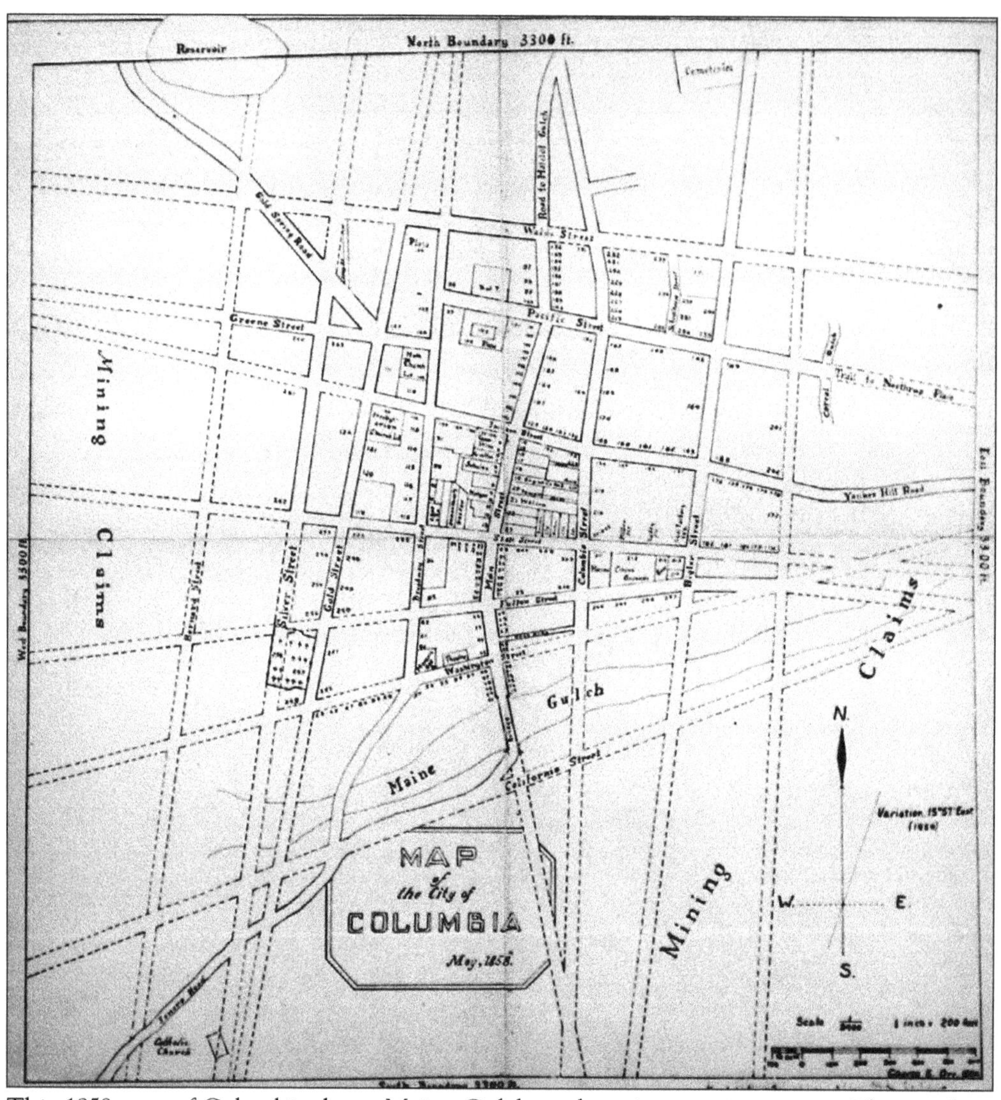

This 1858 map of Columbia shows Maine Gulch as the primary mining area. The numbers represent buildings, both business and residential.

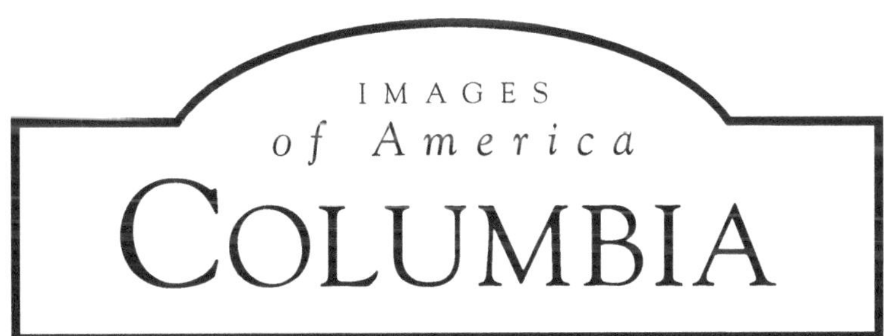

Friends of Columbia State Historic Park

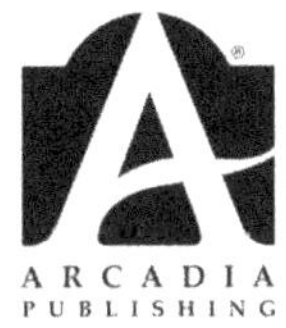

ISBN 978-0-7385-3021-5

Published by Arcadia Publishing
Charleston, South Carolina

Library of Congress Catalog Card Number: 2005927327

For all general information contact Arcadia Publishing at:
Telephone 843-853-2070
Fax 843-853-0044
E-mail sales@arcadiapublishing.com
For customer service and orders:
Toll-Free 1-888-313-2665

Visit us on the Internet at www.arcadiapublishing.com

Contents

Acknowledgments		6
Introduction		7
1.	Mining	9
2.	Water's For Fighting Over	25
3.	Boomtown	35
4.	Wildlife	51
5.	Fire!	69
6.	Reading, Writing, and Religion	83
7.	We Gather Together	97
8.	Life Goes On	109
9.	Revival	121
Photograph Credits		128

ACKNOWLEDGMENTS

It would have been impossible to publish this book without the cooperation of the Department of Parks and Recreation, Columbia State Historic Park and the archives they maintain.

Supervising ranger Kim Baker helped locate photographs in the department's archives and managed the paperwork. Diana Newington, museum technician, was wonderful in her depth of knowledge, willingness to share that knowledge, and most of all in maintaining an open door policy for our work. We thank Kelli Noteman who found time to correct our mistakes and pull the manuscript together. Any errors or omissions remaining belong to the authors.

We also want to thank all those many people, both past and present, who gave photographs, documents, memories, and research to the park. Without their contributions this book would not have been possible. While it would be impossible to mention all of them, certain people and institutions stand out: Aubrey Neasham, Hero Eugene Rensch, Tuolumne County Historical Society, David H. Johnson, and Robert Buckler. Chief among these donors was Barbara Eastman, who spent decades ferreting out little known information on the life and times of Columbia; Otheto Weston, who fell in love with Columbia and its old-timers; and Tom, Maggie, and Julia Conlin, who spent years writing letters to Columbia's citizens asking questions about living here and kept all the information.

And most importantly, we want to mention the four volunteers who put the book together: Audley Buckley, who of the four of us stayed healthy and enthusiastic; John Scofield, who tried to find all the information out there; Steve Bechtold, both researcher and scanner tech, who moved from building to building as computers failed and still managed to scan all the photographs; and Sherrin Grout, who fostered the love of Columbia in so many and had the difficult task of orchestrating this project. And to the spouses, Kalinda Bechtold, Helen Scofield, and Donn Marinovich, without whose support, understanding, and love none of this would have been possible.

The Friends of Columbia State Historic Park (SHP) is a nonprofit organization whose main mission is to raise funds to support projects and programs at Columbia State Historic Park. By purchasing this book, you too have contributed to supporting this wonderful park. For more information or to become a "Friend of Columbia," please visit our web site at www.FriendsofColumbiaSHP.org.

INTRODUCTION

The story of Columbia is the tale of early gold rush adventurers who came to California with gold dust in their eyes. The initial discovery of gold in January 1848 resulted in an economic, social, and cultural upheaval. With luck and hard work, anyone in California could make a good living, even get rich, regardless of ethnicity, education, or social class. Gold nuggets were lying in the streets, or so the story went. The truth was different.

Gold was found in Columbia in March 1850, a wet time of year when streams and creeks were running full. The Hildreth party, traveling through the area, was caught in a rainstorm and stopped to dry out their blankets. One of the members decided to try his luck at panning a stream running near their camp. He found gold. A lot of it. Stories soon spread about the rich diggings. Newspapers reported there was so much gold a man could cover himself in bear grease, roll down a hill, and, when he stood up, would be covered in gold dust. In reality, it took water to mine gold, and in a few months, when the dry season returned, the streams in Columbia dried up. Without water, miners found separating the gold from the dirt very difficult if not impossible. Most miners moved on to other areas. A few took their gold bearing dirt to the Stanislaus River, and a very few merchants stayed, struggling to survive.

With the onset of the wet season the following autumn, the miners returned. Merchants and miners soon realized that for the camp and mining claims to survive and prosper, a reliable source of water needed to be established.

In June 1851, the Tuolumne County Water Company was organized to bring water and prosperity to the town. A permanent source of water, locally controlled, meant the town and it citizens could plan for the future as a community, not just as a transient mining camp. More miners arrived, bringing an increasing number of merchants. Families followed, and a diverse culture was established. Everything from fandango halls to reading rooms could soon be found. Establishing schools, churches, and bands, as well as social and fraternal groups, made the town into a community. For single men, there were fraternal organizations; for the Irish, the Hibernian Benevolent Society; for the Jews, the Hebrew Benevolent Society; for the French, a French consulate; for the Germans, a Schiller Festival; for African Americans, an event celebrating the end of slavery in Haiti.

People who came to Columbia found the promise of prosperity for themselves and their families, but there was a price to pay. Two major fires destroyed the town in 1854 and 1857, not an unusual experience in a California mining town of the 19th century. Townspeople banded together to fight the fires and their causes: arson and accident. New buildings were built with greater foresight, resulting in the type of architecture still seen in town today: brick buildings with iron doors. Also, volunteer fire fighting companies were established, one of which still protects Columbia today.

Remember the water company that made all this possible? Tension over control of the company and the water soon produced hostility between the miners, who were desperate for water, and the company that was struggling to pay off debt and produce profits for investors. While at first the Tuolumne County Water Company was owned and controlled by local residents, within a short time, most of its investors were from out of the county and out of the state. Water rates were raised, miners suffered, and merchants, unable to sell their goods, contributed to the economic tension.

In response, the miners once again organized a water company, the Columbia and Stanislaus River Water Company. Bitter rivalry between the two water companies resulted in civil and criminal troubles. Within a few years, the new company's investors could not pay their bills and it was forced into bankruptcy.

These activities, growing unrest about national politics as the Civil War approached, gold discoveries in other areas, and the increasing difficulty to extract large sums of gold all resulted in people leaving Columbia. Though never completely abandoned, Columbia was never again as prosperous as during its peak with a population of around 6,000. The town was on a downhill slide. People were leaving in great numbers; even some of those buried in the cemetery were disinterred and removed to other areas.

In the 1890s, a brief mining resurgence occurred with hard rock mining in the Stanislaus River canyon and on ridges north of town. In the 20th century, tourists returned to Columbia, including newspaper writers and photographers. Gradually, word spread of this well-preserved town. In 1945, Gov. Earl Warren signed legislation establishing Columbia State Historic Park. Since then, both commercial and residential buildings have been purchased by the state park system, restoration projects have been completed on many of the extant buildings, and some of the buildings that had been destroyed have been recreated. A general development plan that guides these on-going projects will continue to protect and preserve the gold rush streetscape.

One

MINING

A small group of men trudged up the steep slopes of the canyon and crossed the Stanislaus River at the mining camp of Pine Log on their way from Calaveras County to Woods Crossing in Tuolumne County. The group, laden with provisions, crested the rim of the canyon and then dropped down into a gulch. Fording a small stream, they unloaded their provisions and equipment under a large oak at the base of a low hill, planning to camp and rest for the night.

On this day, gray skies opened up and unleashed a soaking rain, forcing the group to stay an extra day to dry out their provisions and equipment. To pass the time, John Walker, a member of this party led by Thaddeus and George Hildreth, decided to try his luck with a pan in the gravels of the stream next to the camp. The date was March 27, 1850, and the California gold rush was already in its third year.

As Walker set about his work, he quickly unearthed a sizable "take" and was able to convince his companions to stay on and continue mining. Within months, hundreds, perhaps thousands, of miners flooded the area hoping to cash in on the "Hildreth" strike.

Other groups or individuals may have mined in the area prior to these "Maine Boys," and most certainly mining was underway in many places nearby, but Walker's chance discovery in 1850 was the first recorded account of a strike in this specific area.

But the excitement almost ended as soon as it started when the stream dried up in May. Gravel had to now be sacked and taken to a water source a few miles away in order to separate out the gold, or water had to be brought in. It wasn't until 1852 that a reliable water source would reach Columbia and mining would begin to take on an industrial flavor.

Mining in Columbia quickly became quite a different scene than the romantic images of the small-scale prospector of 1849, as the mining in this region propelled Tuolumne County to among the top of California's placer gold producing counties. The growth and scope of operations and equipment continued for about 20 years. When the mines finally played out later in the 1800s, Columbia, its people, and its environment were forever changed.

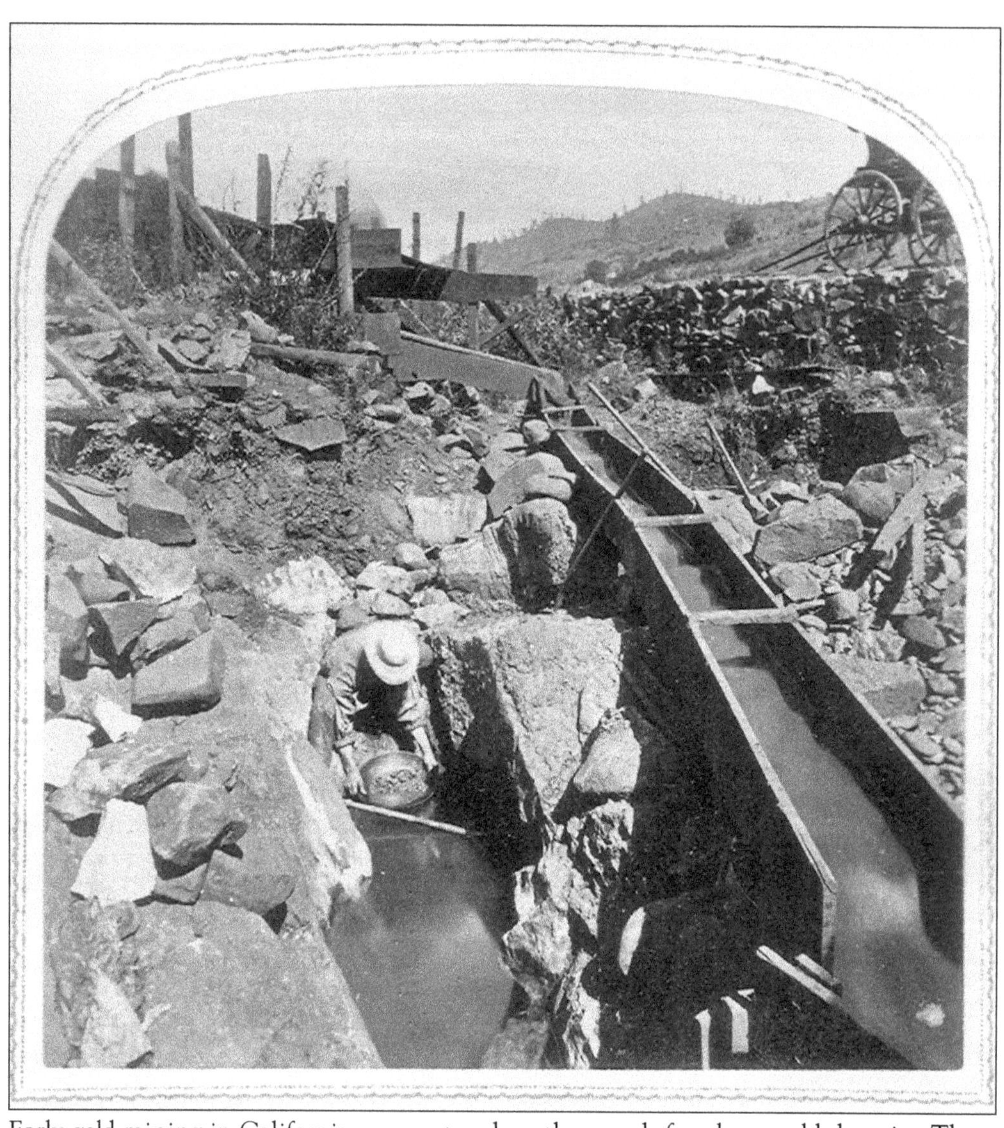

Early gold mining in California was centered on the search for placer gold deposits. These deposits were generally those left by the natural erosion and weathering of quartz veins. Water and weather would break this rock down, and gravity, streams, and rivers would deposit the rock and loose gold in the gravel beds of the rivers flowing to the sea. Columbia was the site of a prehistoric river and while that river eventually changed its course, what it left behind was what would lure men to this flat plain. Early methods of mining during the California gold rush were crude and primitive. Panning was by far the least expensive means of separating gold from the gravel, but it was excruciatingly slow. Early miners in Columbia used this method extensively. Even with the introduction of other processes, many men still had to resort to the pan for the final step in washing gravel. In 1852, when a reliable water source began to arrive, things would change dramatically.

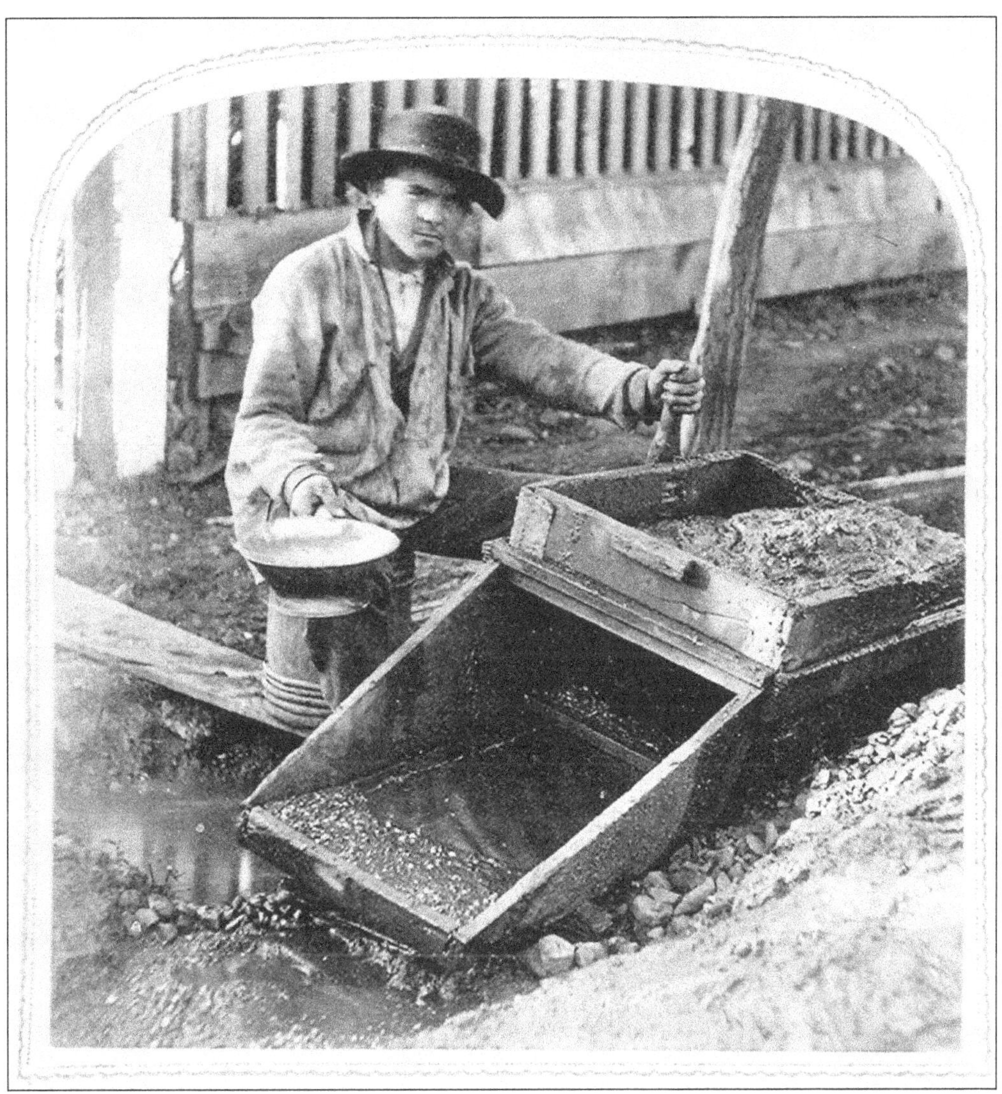

Rockers were the next step in the evolution of the mining industry in California. Likely first introduced in California by Isaac Humphrey, formerly of Georgia, to miners in Coloma in March 1848, the rocker quickly gained popularity as a machine that could wash gravel five to six times faster than the pan. The machines worked very simply. First, gravel and water were added to the "riddle box," where larger rocks would be caught in an iron box with riddles (punched holes). Then, rocking would agitate the gravel and mud, causing the heavy gold to fall to the bottom and catch behind the wooden slats or "riffles" in the bottom of the machine. At the end of the day, the miner would scrape and "pan out" the riffles collecting his gold. Small companies of men quickly formed to work these machines. This image was captured on the streets of Columbia in the mid-1860s, well into Columbia's mining days.

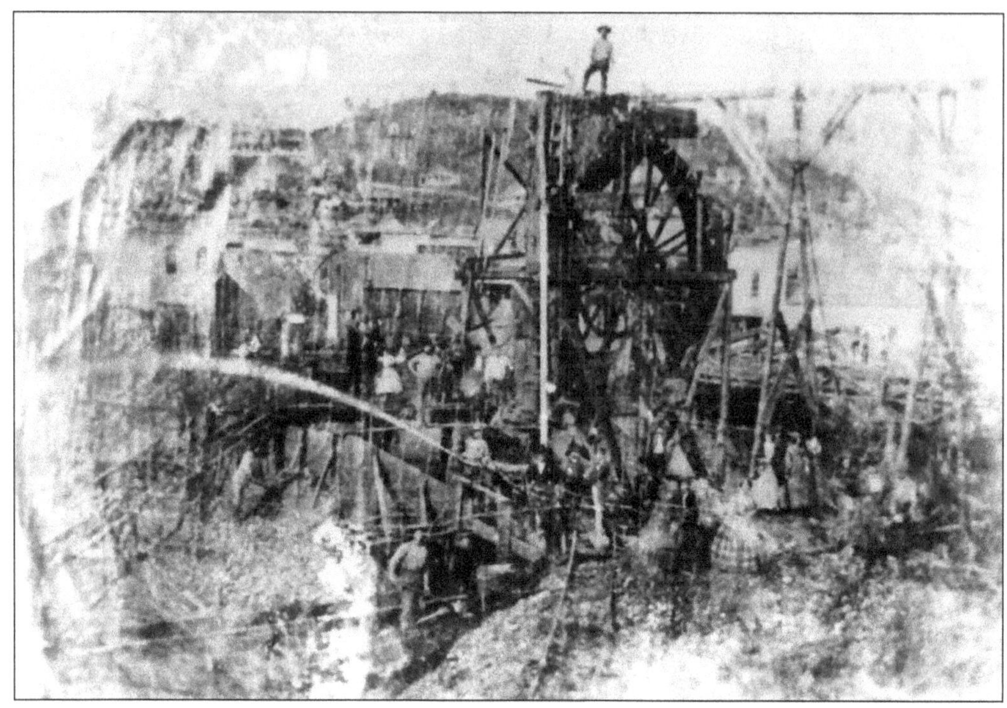

After 1852, more aggressive methods of extracting gold were employed. Meanwhile, original claims were limited to 100 square feet per man. Men combined their claims to form companies. This earliest known image of Columbia mining, taken between 1861 and 1863, shows the bridge over the main gulch still in place, with ladies in hoop skirts and the town visible behind the hoist wheel. By this time the larger companies were taking over.

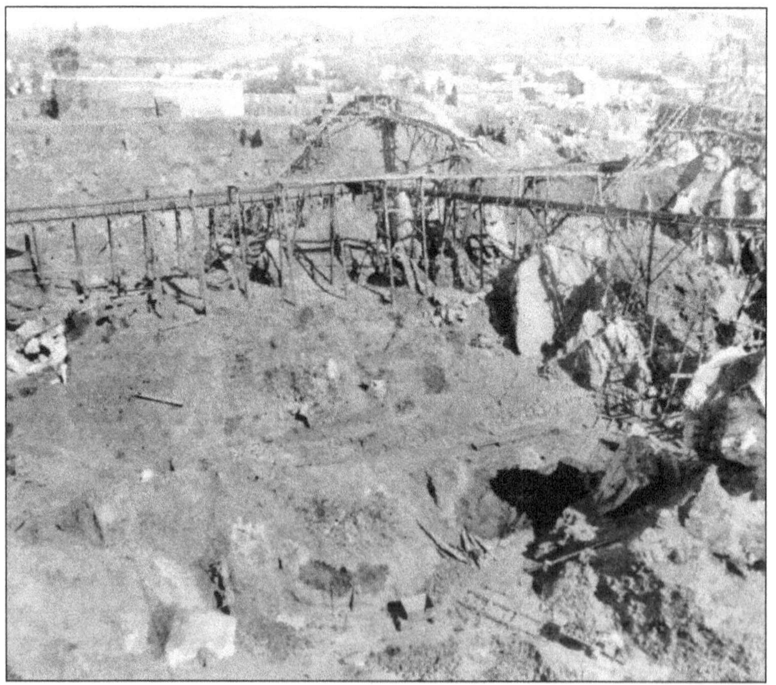

As larger companies formed, investors helped to drive the mines deeper into the ground. Many aspects of these early large mining operations of the late 1850s and early 1860s can be seen here. To put the amount of excavation into perspective, a man pushing a cart can be seen in the lower right corner.

As work progressed in the mines, massive amounts of material and gravel were removed revealing huge limestone formations. Each crack was scraped clean and the gravel was dug and loaded by hand into carts whose wooden tracks wended their way through canyons of limestone, trundling their rich loads to the water at the surface for washing.

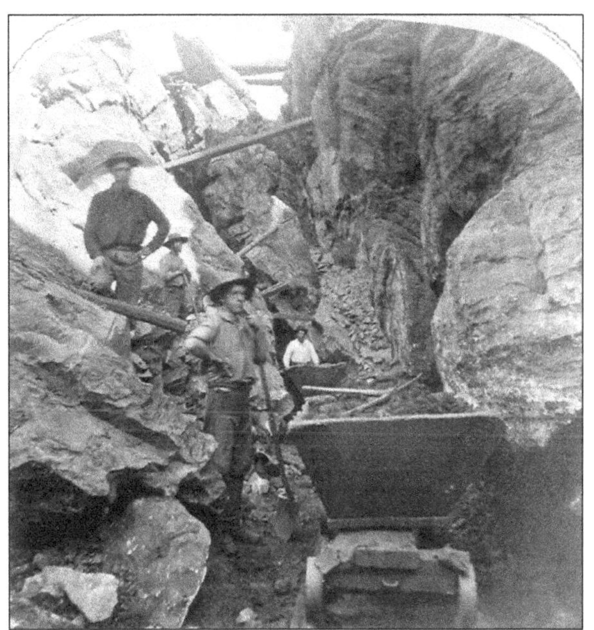

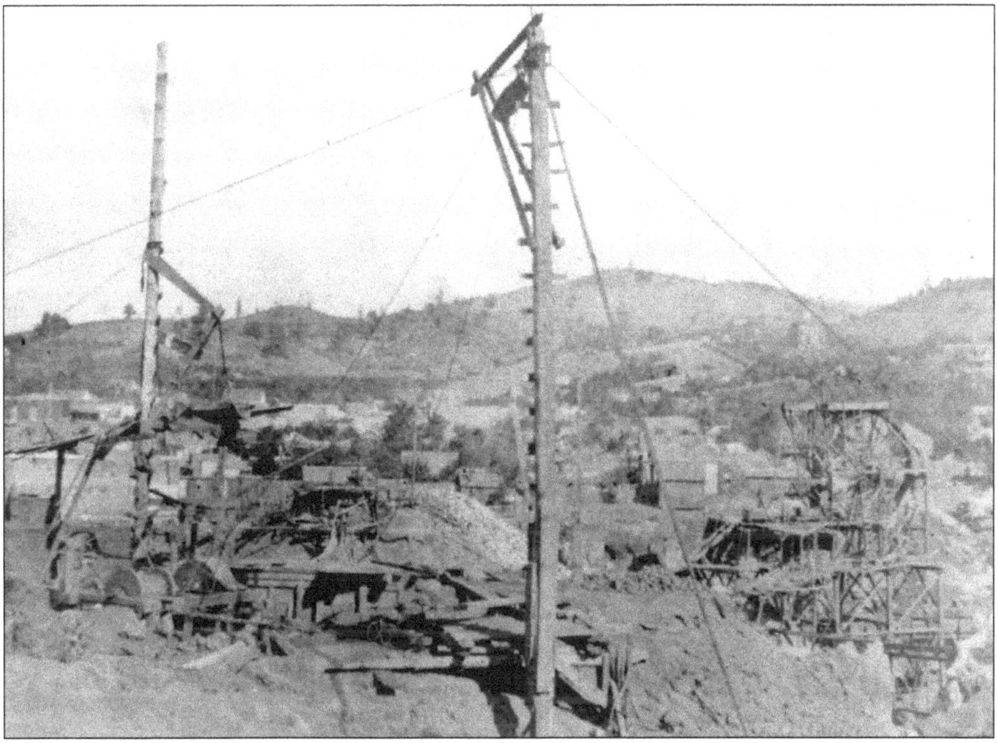

Deeper mines meant encountering larger, sometimes huge, rocks. Boulders had to be moved so that mining could continue under them. Many styles of derricks and hoisting equipment were employed. Identified by the photographer as the "Main Claim," this is probably the "Maine Claim," the original claim of "The Maine Boys," or the Hildreth party. This image shows the hoist pole for the Friedenbur Wheel on the Maine Claim. Visible at the bottom left is the wheel and hoist drum.

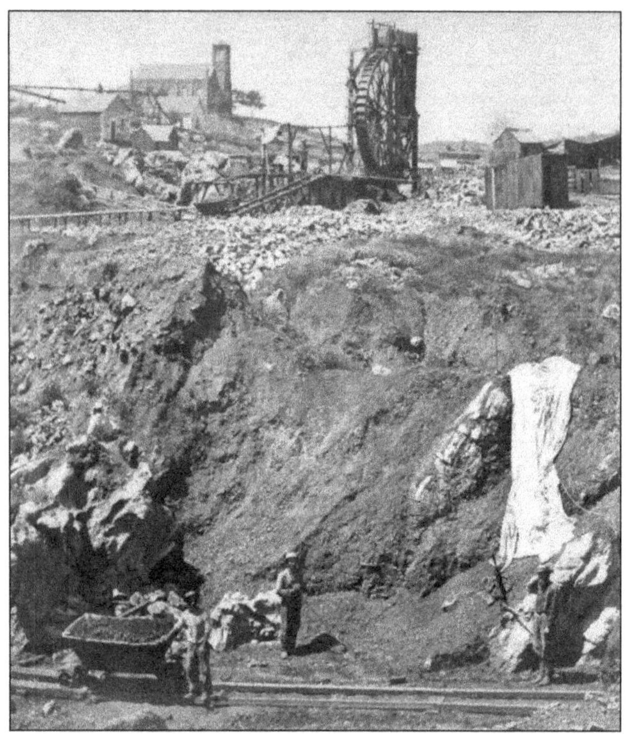

Hydraulic mining methods were designed to wash away hillsides, not excavate pits created when dirt and rocks were removed. Because of this hydraulic mining was not generally employed in Columbia. Most surviving photographs of the excavations are similar to this one. Here miners use traditional hand tools, including picks and shovels, to dislodge the gravel for loading into the cart. St. Anne's Catholic Church presides in the background.

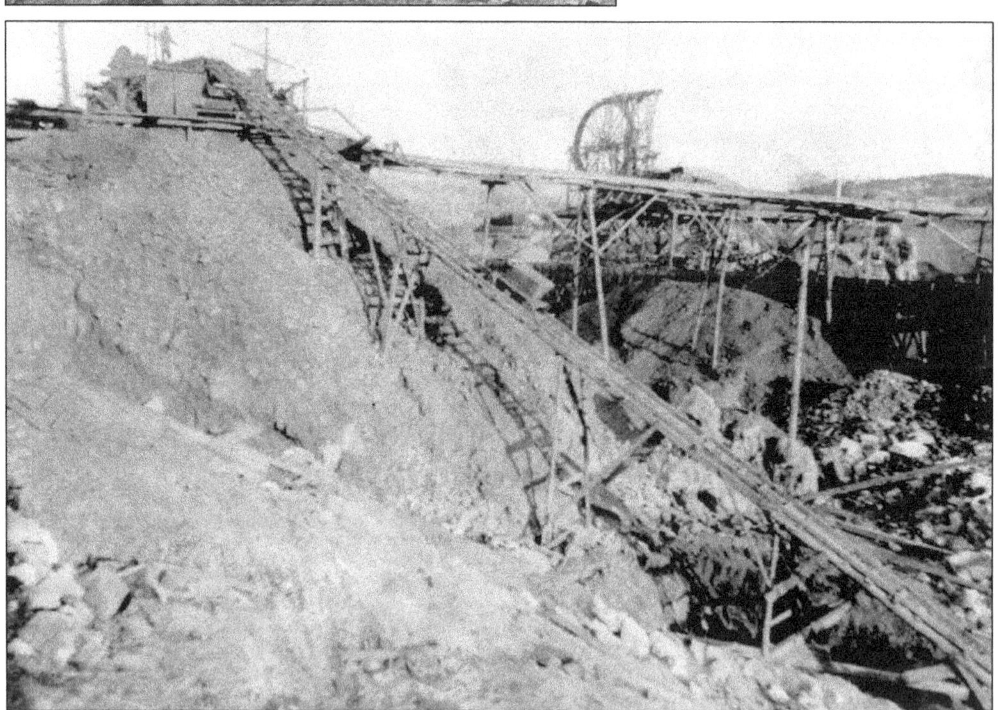

Filled carts, pushed to the bottom of an incline, were connected to a rope and then hoisted out of the gravel beds by a number of inexpensive methods. The carts were dumped and then lowered back down for the next load. As pits deepened toward the end of mining operations, depths of about 100 feet were reached.

Once carts were hoisted out of the gravel beds, they were emptied into a dump box. The two men standing on the dump box behind the sluice man have just emptied the cart shown here. The man with the cap is standing on a sluice box, nothing more than a channel with wooden slats nailed in the bottom to catch the heavier gold while allowing the lighter material to wash away. The round wooden item in right corner is a Chinese chain pump.

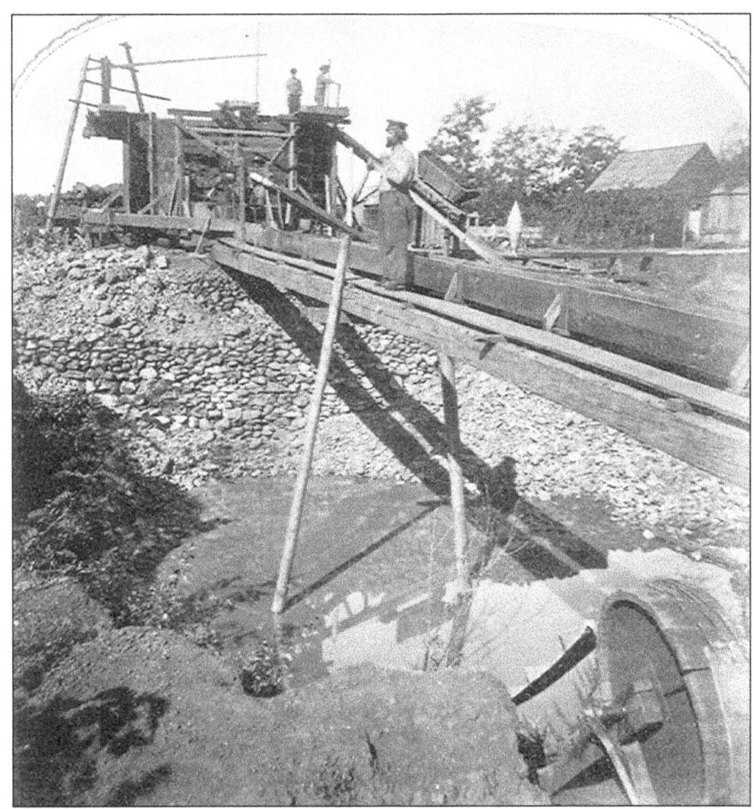

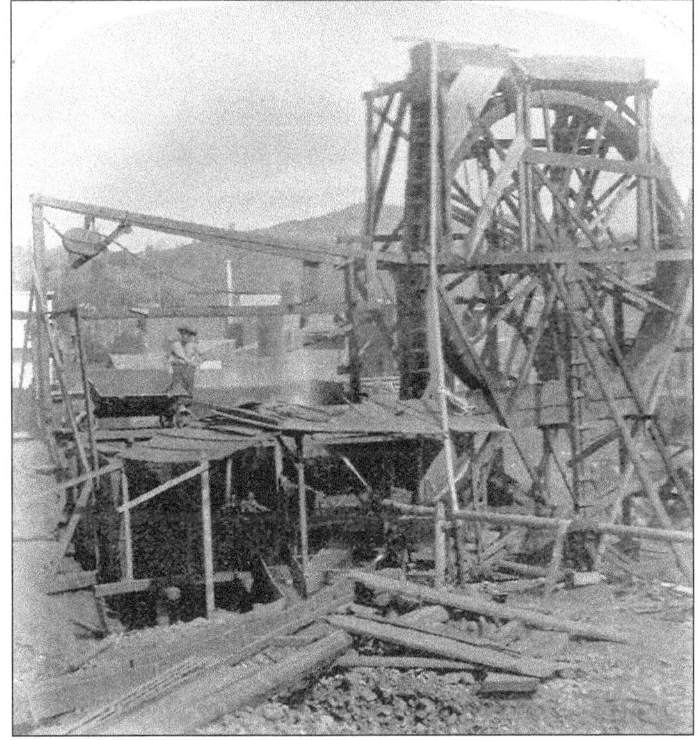

Using water under pressure and piped to the top, the "overshot wheel" was a common waterwheel designed to lift heavy loads. Water developed its pressure by traveling through narrowing pipes from higher reservoirs. The water, piped to the top, allowed the wheels to generate the power to lift carts out of the pits. Water was then recaptured and channeled away from the mines. This wheel is on the Tiger Claim.

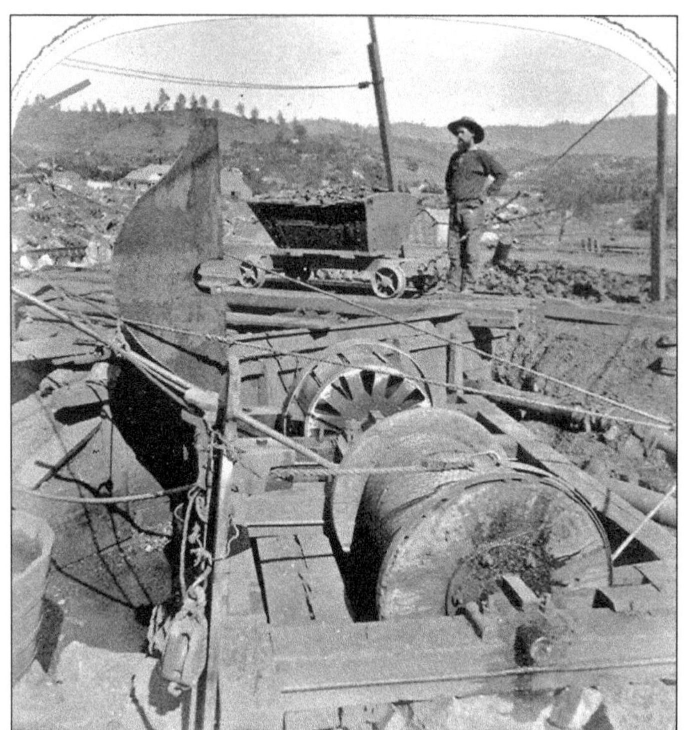

The Friedenbur brothers, early arrivals from Ohio, listed themselves as miners. By 1860, they were advertising custom equipment and carpentry. Pictured above is a close-up of a scene on page 14; this is the only known picture of a Friedenbur Wheel, a waterwheel designed to perform many tasks, such as use on a hoisting rig as shown here. There is no evidence that they were used outside of Columbia.

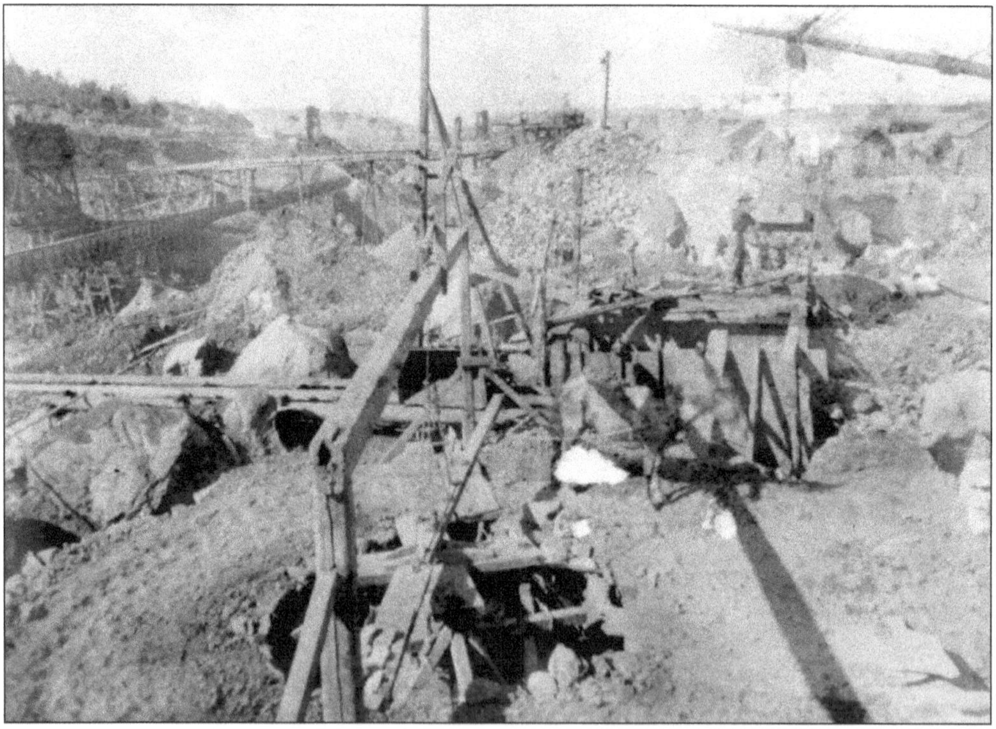

Not all operations utilized expensive hoisting works. Some of the smaller operations employed the ancient method of animals harnessed to a whim to hoist carts or move boulders. Here a horse in front of a dump box walks endless circles to provide the means for hoisting or moving boulders.

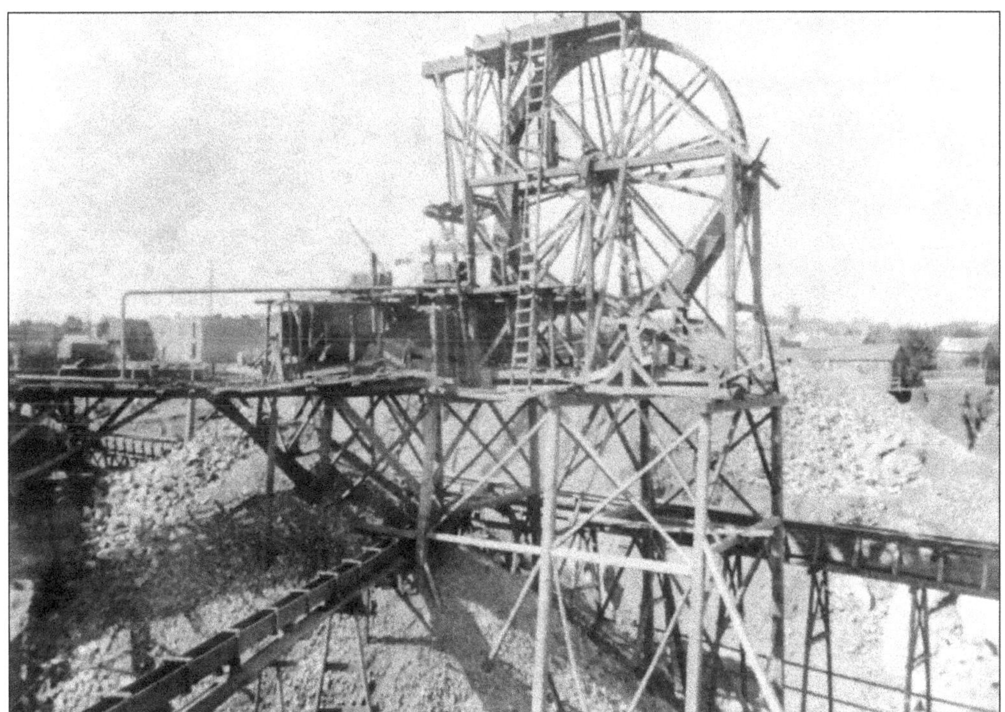

Despite the innovations of the Friedenburs, the "overshot wheel" continued to be the primary lifting mechanism in the mines. Columbia's business district can be seen behind this view of the Daley Claim hoist wheel. These wheels were popular because they were simple to construct or repair. In the mid-1860s, when these images were recorded, the operations had become quite large and involved.

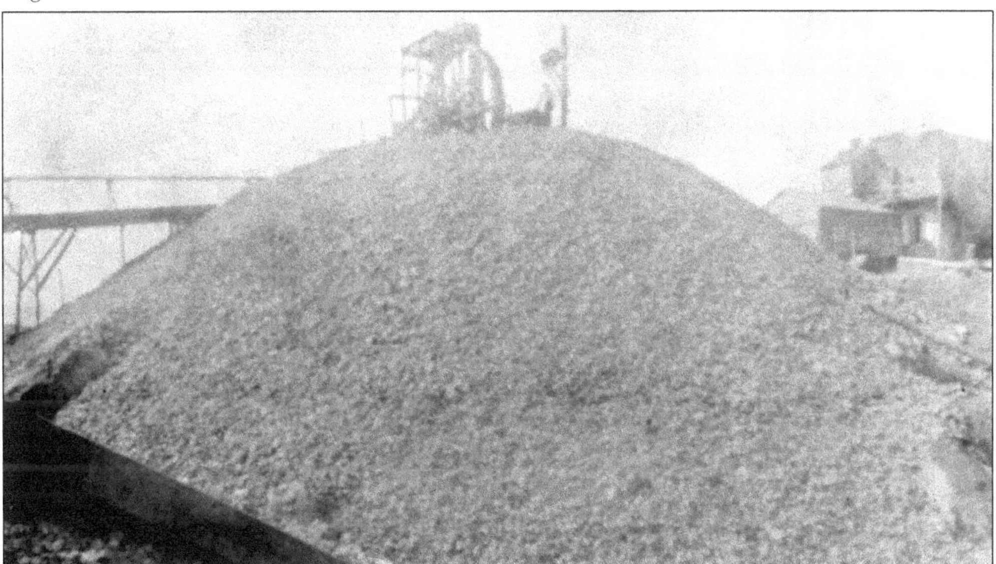

Waste piles, like this one from the Columbia Claim, were prevalent throughout the mining region. This area is now part of modern Columbia's main parking lot on the south side of town. These piles were most likely pushed back into the gravel pits over time, filling in evidence of the extensive operations that had once occurred.

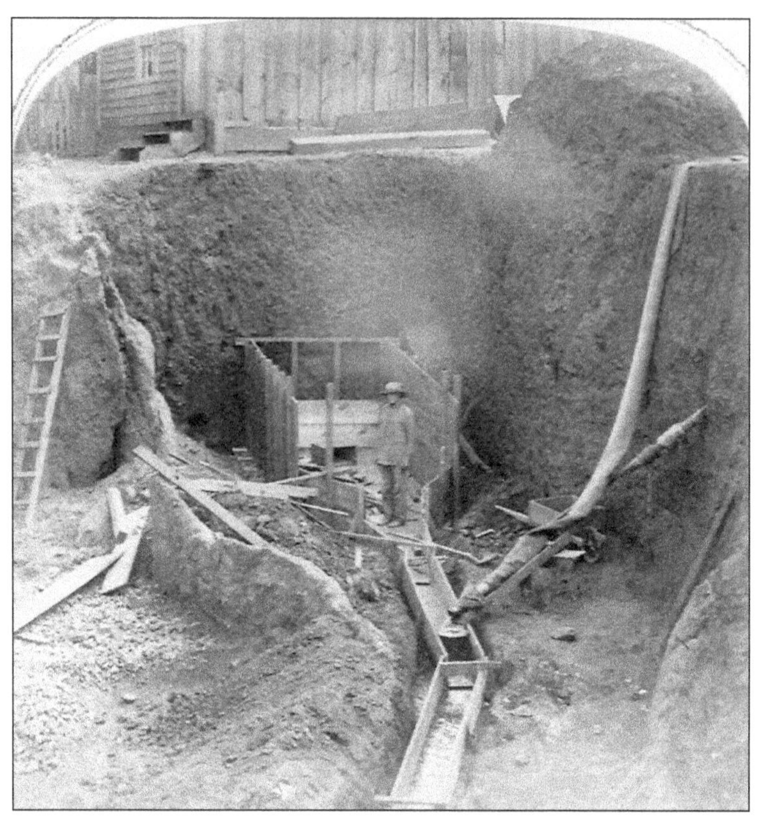

The dump box was the beginning of the involved ore extraction process. Here a dump box is in the process of being built. After being hauled up the inclines, carts were rolled over to the dump box and their contents "dumped" by either being upended or via a dump mechanism built into the cart. Notice how close the excavation is to the structure in the background.

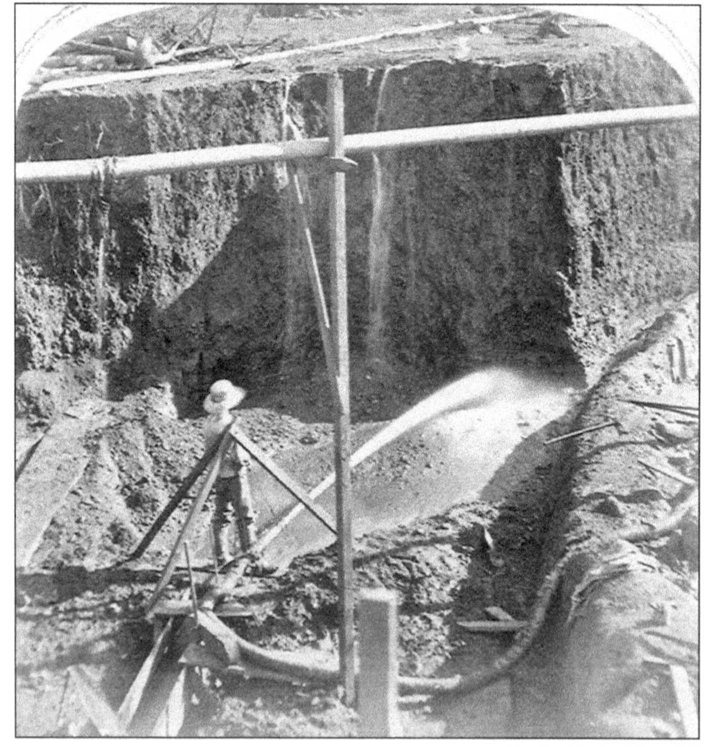

The phrase "Never say never" describes this photograph. While traditional hydraulicking was extremely rare in Columbia, it cannot be said that it never happened. This operation appears to be a different angle of the previous image. While not seemingly done often, the man is excavating with a monitor, washing the gravel back toward the dump box (or sluice) in the previous view (notice the dyke on the man's right side). This is the only known view of mines being worked in a traditional hydraulic method, which is credited to Columbia.

After a cart has been dumped, the gravel rests in the bottom of the dump box, which is nothing more than high wooden walls built to contain both gravel and water. The head of the sluice can be seen in the lower portion of the picture. A sluice fork is being utilized by the man in the box to mix and move gravel toward the sluice.

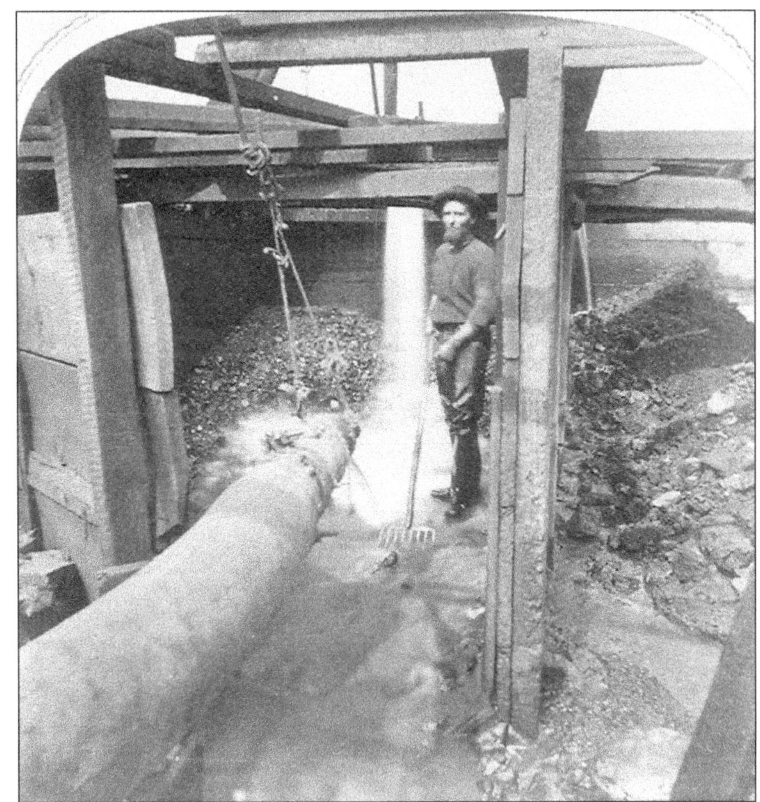

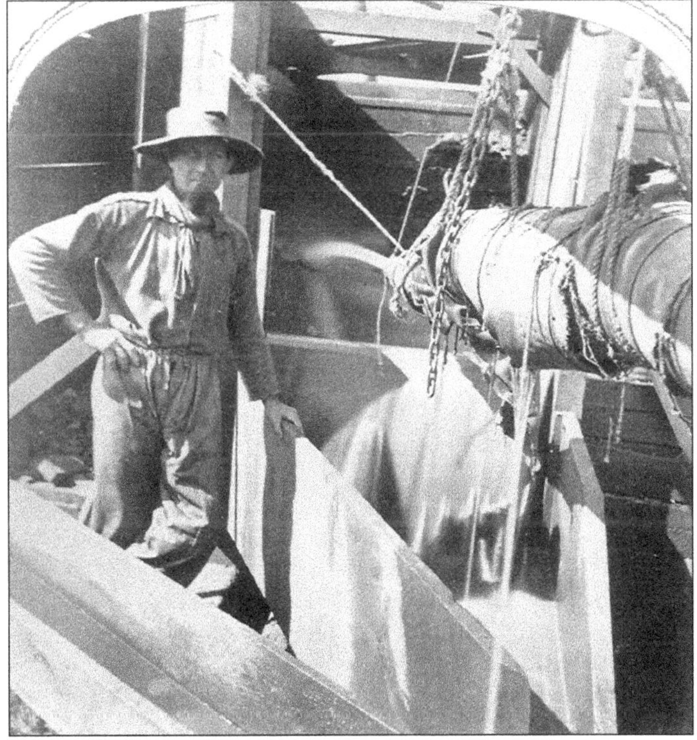

Gravel dumped into the dump box was exposed to a stream from a monitor (nozzle) directed at the mass of rock. The water broke down the gravel and forced it into the sluicing system. Channeled and controlled, the water would not fill the pits, yet provided a strong force to agitate and separate the gold from the gravel. This form of hydraulic mining was popular in early Columbia.

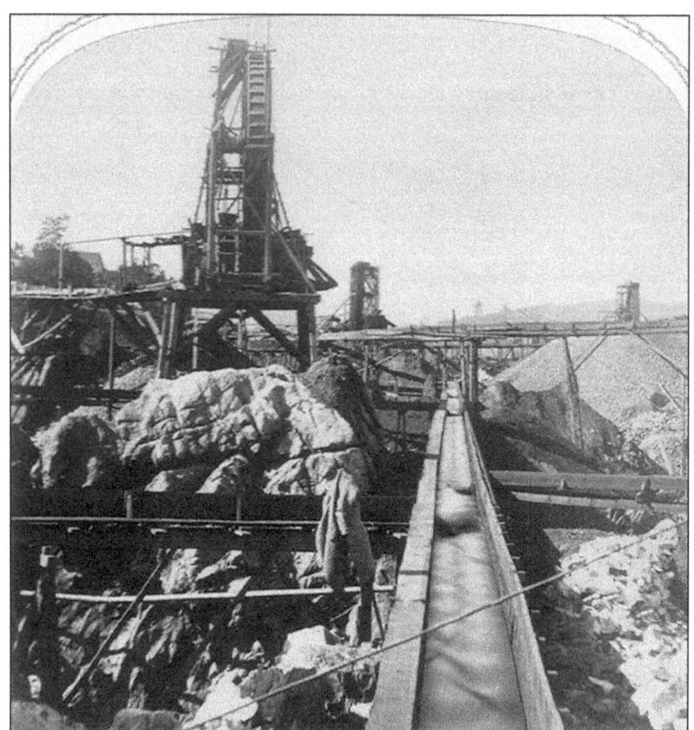

Early in the mining days, claims were located literally on top of each other, and water and gravels had to be moved away in order not fill another claim. Tail flumes served to channel away water so other claims wouldn't flood. As claims were bought or merged into larger operations, waste gravels could be dumped into "worked out" claims. This photograph also shows the extensive fluming and sluicing in and around the workings.

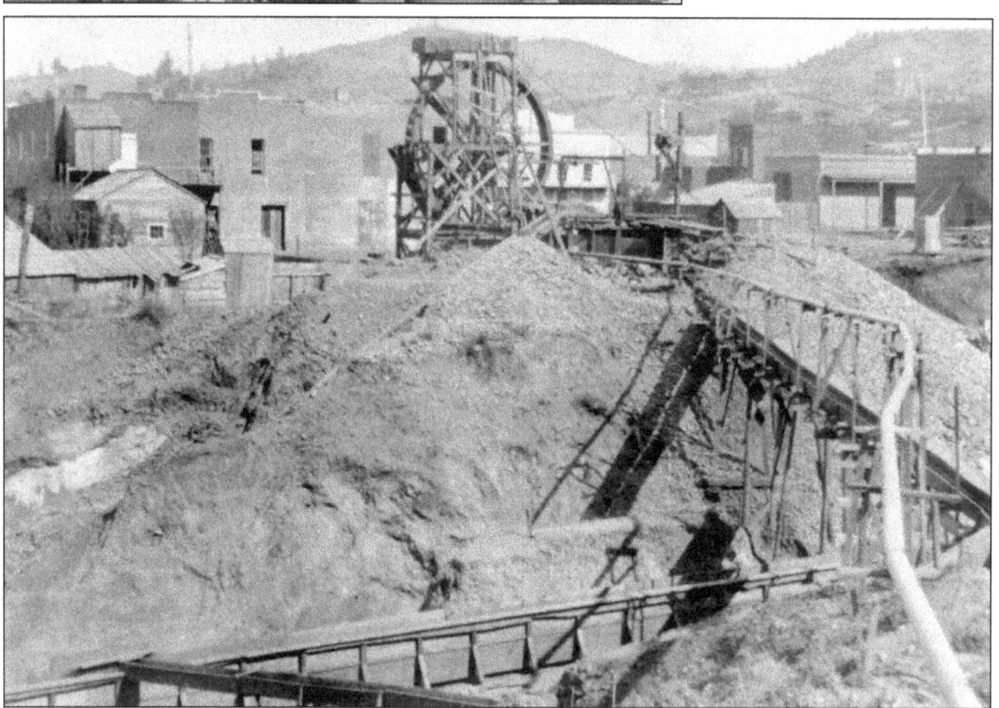

As claims became more and more worked over, mining progressively encroached upon the town itself. Here, the Columbia Claim has placed its hoisting wheel right on the edge of town. The buildings in this photograph fronted Washington Street. The schoolhouse, built in 1860 and still standing today, can be seen on the upper right.

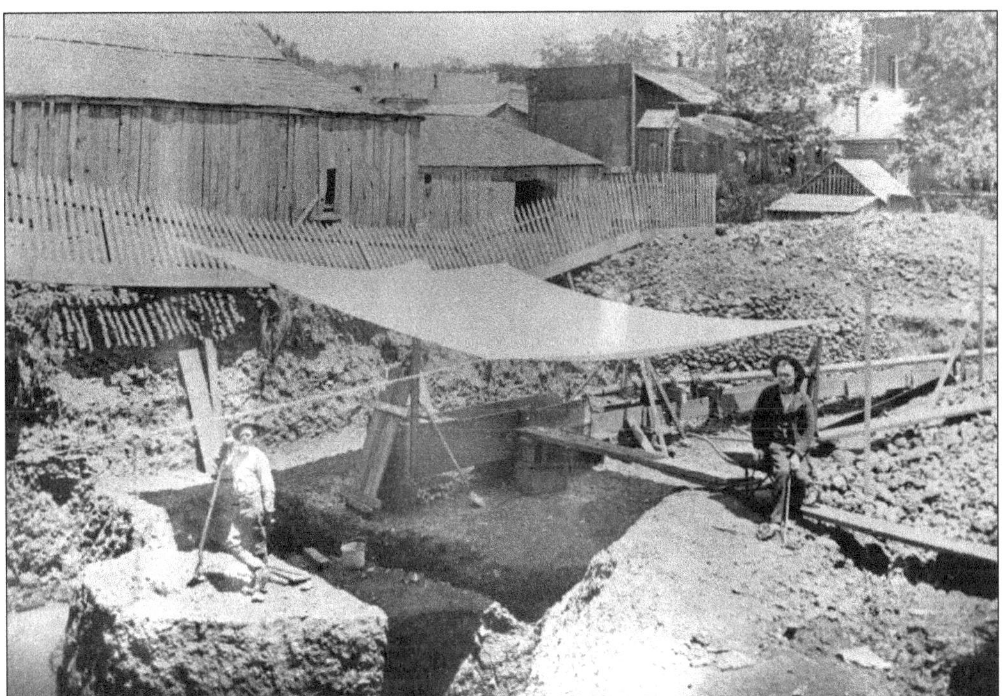

Mines in Columbia began to play out in the late 1860s and miners turned to purchasing lots from businesses leaving town. Buildings were then razed or moved and the ground below them mined. This image shows a small operation in an empty lot behind the Wells Fargo and Mills Bank buildings. This is typical of the smaller independent California operations. Notice the canvas set up to provide shade while the men labored.

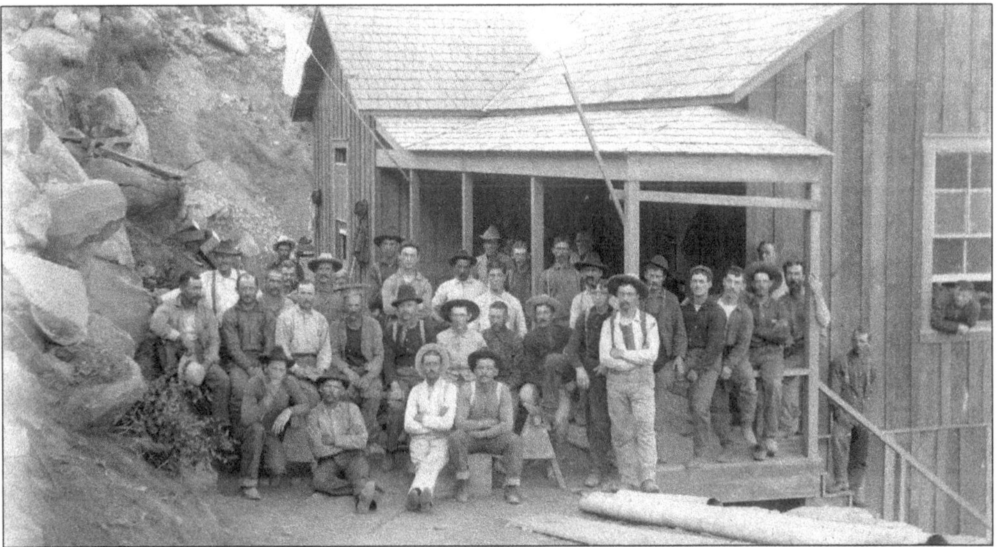

Large operations required large work forces, machinery, and investment. The independent single miner gave way to employers in the mid-1850s. "Easily worked" operations were played out. Gold was difficult to recover in sums that allowed small companies to exist. Toward the end of the 1800s, most California miners were employees working for wages rather than "takes." Here employees of the Densmore Mine pose for a portrait in later years.

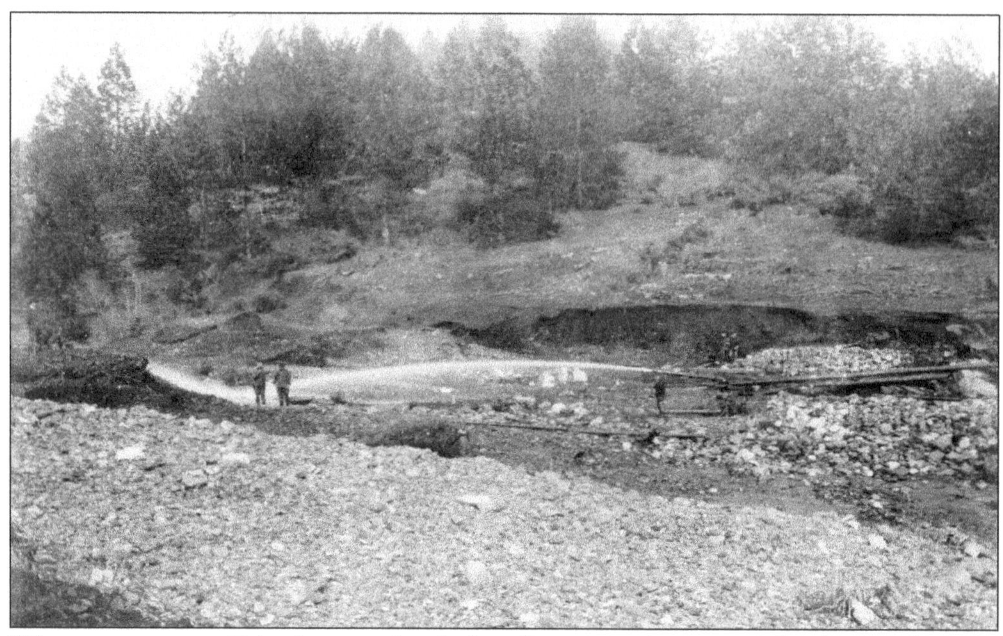

When operations in Columbia were "worked out," areas nearby continued to be mined. In the hills surrounding Columbia, where there were no pits to keep clear of water, hydraulic mining was used extensively. It was simply a matter of washing away ancient river gravels, channeling the water into a sluicing system, and recovering the gold. This image is of the Dondero Gravel Mine on Yankee Hill.

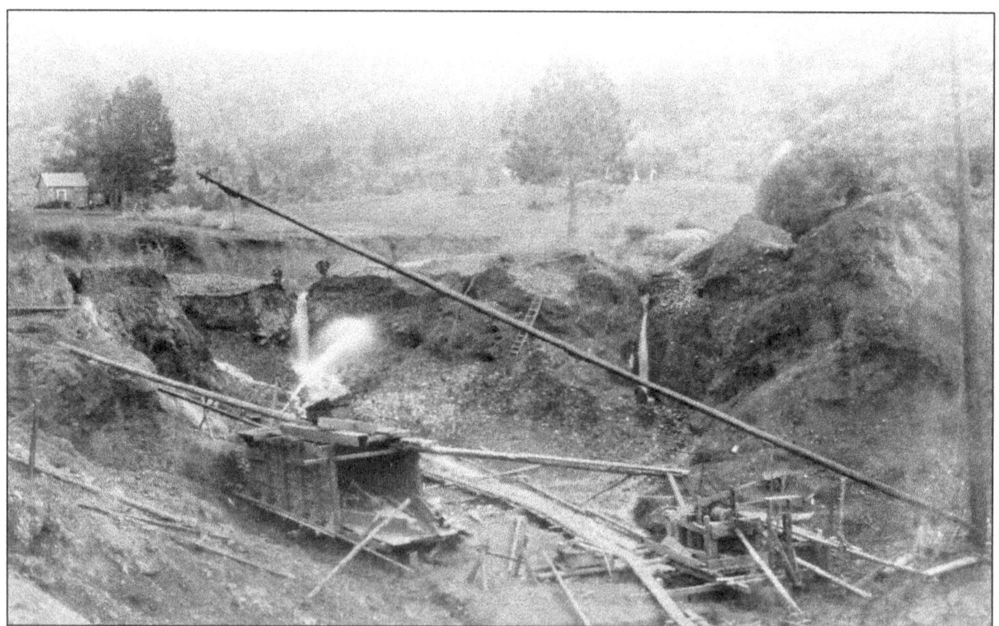

Hydraulic mining was destructive. Whole mountains were washed away, the resulting tailings choking rivers and flooding valleys below. By the late 1800s, farming had overtaken mining as the principle economic force in the state. Farmers were able to lobby Sacramento for the first environmental legislation in the state to control hydraulic run off. This legislation effectively put an end to hydraulic mining, causing mines like the one shown above to cease operations.

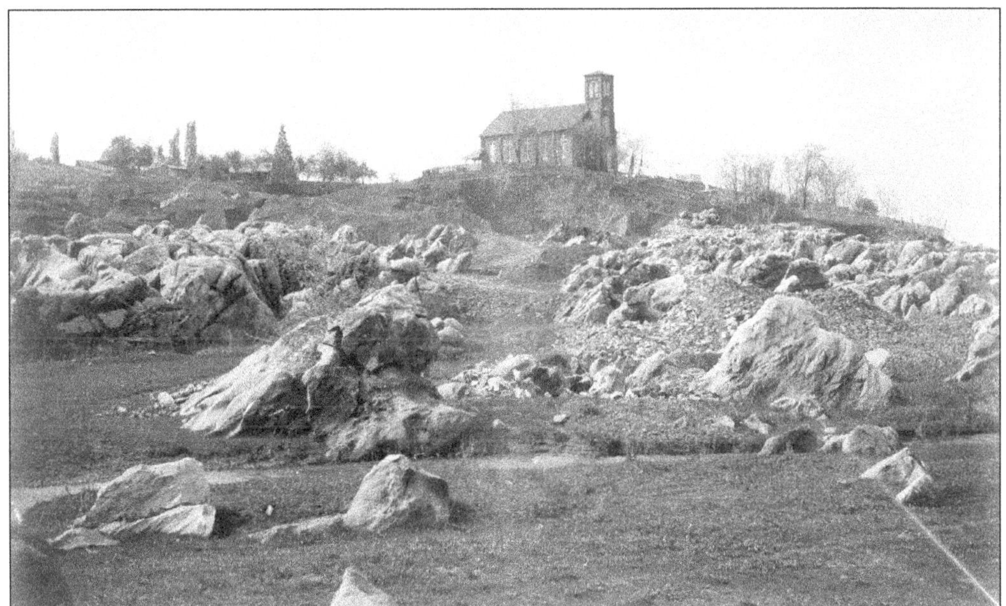

When mining finally ended in Columbia, the landscape was left in devastation. In the quest for riches, even cemeteries had been put at risk. At St. Anne's Catholic Church, pictured above, the mining continued right up to the churchyard, threatening to destroy the church, and disinter the poor souls buried within the yard. Compare this image to the photograph on page 14.

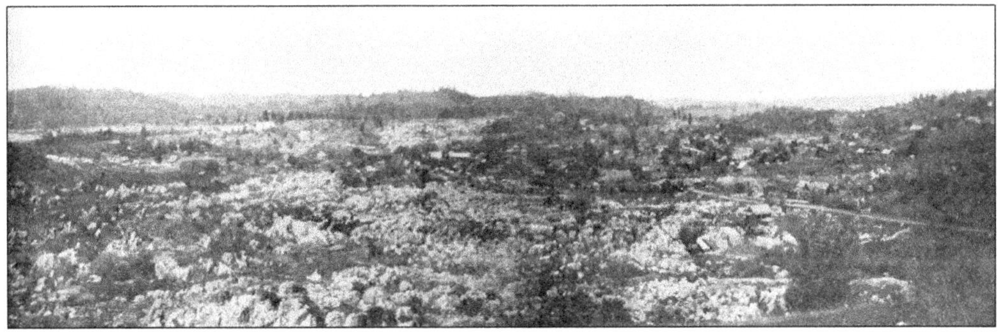

By 1901, boulder fields surrounded the town of Columbia after the large mining operations ceased. Huge rocks poked up from the lower ground level. Every rock and hole had been scraped clean. Gold was removed by miners and pumped into the California economy. In 20 years, Columbians mined over $87 million in gold. That is roughly 400,000 pounds (181,437 kilograms) of gold at a value of $2 billion in today's dollars.

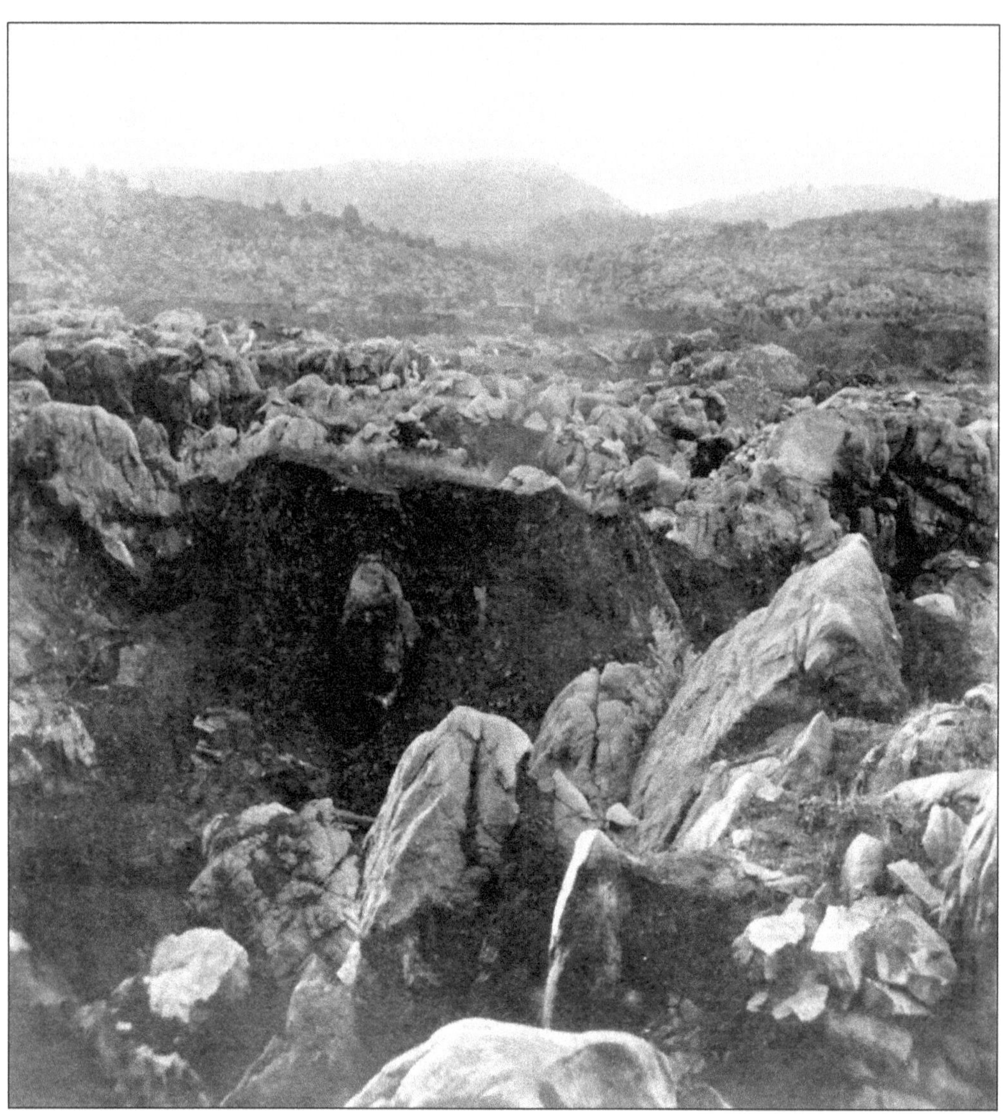

The environmental devastation surrounding Columbia is less evident today due to the growth of brush and trees. For years after the mining ceased, nothing would grow in the boulder-strewn fields. The weird, moon-like limestone formations, formerly underground, were left as silent sentinels to a time when gold ruled men's dreams and motivations. Poking through the brush, these rocks still remain for miles around Columbia.

Two

WATER'S FOR FIGHTING OVER

The quickest and most efficient way to get rich mining for gold was to use water to separate the gold from the dirt. On hearing of the plentiful gold and what seemed to be a close supply of water, Americans swiftly moved to the new gold strike at Columbia. But within a few months, the water supply dried up and most miners left the area. The next winter, following the rains and the return of the seasonal creek, the miners came back and the merchants followed.

Miners and businessmen quickly realized that to stay in Columbia, a reliable source of water was necessary. The Tuolumne County Water Company was founded in June 1851 as an employee owned and controlled company. However, the company's original plans proved ineffective as little water was available. It took almost a year for water to finally arrive in the "diggins" and when it did arrive there was not enough.

While the company was still working to provide enough water to supply the demand, it was forced to charge higher rates to pay for unexpected investments in sawmills, roads, and equipment. These prices, according to the miners, were too high. The water rates fluctuated from $4 to $6 a day, but a good paying claim was producing only $8 a day. Miners found themselves working for wages similar to those they could have earned had they stayed home. And some of these were the same miners who had been stockholders in the water company.

After several protests and strikes against the Tuolumne County Water Company, the miners formed another water company, the Columbia and Stanislaus River Water Company. This ill-fated venture started with ambitious promises but soon ran into significant financial problems. By the time the company's ditch was completed in 1858, there were rumors of imminent financial failure.

In 1859, the Columbia and Stanislaus River Water Company went bankrupt. Sold to pay debts (at about 10¢ on the dollar), it was resold to the "monster monopoly" of the Tuolumne County Water Company. Some of the affected miners, incensed that their hard work had again left them with nothing, formed a group called the "Ditch Breakers" to protest the monopoly. Their actions resulted in destroyed ditches and flumes and threats to employees and officers of the corporation. Local officials formed a committee of conference and, after a payment of $10,000, peace was restored.

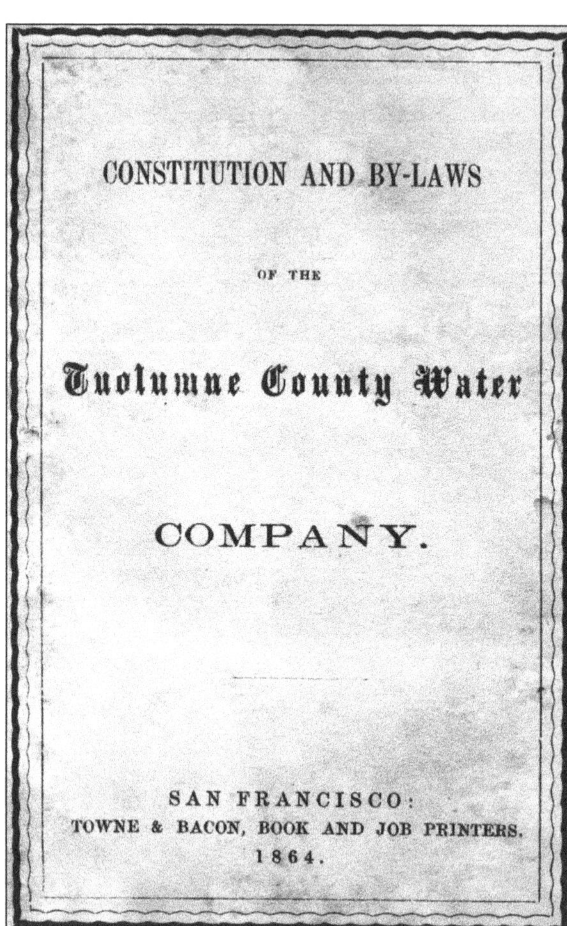

CONSTITUTION AND BY-LAWS

OF THE

Tuolumne County Water

COMPANY.

SAN FRANCISCO:
TOWNE & BACON, BOOK AND JOB PRINTERS.
1864.

As originally written in the constitution of the Tuolumne County Water Company, 200 shares of stock were to be issued. Individual shareholders had one vote, and there were to be no proxy votes. Miners working on the ditch were to get one share of stock as well as $5 a day in scrip for water. Other shareholders had to pay $5 a day or hire someone to work on the ditch, or they would forfeit their share. This was meant to keep the company locally owned. When it was incorporated in 1852, foreigners could not serve as officers. The offices of the water company were in the rear of the D. O. Mills Bank building and remained there until the water company was sold in the early 1900s.

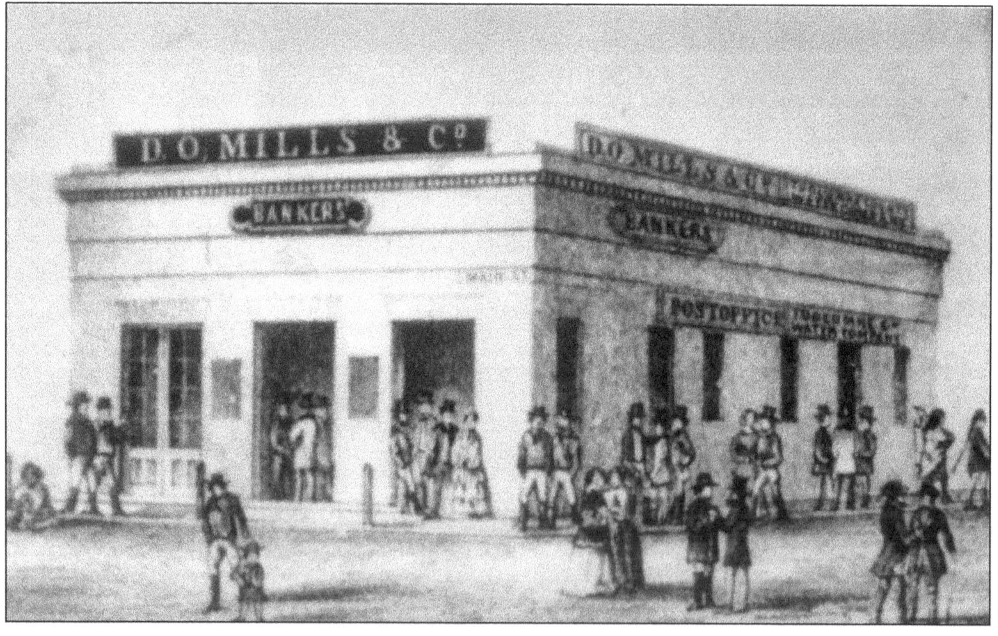

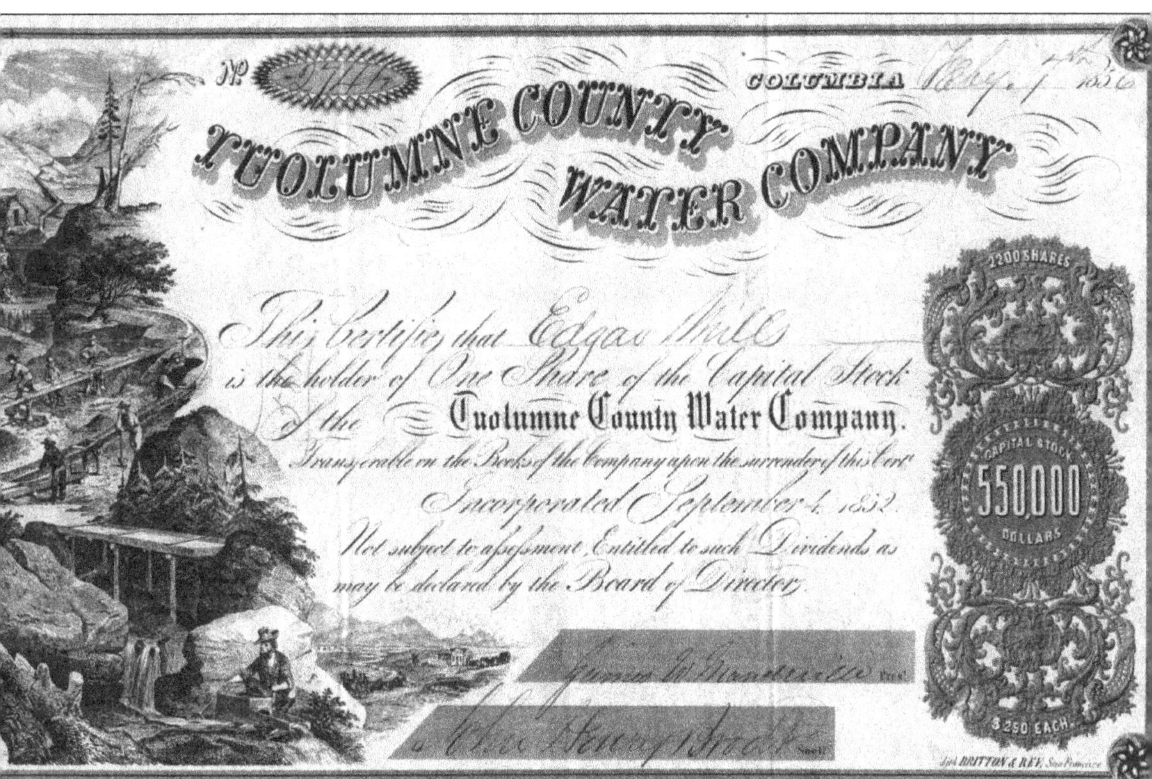

№

COLUMBIA

TUOLUMNE COUNTY WATER COMPANY

This Certifies that Edgar Mills is the holder of One Share of the Capital Stock of the Tuolumne County Water Company.

Transferable on the Books of the Company upon the surrender of this Certf.

Incorporated September 4. 1852.

Not subject to assessment, Entitled to such Dividends as may be declared by the Board of Directors.

Pres.

Secy.

2200 SHARES

CAPITAL STOCK

550,000

DOLLARS

$250 EACH

Lith BRITTON & REY, San Francisco

When originally issued, the shares of Tuolumne County Water Company stock were valued at $25. Within two years the price had increased to $275 and continued to rise. Many miners who had invested in the company were forced to trade their shares for food and supplies when they were unable to find gold. Edgar Mills, the owner of this share, was one of several brothers of D. O. Mills who owned the D. O. Mills Bank in Columbia. For a short time, Edgar Mills was president of the water company. James Mandeville, who signed as president, was on the board for several years.

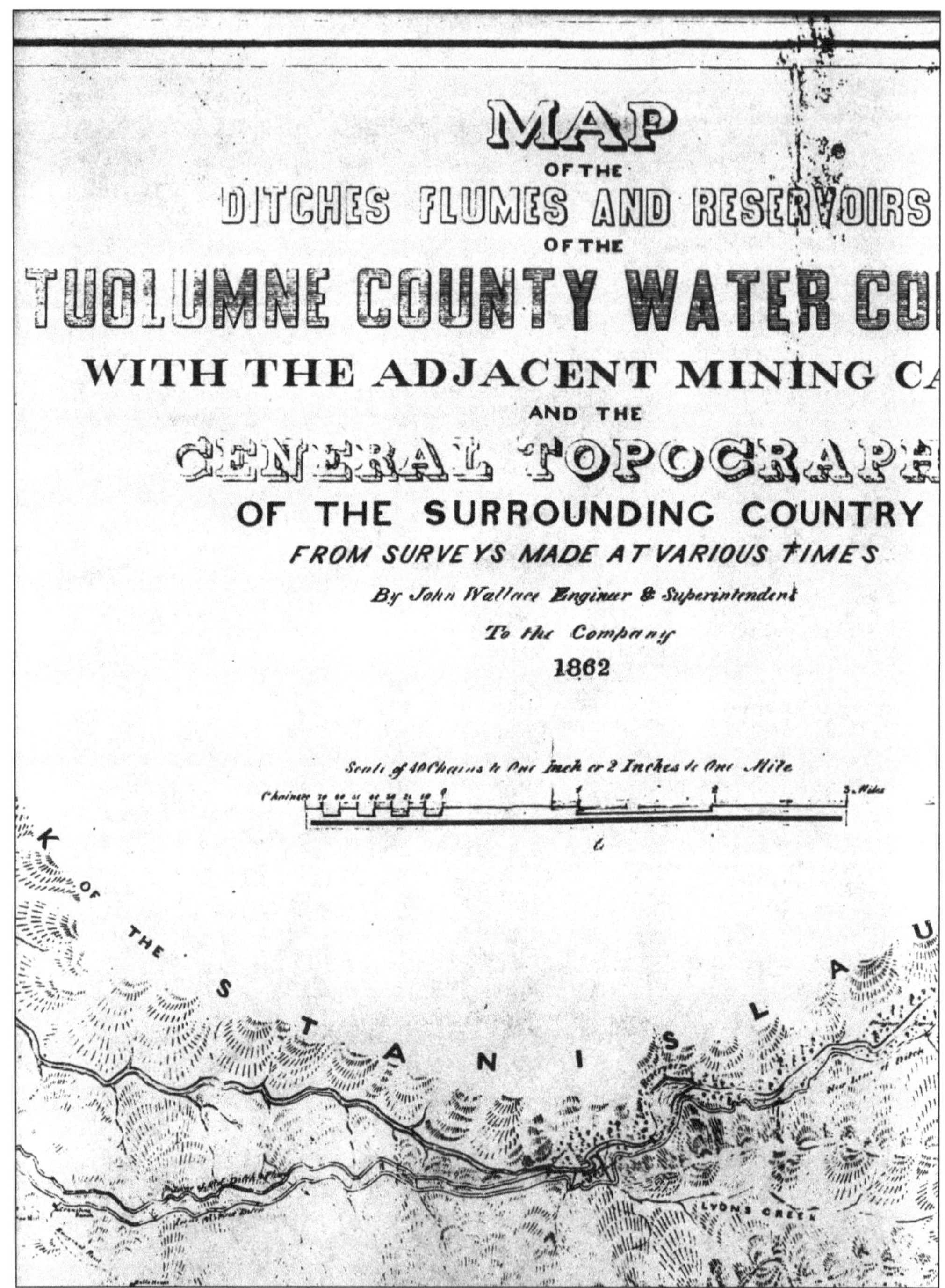

This map shows the extent of the operation involved in bringing water into Columbia for use in mining and the fine surveying and engineering work done by John Wallace. Wallace had studied engineering in England before traveling to California during the gold rush. In 1851, he joined the water company, became assistant engineer, and for a short time, president. Wallace also helped organize the Christian Hill Water Company for "the purpose of supplying ourselves and other residents of Columbia with water for businesses and other uses."

Joseph Benjamin Pownall, a doctor from New Jersey, traveled the southern route to California in 1849. After working as a miner in other areas, he settled in Columbia in 1852, and within a year was a water rent collector for the water company. In 1856, he became secretary of the water company, and later added the duties of treasurer and general superintendent. He continued as secretary until his death in 1890. During the water wars, he was the contact for the private detective hired by the Tuolumne County Water Company to identify the group known as the Ditch Breakers. The detective, Bill Carder, proved ineffective.

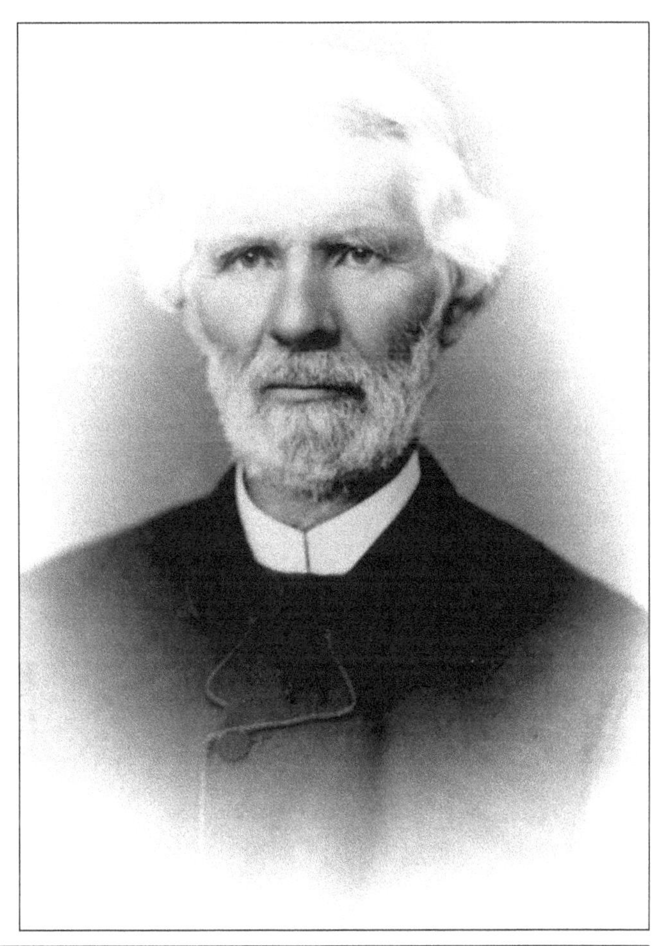

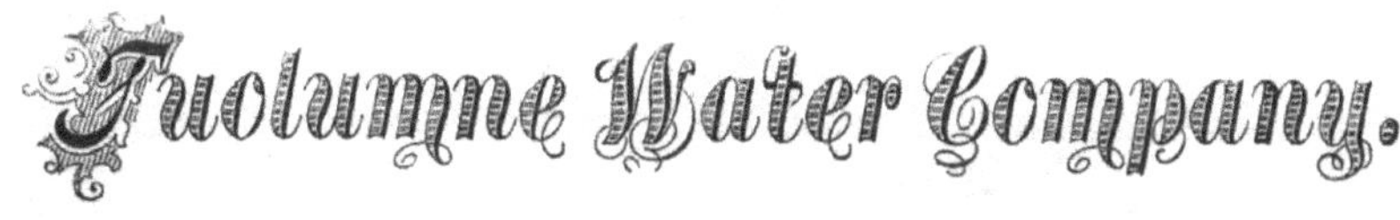

Tuolumne Water Company.

JOS. POWNALL, SEC.

Office on Fulton St.

Columbia, Cal., 187

Tuolumne County Water Company.

No. 3245 Columbia, August 27 1859

Received, of Lemone

Ten — Dollars. 100

for the use of Water, by club

$ 10 — Collector.

N. B.—Please preserve this receipt and give it to the Agent appointed to receive the same.

The dates shown on these two receipts reveal the high cost of water at the end of the 1850s. In only seven days, Lemone used $22 worth of water. At this time, gold claims were not paying as well as they had in the early and mid-1850s. With luck, Lemone may have cleared between $10 and $15 from his claim. Water was even more costly for the miners in the mid-1850s, when they paid between $4 and $6 per day for it. With luck, the miners were finding a half ounce of gold worth about $8 per day. The miners were not happy about "working for wages" and formed the Columbia and Stanislaus River Water Company to compete with the Tuolumne County Water Company.

Tuolumne County Water Company.

No. 3274 Columbia, Sept 3d 185

Received, of Lemone

Twenty two 50/100 Dollars.

for the use of Water, by club

$ 22 50 Collector.

N. B.—Please preserve this receipt and give it to the Agent appointed to receive the same.

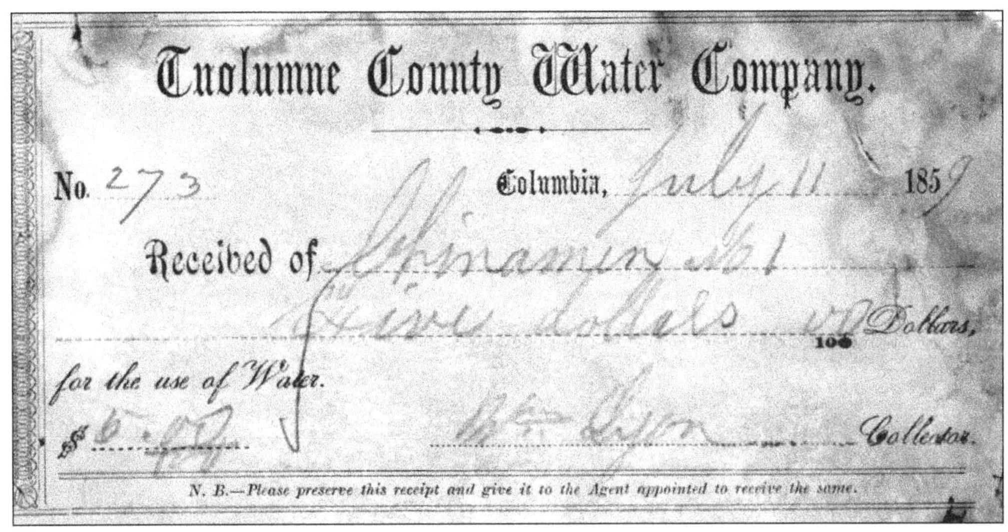

Tuolumne County Water Company.

No. 273 Columbia, July 11 1859

Received of Chinaman No 1

Five dollars 00/100 Dollars,

for the use of Water.

$5.00 Collector.

N. B.—Please preserve this receipt and give it to the Agent appointed to receive the same.

By 1852, Chinese immigrants had settled in Columbia. The rules of the mining district did not allow Chinese to own a claim or work a claim for another person. They could and did, however, own businesses in town and work for the Tuolumne County Water Company. By the time these two receipts were issued, the regulations had changed and these miners were finding a fair amount of gold. More interesting about these receipts is that the rent collector either could not spare the time, or did not care, to learn the miner's name. Other rent collectors used names such as "A Chinaman," "B Chinaman," etc. By the mid-1860s, receipts show that an attempt was made to recognize Chinese miners as individuals with rent receipts issued in their names.

Tuolumne County Water Company.

No. 286 Columbia, July 11 1859

Received of Chinamen No 2

Fourteen dollars 12/100 Dollars,

for the use of Water.

$14.12 Collector.

N. B.—Please preserve this receipt and give it to the Agent appointed to receive the same.

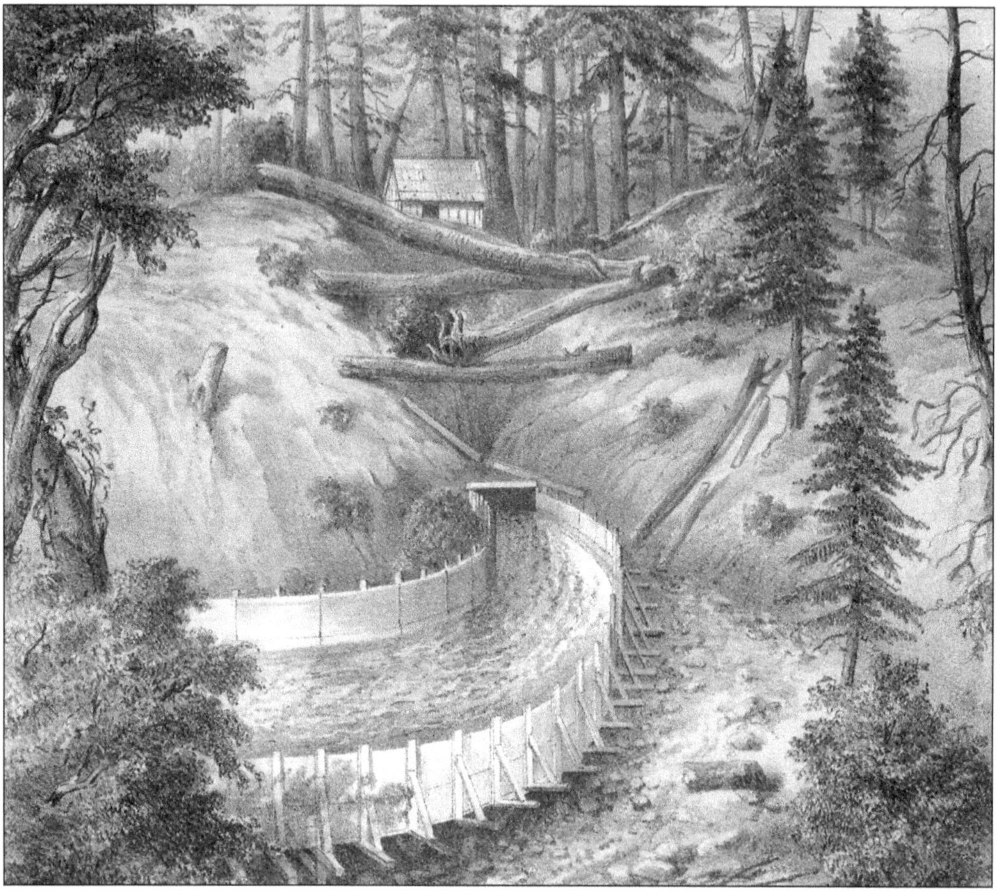

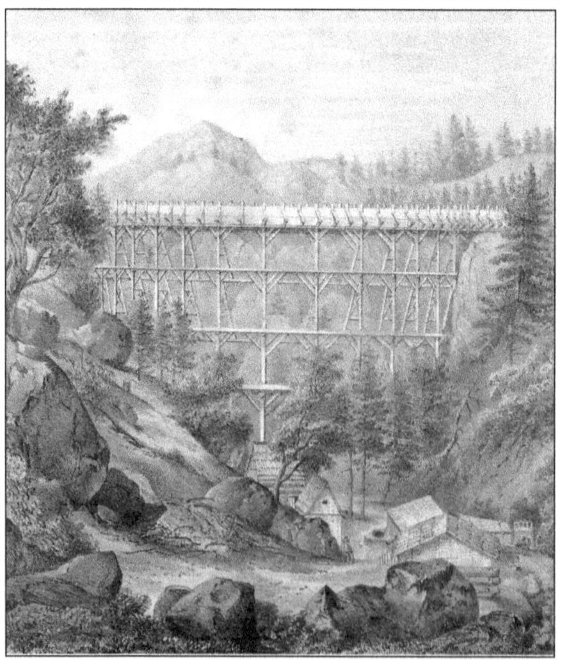

Some of the Columbia and Stanislaus River Water Company's construction problems are seen here. Ditch tenders and work crews lived in log cabins where food and other supplies were brought to them. Work on the tunnel at Spring Gap began a year after the company was formed. It was over 3,000 feet long and had a flume six feet high and seven feet wide to carry the water running through it. The high flume was 1,200 feet long and 200 feet high. Sawmills for supplying lumber for building the ditches and flumes had to be established along the water company's route. During construction, money was continually being borrowed to fund these activities. Many of those mortgages were later purchased by an investor who turned out to be a friend of the Tuolumne County Water Company's D. O. Mills.

Mary Newell Pownall came to Columbia in 1854 to join her first husband, William Newell, who had been secretary of the Tuolumne County Water Company. Just 18 months after her arrival, William Newell died, leaving her to operate his store. She later married Joseph Pownall, also secretary of the water company.

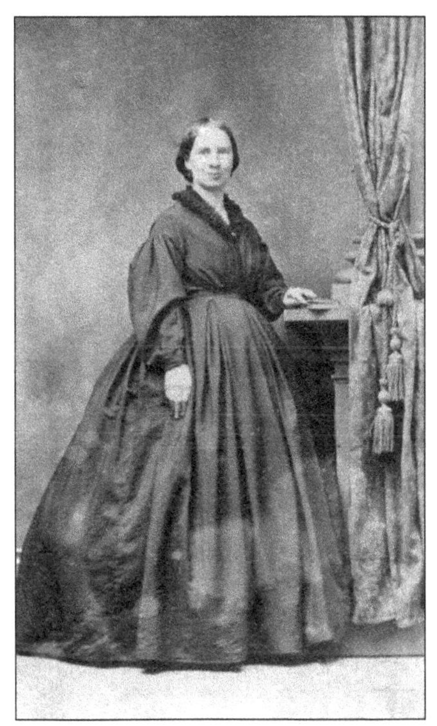

Nov 14" 1860
Gentlemen of the Tuolumne County Water Company
Take Notice
There is a plan matureing for the assassination
of all the prominent members of your company
if ditch matters are not settled within a
certain time As shure as day succeeds night
this is the plan
Act wisely and avoid such
a calamity
A friend to humanity

This note was sent to the Tuolumne County Water Company during the water wars. The note, dated November 14, 1860, reads, "There is a plan matureing [*sic*] for the assassination of all the prominent members of your company," and is signed, "A friend to humanity. " Feelings were running so high between the opposing forces that a plot was hatched to burn the water secretary's house, at that time home to Dr. and Mrs. Pownall.

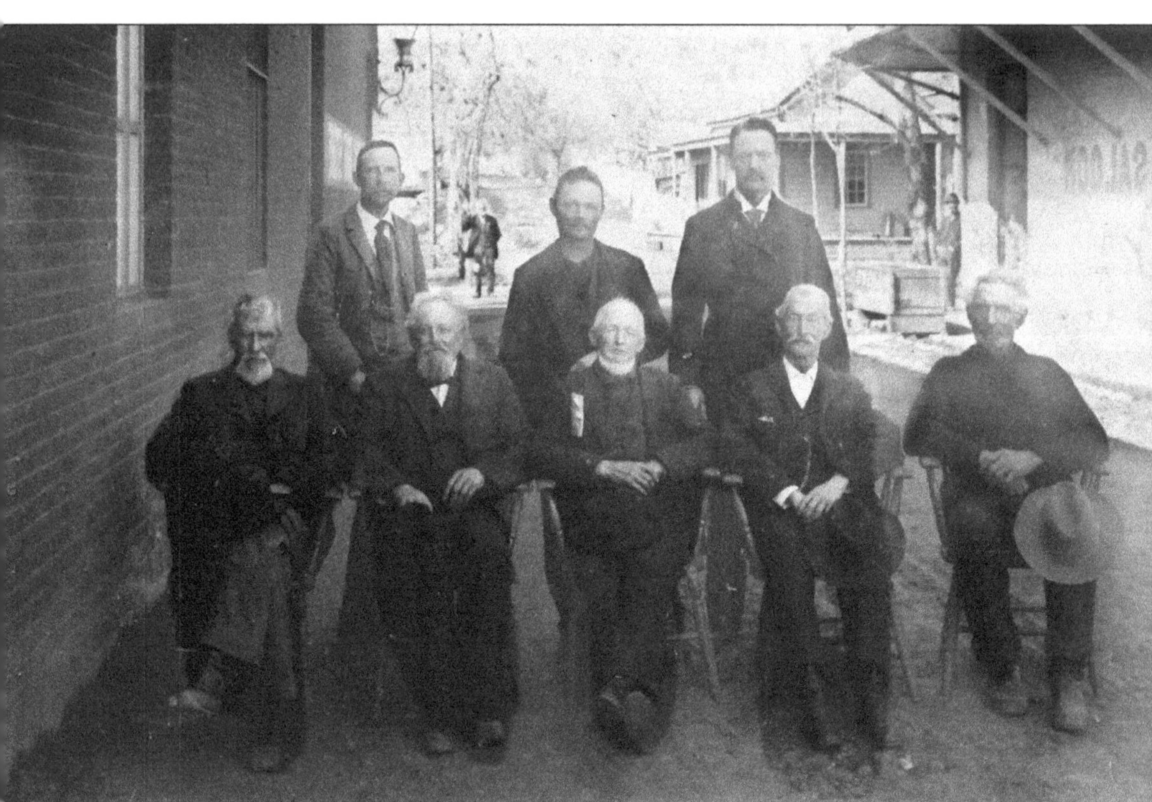

The Tuolumne County Water Company trustees continued to meet at the company offices through 1903, when the company made the decision to liquidate. This picture was taken outside their office on Fulton Street. The photographer did not notice that the image was printed backwards, as the sign on the brick building to the right shows. The trustees, from left to right, are (first row) J. W. Ellis, G. W. Hale, William Mansfield, B. Hamman, and George Wight; (second row) Benjamin Pownall, Tom Conlin, and Judge Clary.

Three

Boomtown

The news of the Hildreth party's discovery spread quickly. Miners, merchants, entertainers, and opportunists poured into the little flat and began pulling riches out of the ground or the pockets of the miners. The citizens voted to change the name of the settlement from Hildreth's Diggings to American Camp and finally to Columbia.

Columbia was a boomtown. The population exploded from a little camp to 6,000 or 7,000 permanent citizens. In the spring of 1853, extracted gold was valued at $100,000 per week and claims averaged a rich one ounce per day. On April 1, 1854, a gold specimen valued at $4,900 was found.

As more people arrived, demand for various businesses, services, and entertainments grew. In late 1852, Columbia offered produce and grocery stores, dry goods stores, meat markets, drug stores, bakeries, and a coffee shop. Business could be conducted in banking and gold offices or the express offices. There were livery stables, a blacksmith, and a wheelwright shop. Other goods and services could be purchased from the carpenter shop, boot and shoe shop, tin shop, printing office, book and stationery store, daguerreotype studio, silversmiths, laundries, and barber shops. Professional services could be sought at many doctor and law offices. By 1854, there were 235 buildings and 109 businesses.

When fire struck on July 10, 1854, and destroyed much of the town, the citizens were not discouraged. Within a few days, 100 brick buildings were under construction.

Many California gold rush towns had passed their peak by 1857, but gold was still being taken out in large amounts at Columbia. In one week, $17,000 in gold was taken from local mines. The 4,500 miners that lived in and around Columbia reported earning $8 to $10 per day. In October, a 29-pound gold nugget worth $1,500 was found. On May 23, the *San Francisco Evening Bulletin* reported that Columbia was "the most beautiful and flourishing town in the Southern Mines . . . in the suburb . . . are pleasant dwellings, surrounded by luxuriant flower gardens." A 22-foot-wide bridge that could support the heaviest wagons was built at the foot of Main Street, and the Columbia Gas Company laid lines for street lights and businesses.

From the first discovery of glittering flakes through the exciting sparkle of the boomtown era, Columbia earned her nickname, "Gem of the Southern Mines."

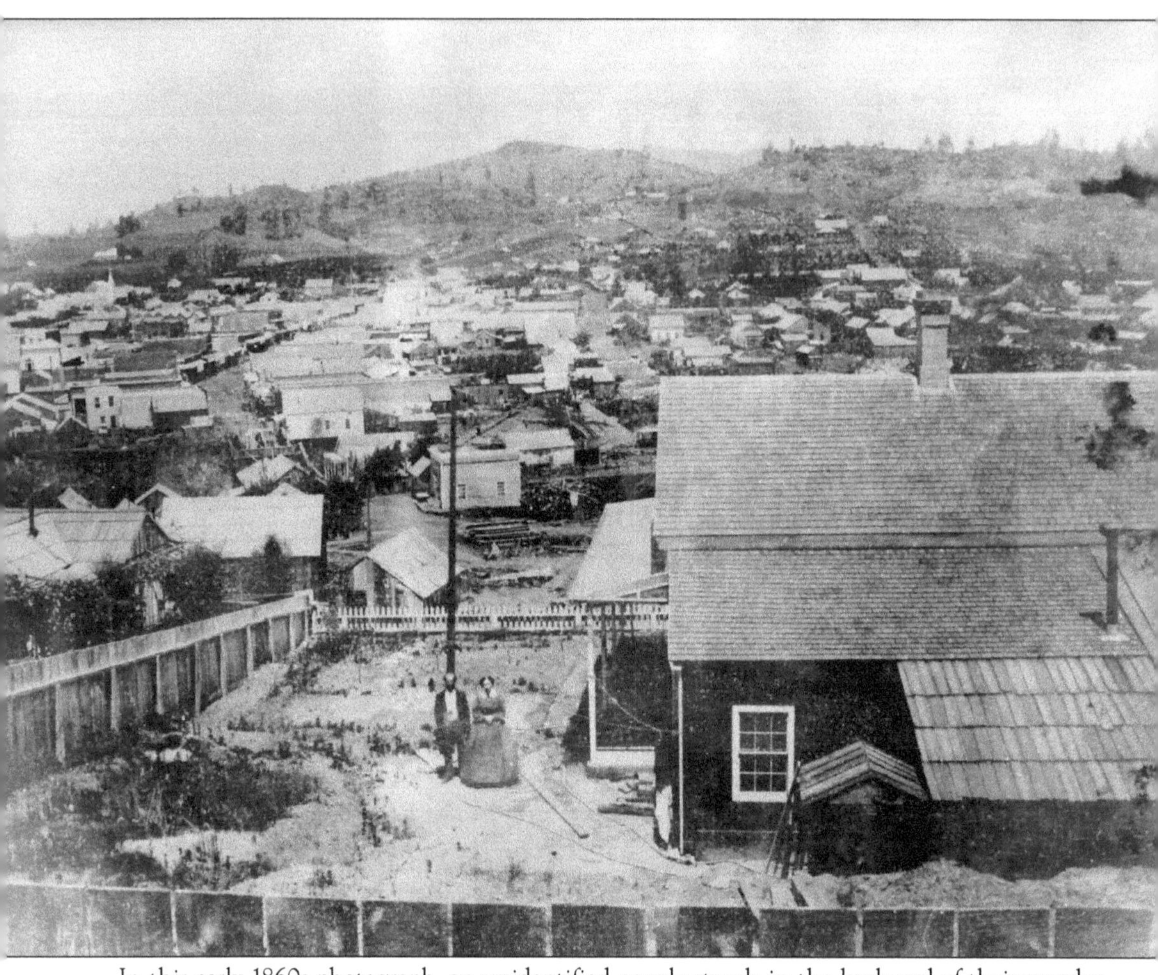

In this early 1860s photograph, an unidentified couple stands in the backyard of their wooden house. In the same area, looking north from Kennebec Hill, similar dwellings and sheds are visible. Main Street runs north from the deteriorating 1858 bridge, which crosses the main gulch, and is seen in the center of the picture. Many businesses were located on the east and west sides of Main Street. Broadway Street, to the west, also appears to contain many buildings as do Fulton and State Streets. Most of these were rebuilt after the disastrous fire of 1857. The large white building seen on the north side of Washington Street housed Cardinell's Theater and the second assembly hall, built in the fall of 1857. Destroyed in the 1861 fire, neither was rebuilt, nor was the Donnell & Parson's brick building on the south side of Washington Street. In this photograph, Columbia still appears as a prosperous town, although the years 1857 and 1858 had already seen the peak in population and gold production.

William Knapp was a prosperous young man. Born in Columbia, he was one of Sewell and Caroline Gilman Knapp's six children. Following in his father's footsteps, he helped in running the family's general store, located at the corner of Main and State Streets. William bought the store from his father and, with R. C. Davis, operated the store under the name Knapp and Davis.

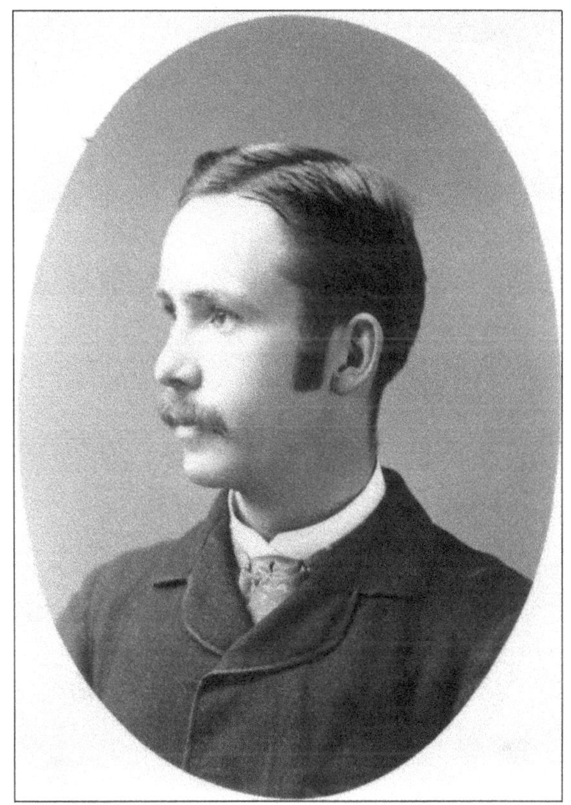

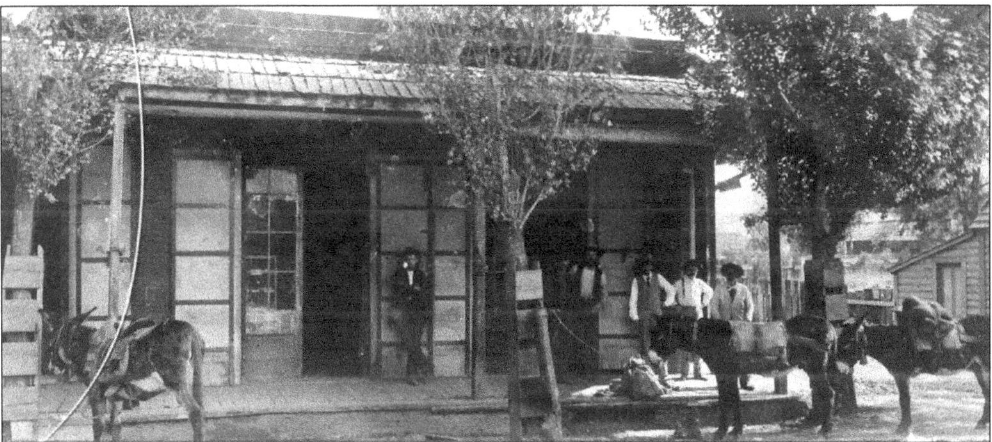

The Sewell Knapp Building, with unknown men in front, is an example of the typical architecture of the 1850s. Made of brick, it had an overhang with wooden shingles, tall inside doors with glass panels, and outside iron doors, which could be closed for fire protection. The pack mules were owned by Joaquin Dilucci, who brought supplies to Columbia even when wagons were unable to travel muddy roads or cross swollen rivers.

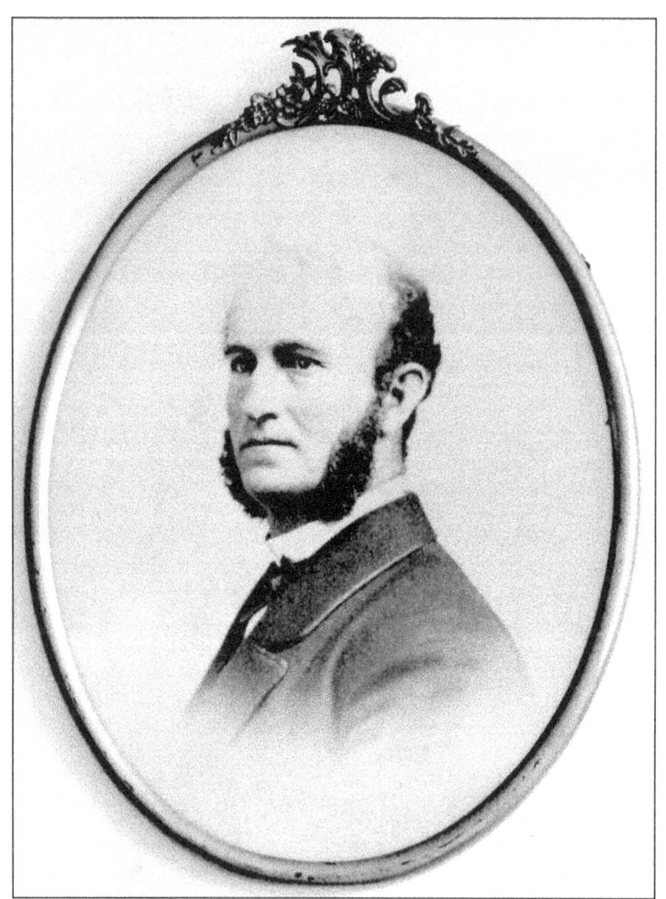

Darius Ogden Mills was a Buffalo, New York, banker. With the profit he realized from a shipping venture, he and his brother traveled to California and started the D.O. Mills Bank in Columbia in 1852. Their first building was made of wood, which was destroyed in the 1854 fire and replaced with this brick building. The bank was considered the most beautiful in the Mother Lode, with steps of Columbia marble and counters of Honduras mahogany with black walnut inlays and decorated with hand carvings. The large gold scales could weigh up to $40,000 at a time. With his primary bank in Sacramento, Mills left his brother to run the business in Columbia. Although the Mills brothers sold the business in 1857, a bank continued in the building until 1865.

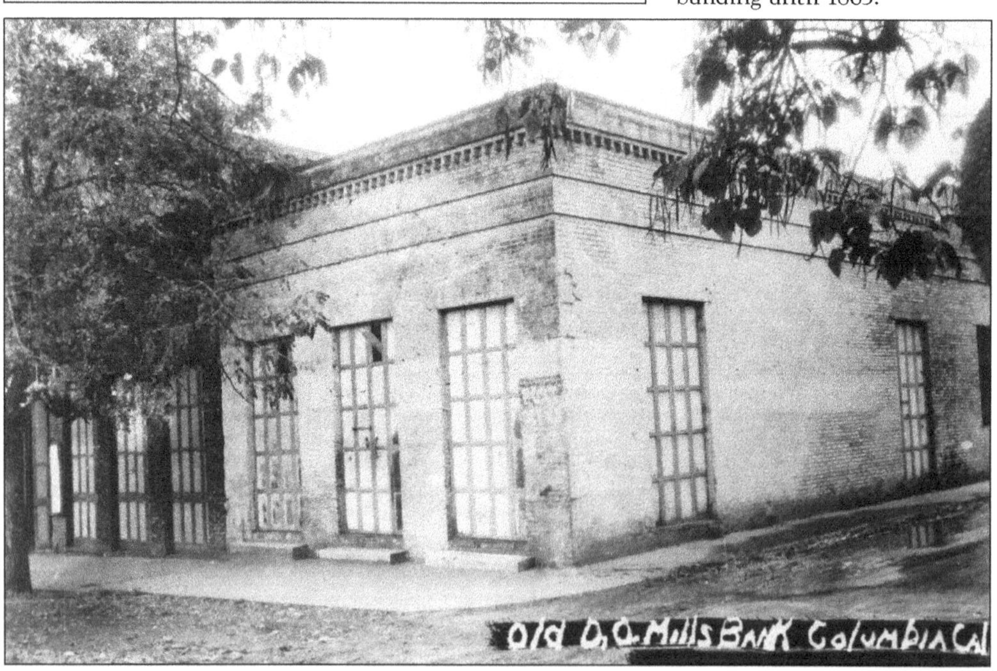

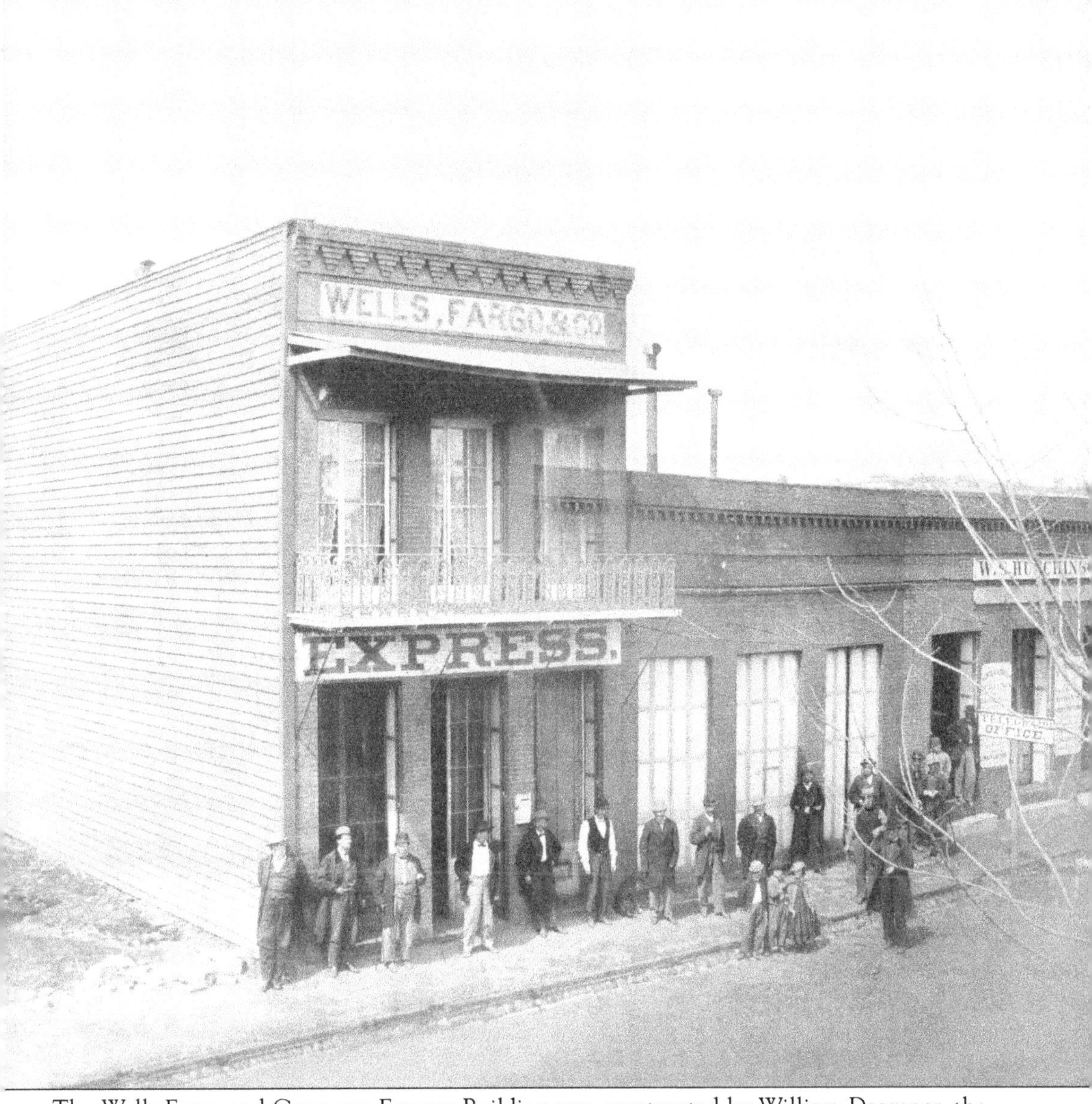

The Wells Fargo and Company Express Building was constructed by William Daegener, the first Wells Fargo agent in Columbia in 1858. The brick building was hot and humid during the summer and cold and damp during the winter because of poorly made bricks. Wooden siding was attached to the bricks in the hope that this would make the building more comfortable. Business was conducted downstairs, and the Daegener family lived on the second floor.

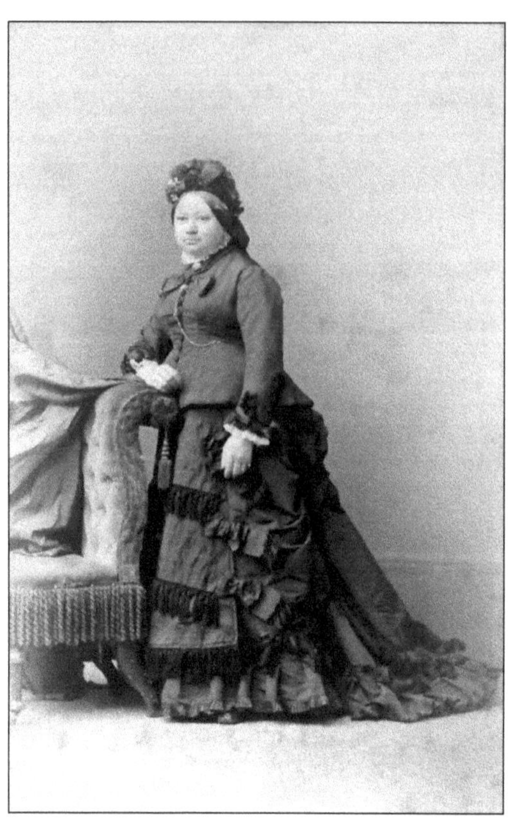

Maria Schultz Daegener and her husband, William Daegener, Wells Fargo's first agent, were from Prussia. In 1855, Maria Schultz joined Daegener in San Francisco where they were married before coming to their new home in Columbia. In 1858, the family moved upstairs in the new Wells Fargo building. The Daegeners left Columbia in 1872 and moved to a ranch near St. Helena.

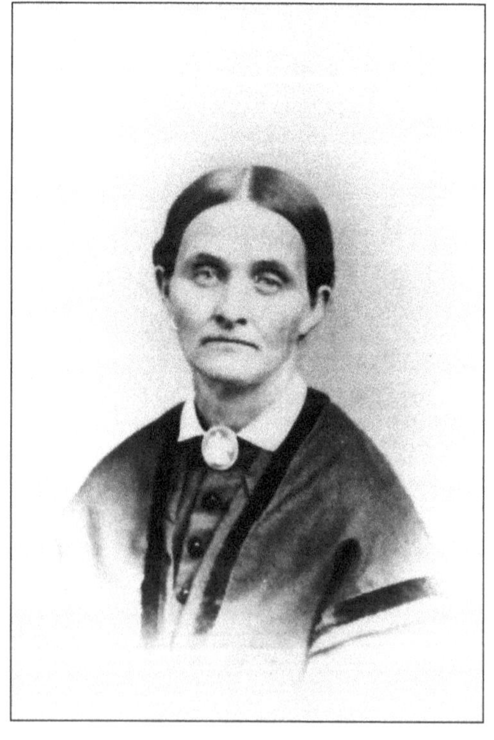

This photograph of Almira Foss Sleeper shows a woman in middle life. Mrs. Sleeper was the wife of William Osgood Sleeper. Leaving his family in Maine, William came to California in 1852 but sent for them after becoming prosperous as "W. O. Sleeper, Banker." After the bank closed in 1867, the Sleepers moved to San Francisco and later to Santa Rosa.

Henry Sevening, born and educated in Germany, came to San Francisco in 1852. After engaging in other businesses in Jamestown, he moved to Columbia with his wife, Louise Wedel, in 1860 and continued to be a successful merchant. In May 1872, Henry was appointed as the second Wells Fargo agent, taking over from William Daegener. He remained until 1884, when he and his family moved to Alameda.

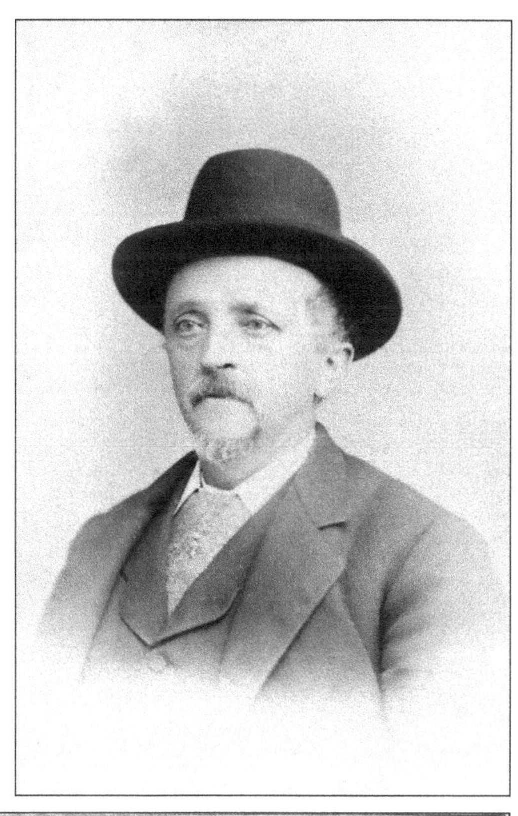

FORWARDING RECEIPT.

WELLS, FARGO & CO'S EXPRESS.

Value, $ 50 00 Columbia June 19 1875

Received of S. Knapp

Coin *Package* **Valued at** Fifty Dollars

Addressed A. S. Mizner

Bishops Creek

Which we undertake to forward, by usual conveyance, to the nearest point to destination reached by this Company, subject to the following conditions, namely: This Company is not to be liable for any loss or damage except as forwarders only, nor for any loss or damage by fire, by the dangers of navigation, stage or railway transportation (unless specially insured by this Company and so specified herein); nor by the act of God, nor of the enemies of the Government, the restraints of Government, mobs, riots, insurrections, pirates, or from or by reason of any of the hazards or dangers incident to a state of war. Nor shall this Company be liable for any default or negligence of any person, corporation or association, to whom the above described property shall or may be delivered by this Company, in the performance of any act or duty in respect thereto, at any place or point off the established routes or lines of this Company, and any such person, corporation or association is not to be regarded, deemed or taken to be the Agent of this Company for any such purpose, but on the contrary, such person, corporation or association shall be deemed and taken to be the agent of the person, corporation or association from whom this Company received the property above described. It being understood that this Company relies upon the various Stage, Railroad and Steamboat lines of the country for its means of forwarding property delivered to it to be forwarded, it is agreed that it shall not be liable for any damage to said property caused by the detention of any stage, train of cars, or of any steamboat upon which said property shall be placed for transportation; nor by the neglect or refusal of any Stage, Railroad or Steamboat Company to receive and forward the said property. **Nor shall this Company be liable in any case for an amount exceeding FIFTY DOLLARS, unless the true value thereof is herein stated**; nor for any amount upon any property or thing unless properly packed and secured for transportation; nor upon any fragile fabrics, unless so marked upon the package containing the same; nor upon articles consisting of or contained in glass. And it is also understood that the stipulations contained herein shall extend to and inure to the benefit of each and every company or person to whom, through this Company, the above described property may be intrusted or delivered for transportation. **The party accepting this receipt hereby agrees to the foregoing conditions.**

READ THE CONDITIONS OF THIS RECEIPT.

For the Company,

Charges, $ Pd H. Sevening

J. G. Hodge & Co., Manufacturing Stationers.

This Wells Fargo and Company Express receipt for $50 is dated June 19, 1875, and is signed by Henry Sevening, Columbia's Wells Fargo agent. Mr. S. Knapp, of the Knapp General Store, was sending $50 to A. S. Meizer at Bishop's Creek. It is of interest to note the large letters near the bottom stating, "Read The Conditions of This Receipt."

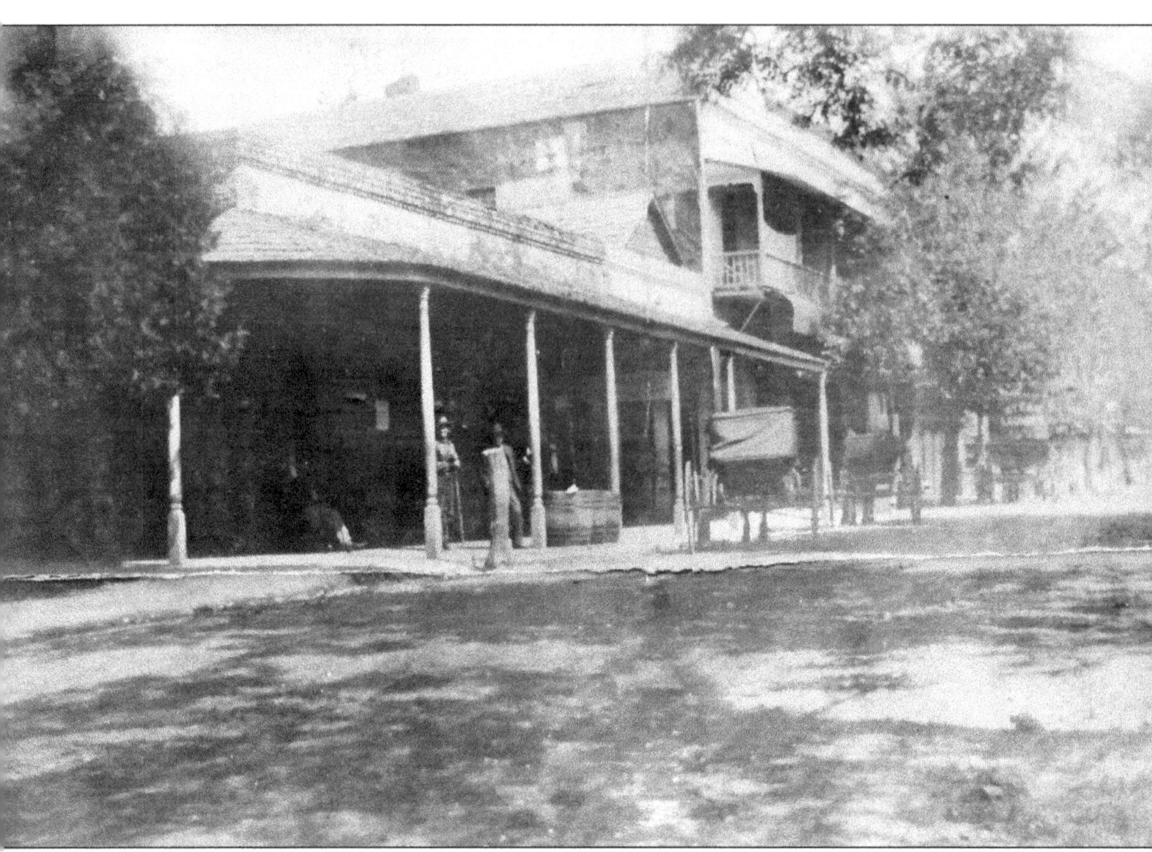

This two-story building is the City Hotel. The original frame building was purchased in 1854 by George Morgan, a native of England, who soon added another frame structure called the "English Ale and Porterhouse Saloon." A two-story brick building was constructed in 1857 and named "The What Cheer House." That building is the center of the City Hotel seen here. The middle or original section was 24 by 54 feet and had three broad, high doorways in the front. Additions on the north and south side of the center building had two high, broad doorways. Every doorway was equipped with double folding, solid sheet-iron doors on the outer side that could fold back against the outer wall. Four of the original double doors opened inward and had solid wood panels below with glass panels above that let the light in. A large hall upstairs was used for theatrical and concert performances. Known as Morgan's City Hotel in 1874, the two-story building became the City Hotel by 1890.

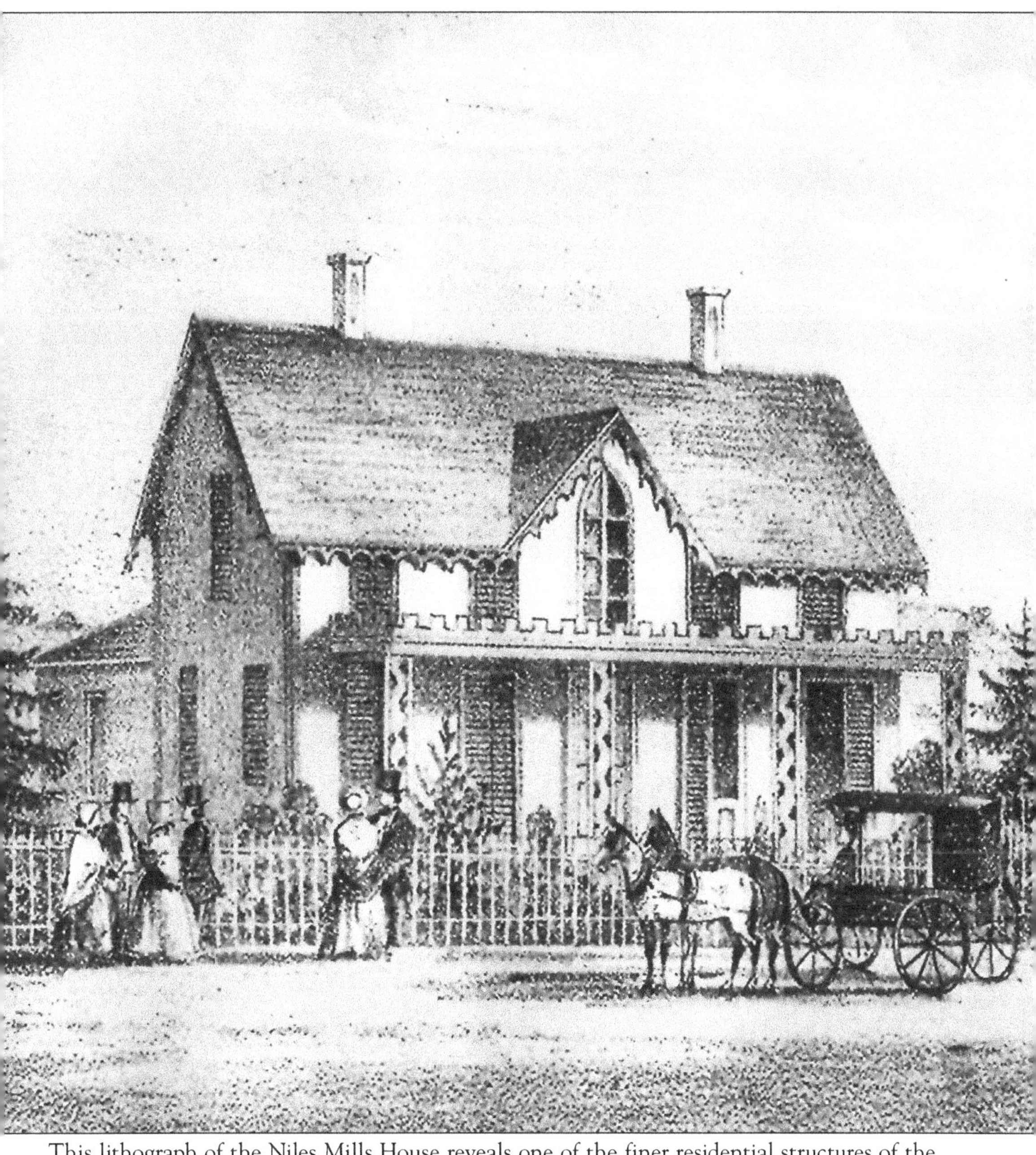

This lithograph of the Niles Mills House reveals one of the finer residential structures of the 1850s period in Columbia. Located on the east side of Gold Street between Jackson and Green Streets, this two-story framed building was owned by banker Niles Mills, brother of D.O. Mills, the founder of the 1852 D. O. Mills Bank. Although most businesses were made of brick, the town residents, who were predominantly from New England, brought their style of architecture with them. Their homes were typically one-and-one-half to two-stories high, had shingled, gabled roofs, and wood siding. The pine lumber siding was usually provided by a local mill. A one-story open veranda across the front provided an area where Mills could socialize with friends and business associates, some of whom have just arrived in their horse-drawn buggy. The Mills home was well known for its gardens, picket fence, shrubbery, and lovely shade trees.

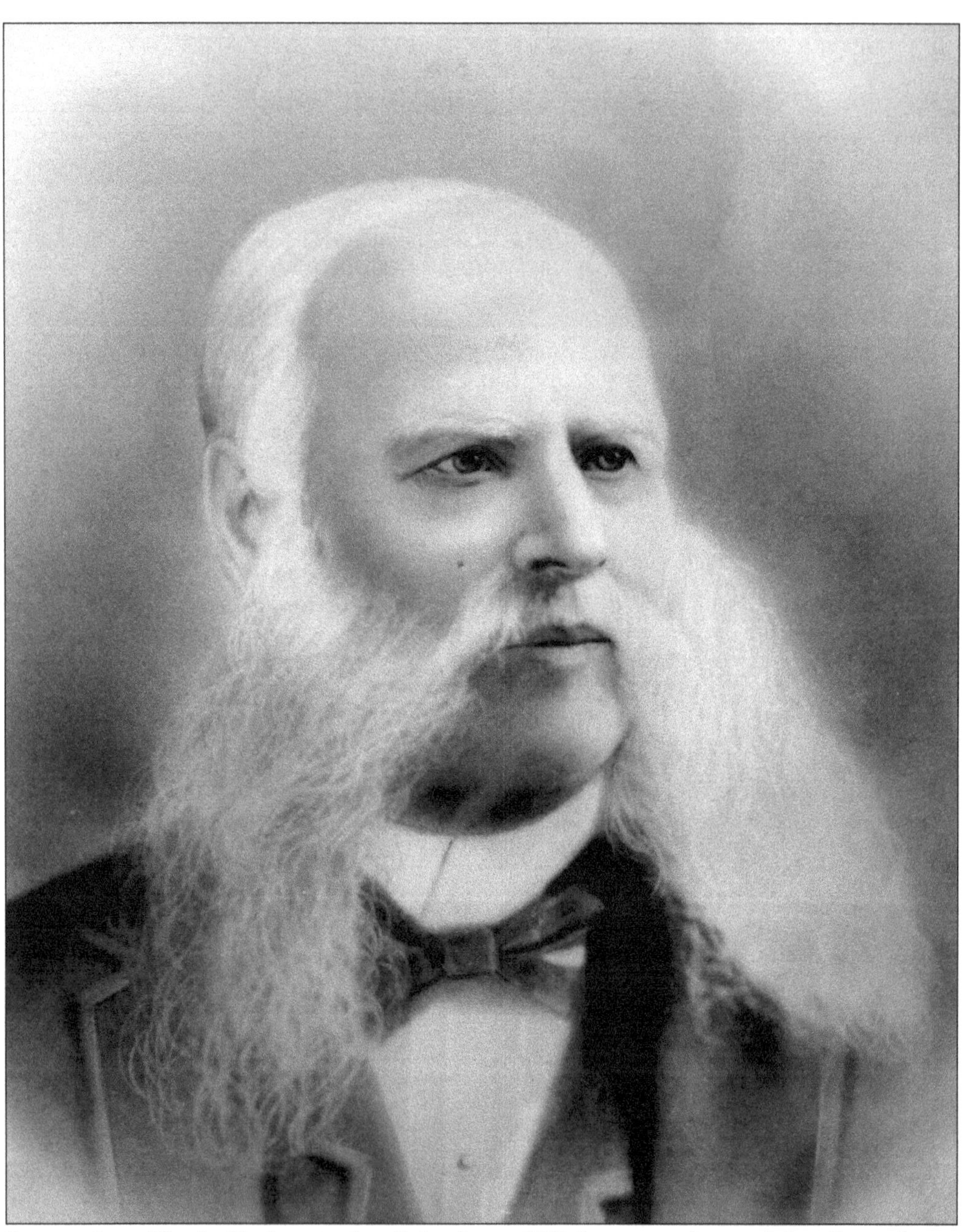

Prussian-born Charles Koch arrived at Columbia in 1851. Leasing a place on Main Street, he set up a barbershop where he plied his lucrative trade of cutting hair, trimming beards, giving shaves, pulling teeth, and using his own leeches for bloodletting. Eventually, he purchased the building and added a bathhouse with two tubs, which were supplied with hot water by a Harris and Toner water heater. Koch formulated many of his own recipes for hair dyes, shampoos, inflammations, rheumatism, fever, general injuries, and something called "Barbers Ich." Because Koch knew little English, John Kaylee, a friend and fellow barber from Knights Ferry, wrote many of these recipes out for him. One of the recipes reads, "For Barbers Ich, take the ashes from a cigar and wet with spit and make a paste of the ashes. Put on the sore, and it will kill the Ich." Living at the back of the shop, Koch barbered for 47 years.

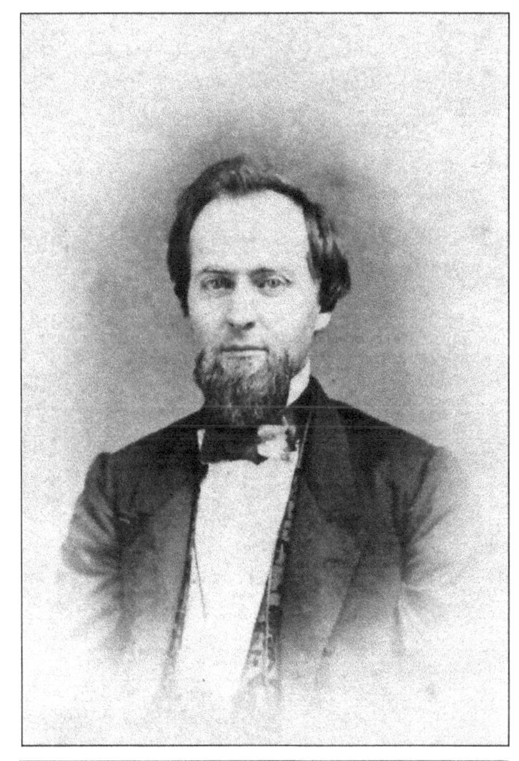

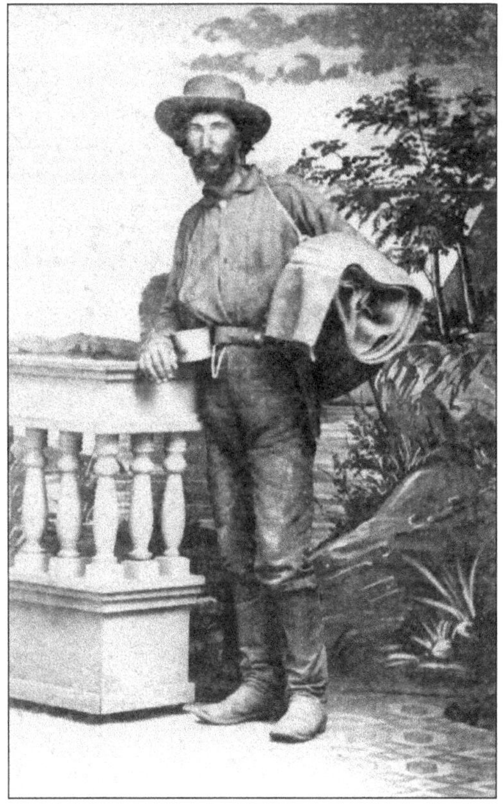

John Ross Hicks was born in New York and arrived in Columbia in 1858, where he acquired the photography shop on Main Street called "Cameron's Old Stand." Although there were five or six other photographers already in Columbia, citizens wanting "images" provided enough business for all. Hicks continued in business until 1867 and moved to San Francisco a short time later where he operated a shop known as "Hicks and Company." This sample of his work, taken in 1864, is of Joseph Spier, a sign painter in Columbia. Spier painted the interior office sign at Wells Fargo and the scenes used in special ceremonies held by the Masons at the Masonic Hall.

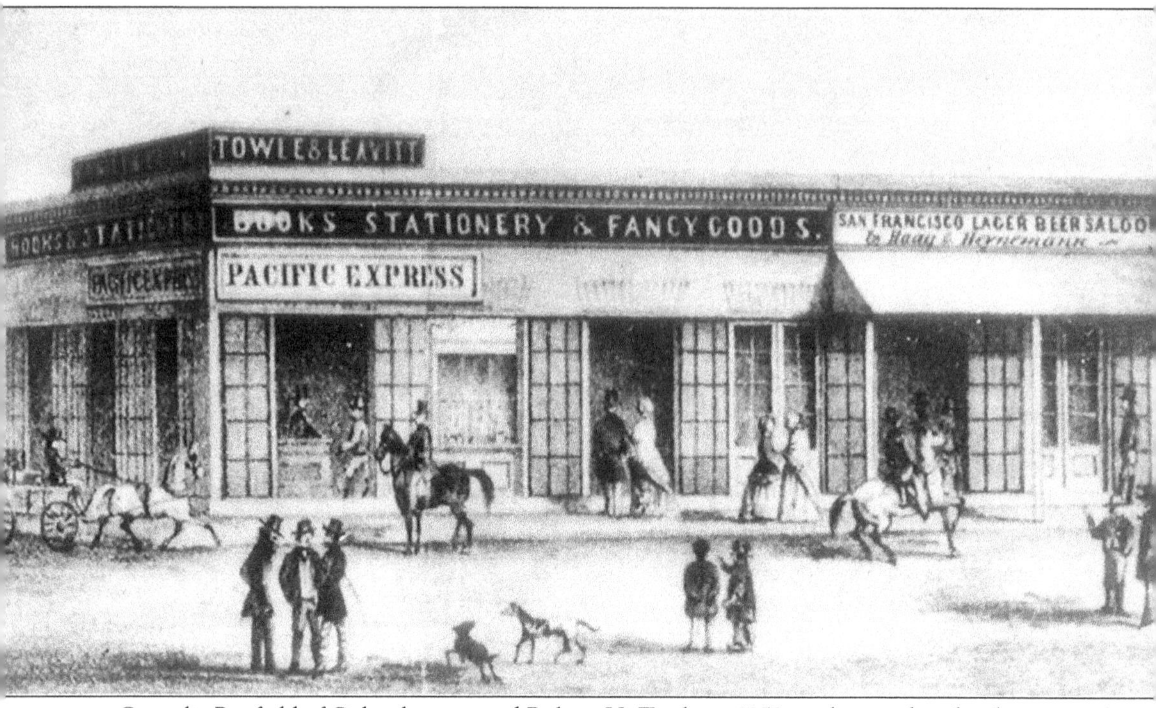

Cornelia Penfield of Columbia married Robert H. Towle in 1858, and carried on her business of selling books, stationery, and merchandise here at the Towle and Leavitt Building. The property was originally several lots with a wooden building on the site. Prior to its destruction by fire in 1854, various shops were located there, including a barbershop, a watch and jewelry shop, and a stationery and book business. After the fire, jeweler Zelie Jalumstein had J. N. Bean construct a brick building with two stores. Charles Brown operated a bookstore in the north store and Jaluemstein his jewelry shop in the south store. By 1855, R. H. Towle and Albert Leavitt had formed a partnership, bought the building, and operated a book, stationery and jewelry store, as well as a lending library of 1,000 books. Soon after the opening, they brought out their famous lithograph of Columbia showing the fronts of many buildings and a large view of Columbia in the center. Towle soon left to open his own shop.

Cornelia M. Towle — Sole-Trader.

Know all Men by these Presents, That I, Cornelia M. Towle Wife of Robert Towle of the City of Columbia in the County of Tuolumne & State of California intend and do by the presents avail myself of the benefit of the act of the Legislature of the State of California entitled, An Act to authorize married women to transact business in their own name as Sole traders. Passed April 12th 1852, and I hereby declare that I intend to carry on and do business in my own name and on my own account in the City of Columbia in the County of Tuolumne & State of California, and the business I intend to do and carry on as aforesaid is, buying and selling Books, Stationary and Merchandize, and the sum of money invested in said business is less than five thousand dollars, and no part of the money invested in said business has come from any funds belonging to my said husband. In Witness Whereof I have hereunto set my hand this the 13th day of October A.D. 1859.

C. M. Towle

Subscribed and sworn to before me this the 13th day of October A.D. 1859.
O. H. Allen Notary Public.
(Seal)

Recorded Oct. 13. 1859 at 4 h. P.M. by request of Robert Towle.

The Sole Trader Act Affidavit of Cornelia Towle represents one of several privileges women acquired during the gold rush. This act, passed by the California State Legislature on April 12, 1852, authorized married women with $5,000 in their own name to transact business in their own name as a "Sole Trader." She would be "individually responsible in her own name for all debts contracted by her on account of her said trade." The entire declaration was to be advertised in a local paper for three weeks prior to plying her said business. The act further stated that "The property, revenue, monies, and debts, and credits so invested, shall belong exclusively to said married woman and shall not be liable for any of the debts of her husband," and also that she would be responsible for the maintenance of her children. Cornelia Towle stated that she would be buying and selling books, stationery, and merchandise.

THE UNITED STATES OF A

To all to whom these presents shall come, greet

CERTIFICATE

Whereas, William Mansfield President of the Board of Tru

of the inhabitants of Cities and Towns upon the Public Lands

Stockton

William Mansfield President as aforesaid

and forty acres

Know ye, That the United States of America, in consideration of the premises, and in conformity with the several Acts of Cong

William Mansfield President as aforesaid

Mansfield President as aforesaid, in trust as aforesaid

BY THE PRESIDENT:

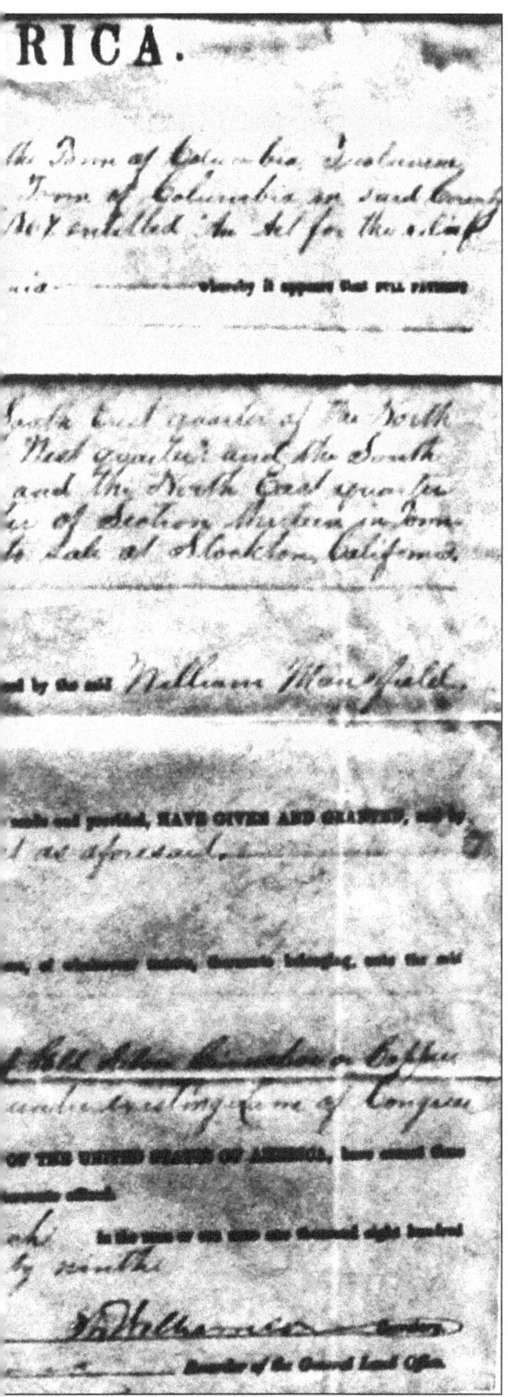

RICA.

Town of Columbia in said County

whereby it appears that full payment

South East quarter of the North

West quarter and the South

and the North East quarter

of Section

sale at Stockton California

by the said William Mansfield

HAVE GIVEN AND GRANTED

as aforesaid

OF THE UNITED STATES OF AMERICA, have caused these

Recorder of the General Land Office.

This 1875 land grant is of great interest as Columbia incorporated several times: in May 1854, in 1857, when the city limits were expanded, and finally in 1870, when citizens petitioned under a new law. While these various incorporations of Columbia were accomplished, the town did not own the land until 1875. At this time, the town was governed by a board of trustees, and its president, William Mansfield, was granted certificate No. 5689 to hold "in trust for the use of the inhabitants of Columbia, an area of six hundred and forty acres of public land excepting valid mining claims thereon." Certificate No. 5689 is dated March 20, 1875, and is signed by U. S. Grant and S. D. Williamson, secretary. Columbia now officially owned the land that had been incorporated four times. However, the town had so few people that it unincorporated in 1876.

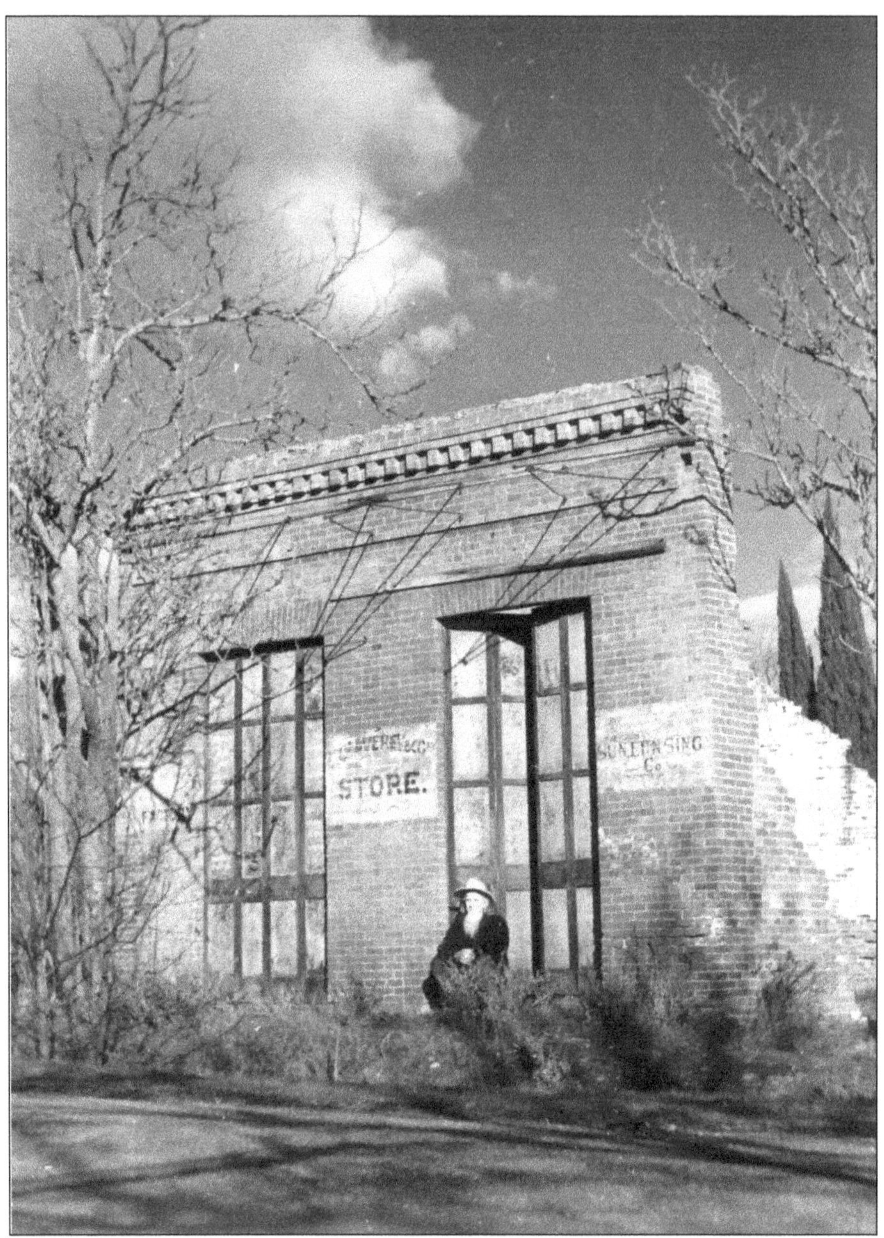

Hubert Brady stands in front of the "China Store" building, which was located north of Jackson Street on the east side of Main Street. Originally, partners Louis Claverie, Charles Meysan, and Victor Penchard, all Frenchmen, sold groceries, hardware, and liquors in a framed building at this location. After the big fire of August 25, 1857, a small brick store was quickly constructed and continued to sell the same products as the earlier store. The partnership dissolved in 1861 with Charles Meysan becoming the sole owner. Meysan added an expanded line of fine liquors to the stock on hand, and his store was very popular with the miners. Because the 1857 fire was thought to have started in a Chinese residence, the Chinese, already living north of Jackson, were forced to move farther north out of town. As gold became scarce and many townspeople left, the Chinese moved back into the area. In 1869, Meysan sold the store to Sun Yu Wo, and it became known as the "China Store."

Four

WILDLIFE

In early camps, the saloon was the miner's main recreation. Here he could meet people, relax, and pass the time when not working his claim. Gambling and drinking were popular but soon the saloons began to offer other forms of recreation, such as dance floors, bowling alleys, billiard rooms, and stages for live entertainment. In 1855, Columbia had two theaters, two fandangos, six gambling saloons, ten public houses, and as many as 40 places where liquor could be bought by the glass. The Chinese had their gambling houses, the Mexicans brought bullfights, and the town even had a bull and bear pit.

Theaters attracted some of the best talent from San Francisco. Singers, minstrels, and performances of Shakespeare were common. The Chapmans, a theatrical troupe, were very popular. During one performance, in fact, the adoring miners threw bags of gold dust onto the stage. When the Chapmans moved on to Sonora, over 1,000 miners escorted them. In 1881, the Chinese had their own theater with lavish costumes and a stage that was 30 feet by 80 feet and 28 feet deep and could accommodate a troupe of 40. A play called "Three Rival Suitors" took 90 days to perform. The theater burned down in 1882.

Before courts were established, miners' committees, sometimes called vigilance committees, were formed to handle any problems that arose. Theft of property might be punished with 25 to 100 lashes and/or the loss of both ears. Murder might result in hanging the killer from the nearest tree or flume. Sometimes the committees dealt with other concerns, such as on April 15, 1852, when a committee met to formulate plans for the exclusion of Asians and South Sea Islanders from the district mines.

Courts were established in Tuolumne County in 1852, and Joseph Carley was elected as the first justice of the peace in Columbia. His first cases were heard in a room behind a saloon, but his first actual court was located near the present-day Fallon House. A justice court was in continuous operation in Columbia from 1852 until 1989, when justice courts were phased out in California.

Meanwhile, the entertainment forms of the early gold rush days mellowed as women and children moved to California. Churches and schools were established and Columbia grew more respectable. Today, theater and musical events continue to be popular in the area and gaming is once again legal at the Me-Wuk Casino in Tuolumne.

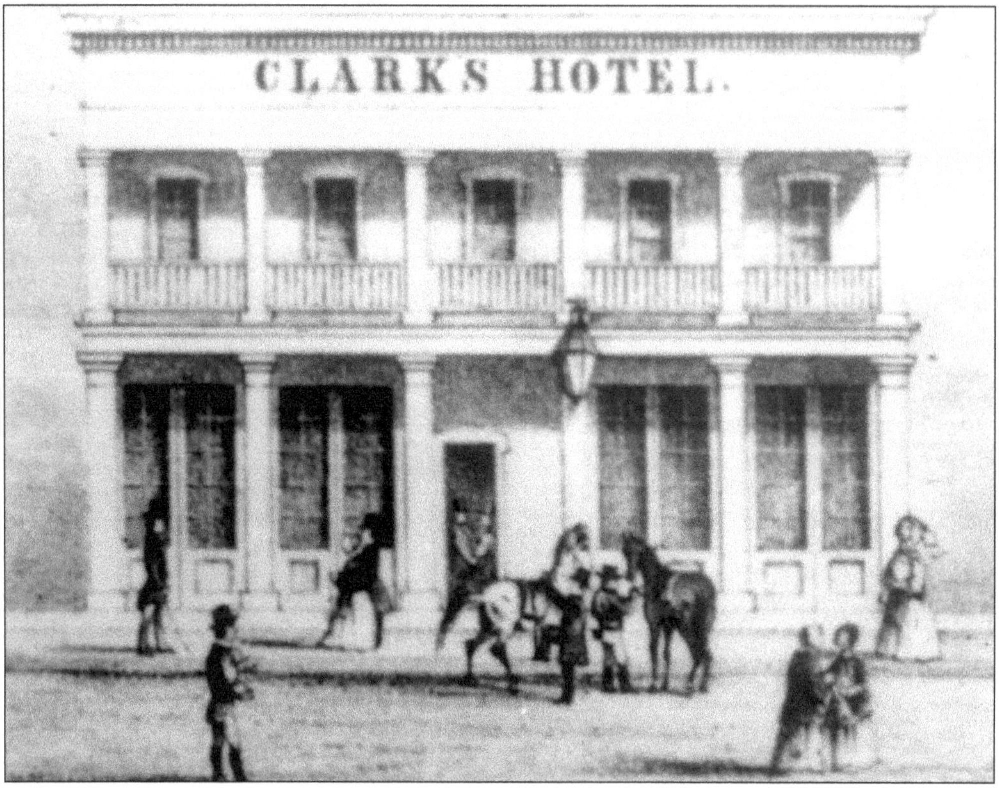

Clark's Hotel was built in 1854 after a fire had destroyed the original building. The hotel was owned by J. H. Clark and was also known as the Broadway Hotel. Located on the west side of Broadway (Parrotts Ferry) at the head of Fulton Street, it survived the fires of 1857 and 1861 only to be torn down sometime after 1867 so the property could be mined for gold.

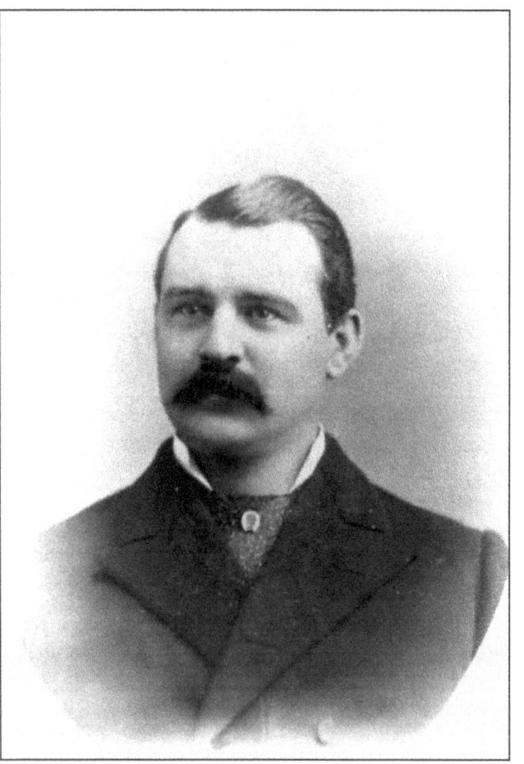

Jack Noonan was a bartender at Clark's Hotel. Originally from Maine, Noonan had served in the navy during the U.S.-Mexican War. On December 20, 1865, he attempted to save Thomas Horn, a prisoner who was trapped in the Sonora jail during a fire. Twice Noonan tried to pass through the fire to get to Horn's cell, but the heat and flames were too intense. Horn was thought to have started the fire himself.

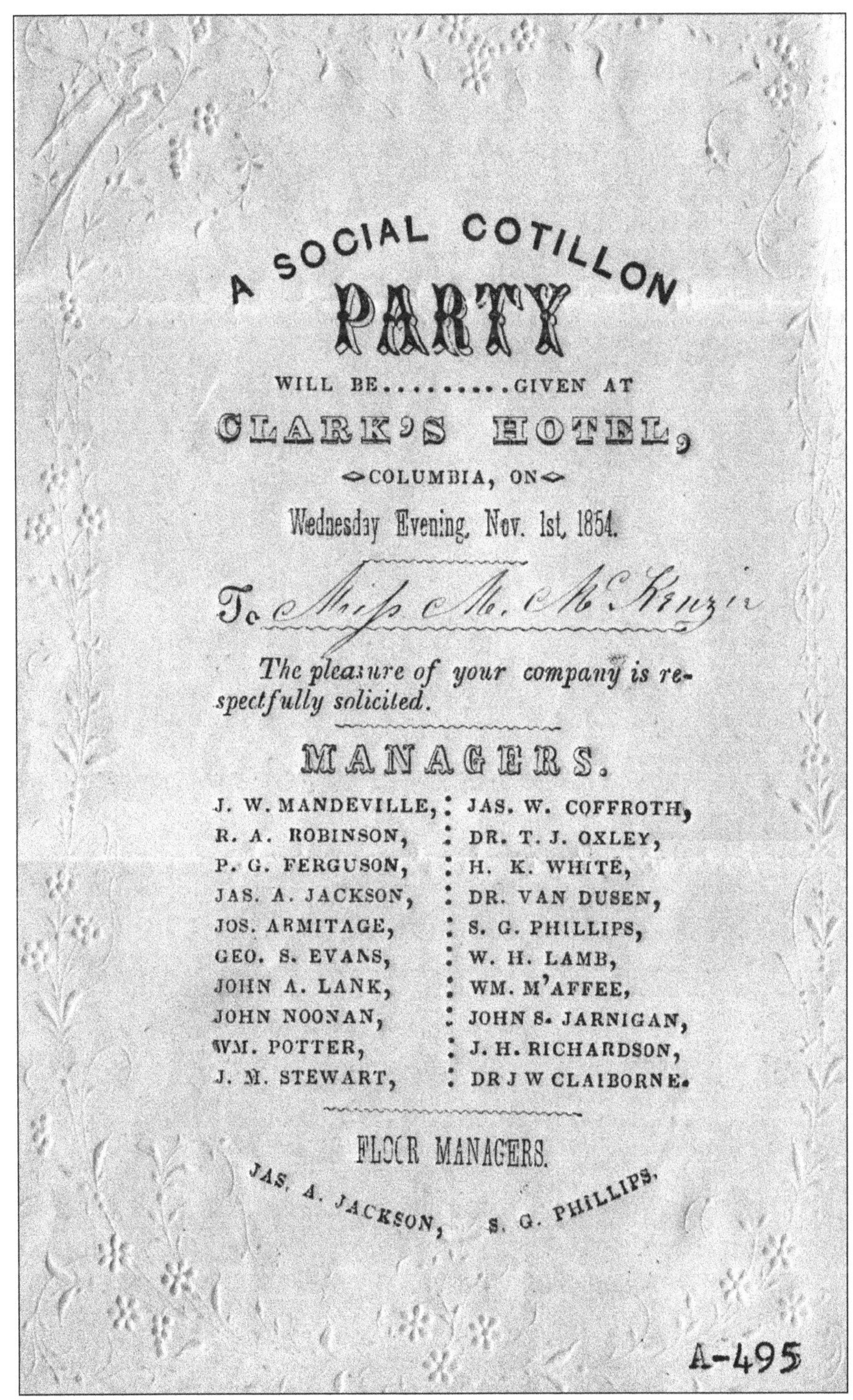

A SOCIAL COTILLON
PARTY
WILL BE.........GIVEN AT
CLARK'S HOTEL,
COLUMBIA, ON
Wednesday Evening, Nov. 1st, 1854.

To Miss M. McKenzie

The pleasure of your company is respectfully solicited.

MANAGERS.

J. W. MANDEVILLE,	JAS. W. COFFROTH,
R. A. ROBINSON,	DR. T. J. OXLEY,
P. G. FERGUSON,	H. K. WHITE,
JAS. A. JACKSON,	DR. VAN DUSEN,
JOS. ARMITAGE,	S. G. PHILLIPS,
GEO. S. EVANS,	W. H. LAMB,
JOHN A. LANK,	WM. M'AFFEE,
JOHN NOONAN,	JOHN S. JARNIGAN,
WM. POTTER,	J. H. RICHARDSON,
J. M. STEWART,	DR J W CLAIBORNE.

FLOOR MANAGERS.
JAS. A. JACKSON, S. G. PHILLIPS.

A-495

This invitation to Miss McKenzie was for a social cotillion party given at Clark's Hotel on November 1, 1854. P. G. Ferguson and John Noonan are listed as managers. Note that in the invitation, cotillion is spelled cotillon. Some dictionaries show this as an approved second spelling.

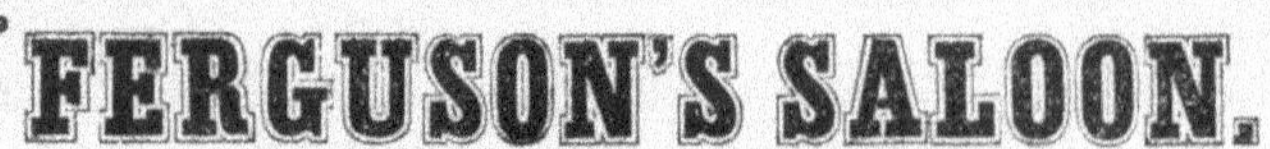

FERGUSON'S SALOON.

CORNER OF MAIN AND FULTON STS.,

COLUMBIA.

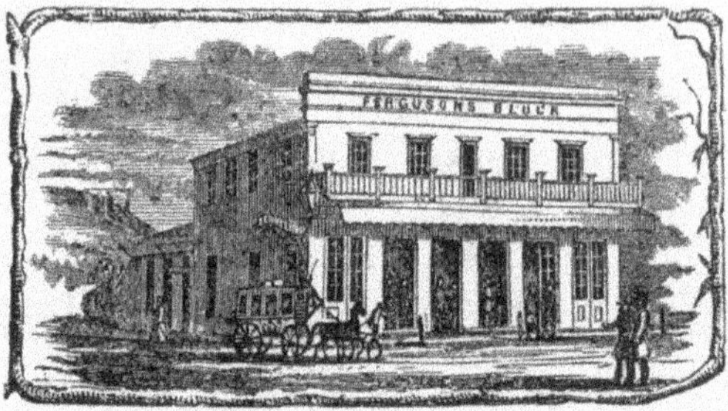

THIS Saloon is the largest and most elegant of any other in the Southern Mines. No expense having been spared, and the best Artists consulted, and employed in its decorations and appointments, to render it every way comfortable and worthy. It is supplied with Griffith & Decker's best

BILLIARD TABLES,

which are at all times in perfect order for Amateurs. A comfortable apartment is attached to the main Saloon, where gentlemen wishing to be private can retire to.

THE

JENNY LIND RESTAURANT

IS UNDER THE SAME ROOF, WHERE

Meals can be had at all Hours.

GOOD LODGING APARTMENTS

are connected with the House, and good and trusty servants in readiness to wait upon its patrons.

THE BAR is supplied with choice **Liquors & Segars,** and presided over by J. B. DOUGLASS, the well known and popular Bar-Keeper.

P. G. FERGUSON returns his sincere thanks to his numerous friends for the liberal patronage they have been pleased to bestow upon him, and hopes by unremitting attention, to merit a continuance of the same.

This page is from the Columbia Businessman's Directory of 1856. S. Ingersol operated this saloon with P. G. Ferguson from 1852 to 1854. Ferguson's Saloon was advertised as being "the largest and most elegant of any other in the Southern Mines." It boasted beautiful decorations, billiard tables, a restaurant, and good lodging. The bar had choice "Liquors & Segars," and the bartender was J. B. Douglass who was later to open his own business, the Douglass Saloon. Ferguson, a native of Canada, was secretary of Columbia Gas Works from 1857 to 1859. He was also the town assessor for awhile. The Ferguson Saloon also had a restaurant called the Jenny Lind that was operated by an African American by the name of William O'Hara, who later became a prosperous businessman in Bodie.

Christmas Ball.

GIVEN AT FERGUSON'S SALOON,

Columbia, Dec. 25th, 1855.

Your attendance is respectfully solicited.

Managers.

Columbia.

Henry Smith, Jas. A. Jackson, T. J. Oxley, Jas. W. Coffroth, John L. Conner, O. Bonney.

Sonora.

R. A. Robinson, L. Quint, S. G. Phillips, H. G. Platt.

Shaw's Flat.

Wm. McAffee. E. Wellington, Mr. Janagan.

Springfield.

Chas. Wolcott, Dr. Van Dusen, Henry Bullock.

Jamestown.

Benj. Randall, F. B. Clark.

Jacksonville.

Charles Deering, Isaac Desler.

Gold Springs.

Moses A. Lewis, John Jolly.

Murphey's.

George D. Brush, William Sperry.

Floor Managers.

Henry Smith, R. A. Robinson, Jas. A. Jackson.

A Christmas ball was given at Ferguson's Saloon on December 25, 1855, as this invitation shows.

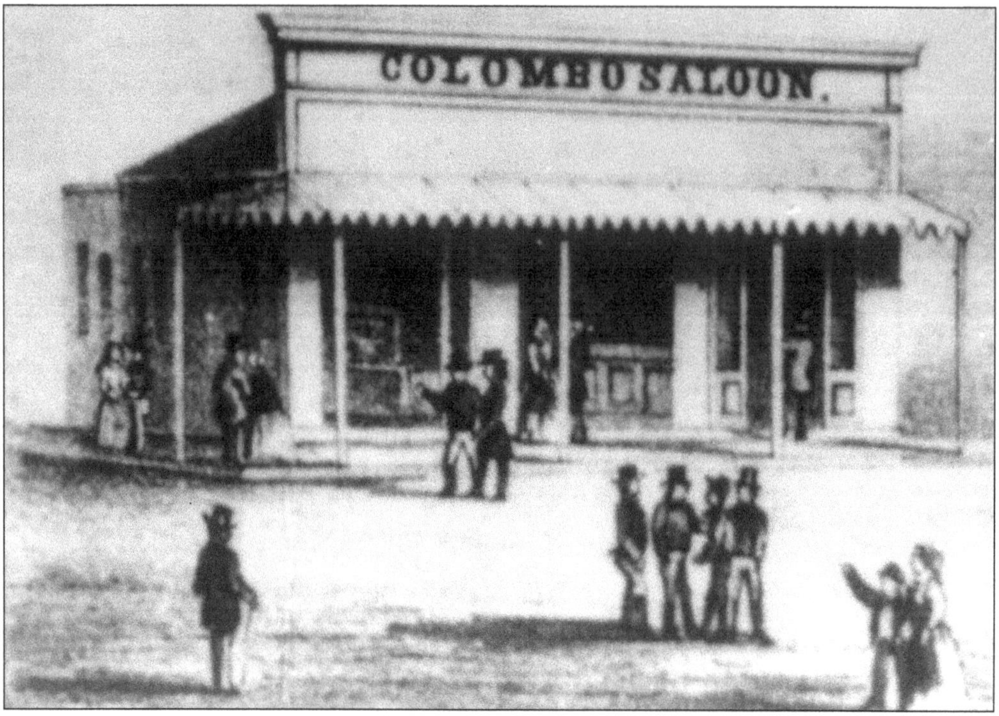

Gambling was part of Columbia from its earliest days. The Columbo Saloon was a wood-frame structure located at the southeast corner of Main and State Streets at the site of the present-day blacksmith shop. The Columbo had a very nice restaurant and advertised "The best eatables the market affords." Board was $9 per week. Another of the saloons, the Long Tom, stretched a full block in length and contained 12 tables that were rented to gamblers who wanted to "buy" a table where they could work. These gamblers were monitored by the proprietor and would be banned if they received too many complaints. There was something for everyone: roulette tables and card tables, games of brag, euchre, lansquenet, monte, and fan tan.

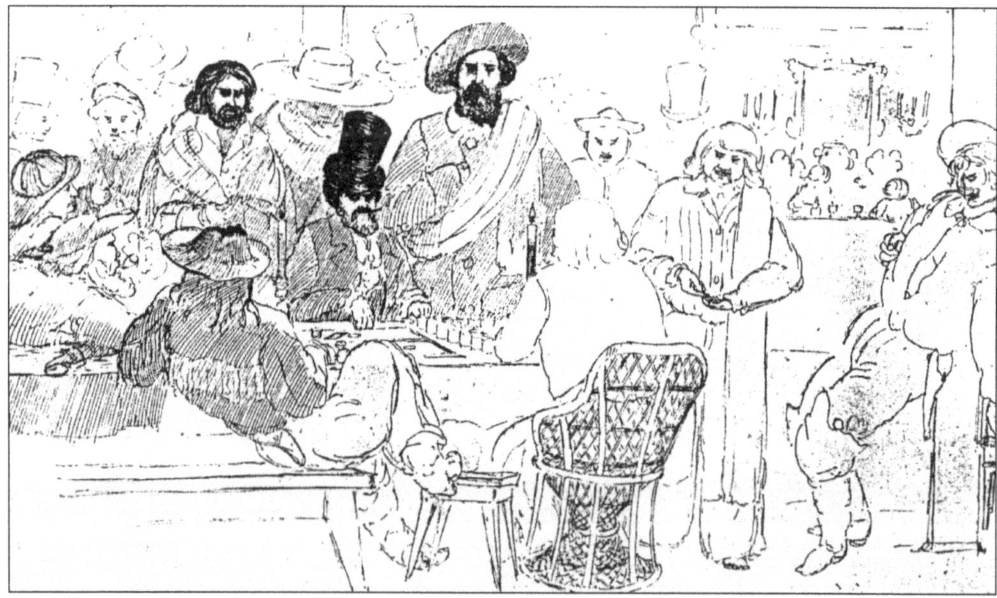

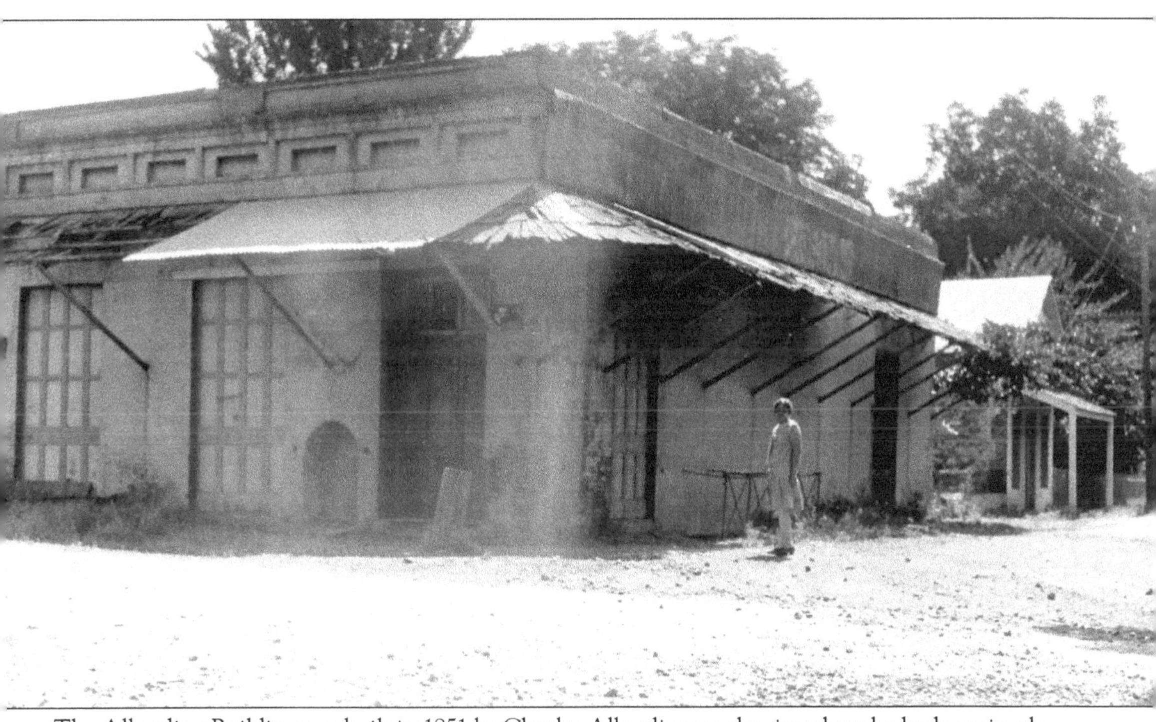

The Alberding Building was built in 1851 by Charles Alberding on the site where he had previously owned and operated a general merchandise store in a wooden frame building. The brick building that stands there today was built in 1856. In 1859, it served as a bakery and coffee saloon. Through the years, the building changed hands many times and has been known as the Alberding Saloon, the Italian Saloon, and the Oyster Saloon. In 1861, it was known as the St. Charles. In the 1930s, it was called the Pioneer Saloon, and had a barber shop in the corner. Since its restoration in 1968, it has been known as the St. Charles Saloon.

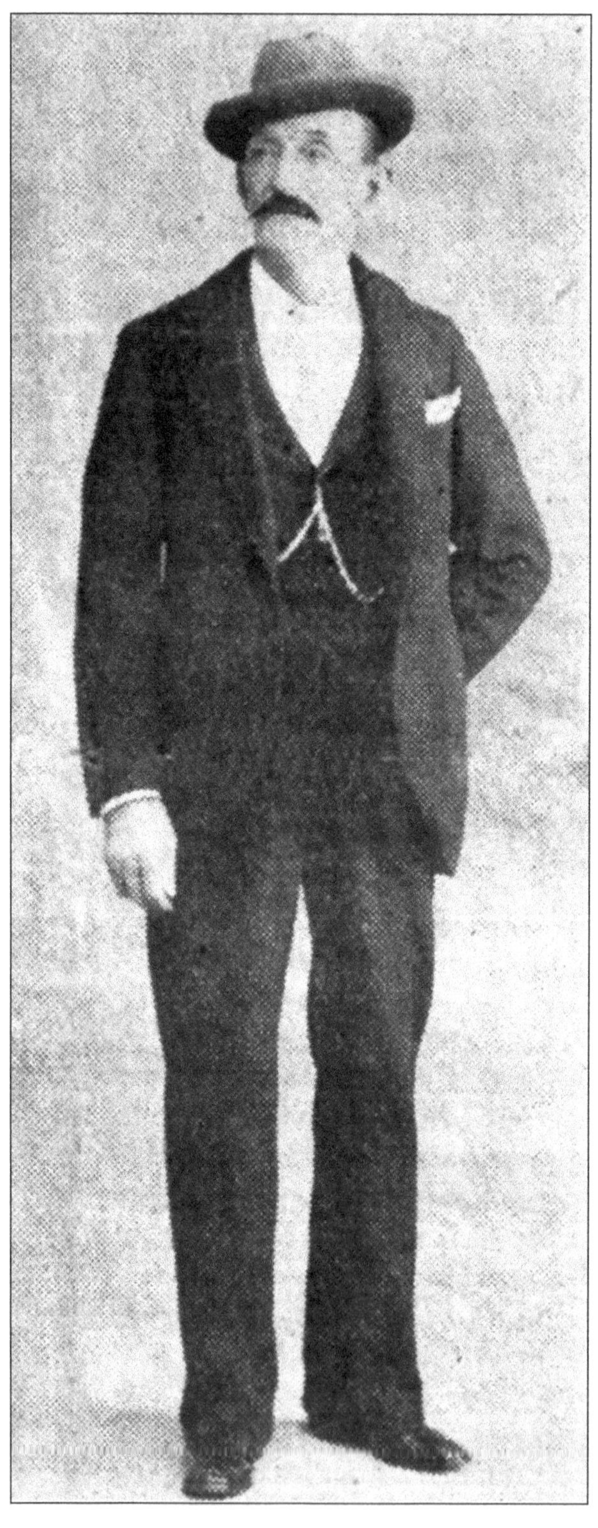

John "Jack" Douglass was born in New York City in 1830. He arrived in California in 1849 and Columbia in 1852, where he worked for several saloon owners before opening his own establishment, the Douglass Saloon, on the corner of Main and Fulton Streets. Douglass was known as "Honest Jack," and miners often came into his saloon, threw bags of gold onto the bar, and asked him to put them in his safe. Most miners never asked for a receipt because Jack was thought to be the most honest man in town. He was very active in town affairs and a working member of the fire department. Unfortunately, his saloon burned down three times, and after the last fire, he moved to Stockton and opened a Douglass Saloon there.

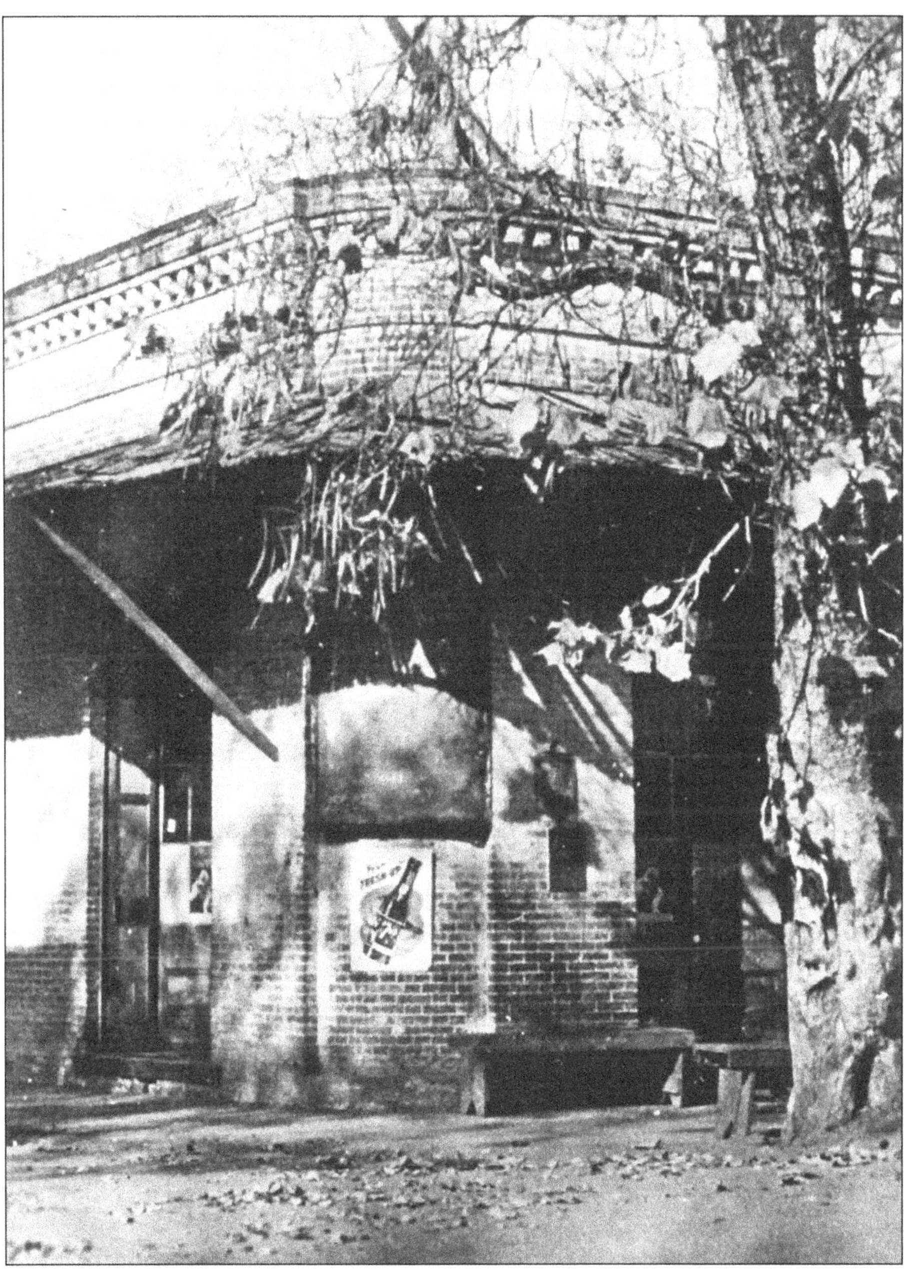

H. Piley and Company had a meat market on this site in the early 1850s. Piley sold the building to Soderer and Marshall in 1854. When it burned later that year, they built another wood-frame building, which also burned in 1857. Soderer and Marshall then built the brick building that still stands today. In late 1857, John Douglass opened a saloon in a small corner of the building, which was well known for both its collection of paintings on the walls and its collection of gold specimens. Local residents and travelers gathered here awaiting the arrival of stages from the Mokelumne Hill and Stockton Stage Line and the Columbia and Stockton Mail and Express Line. Douglass was agent for both stage lines. The building changed hands and names several times through the years. By 1948, it had become known as the Stage Drivers Retreat. The building was restored and opened once again in 1968 under the name Douglass Saloon.

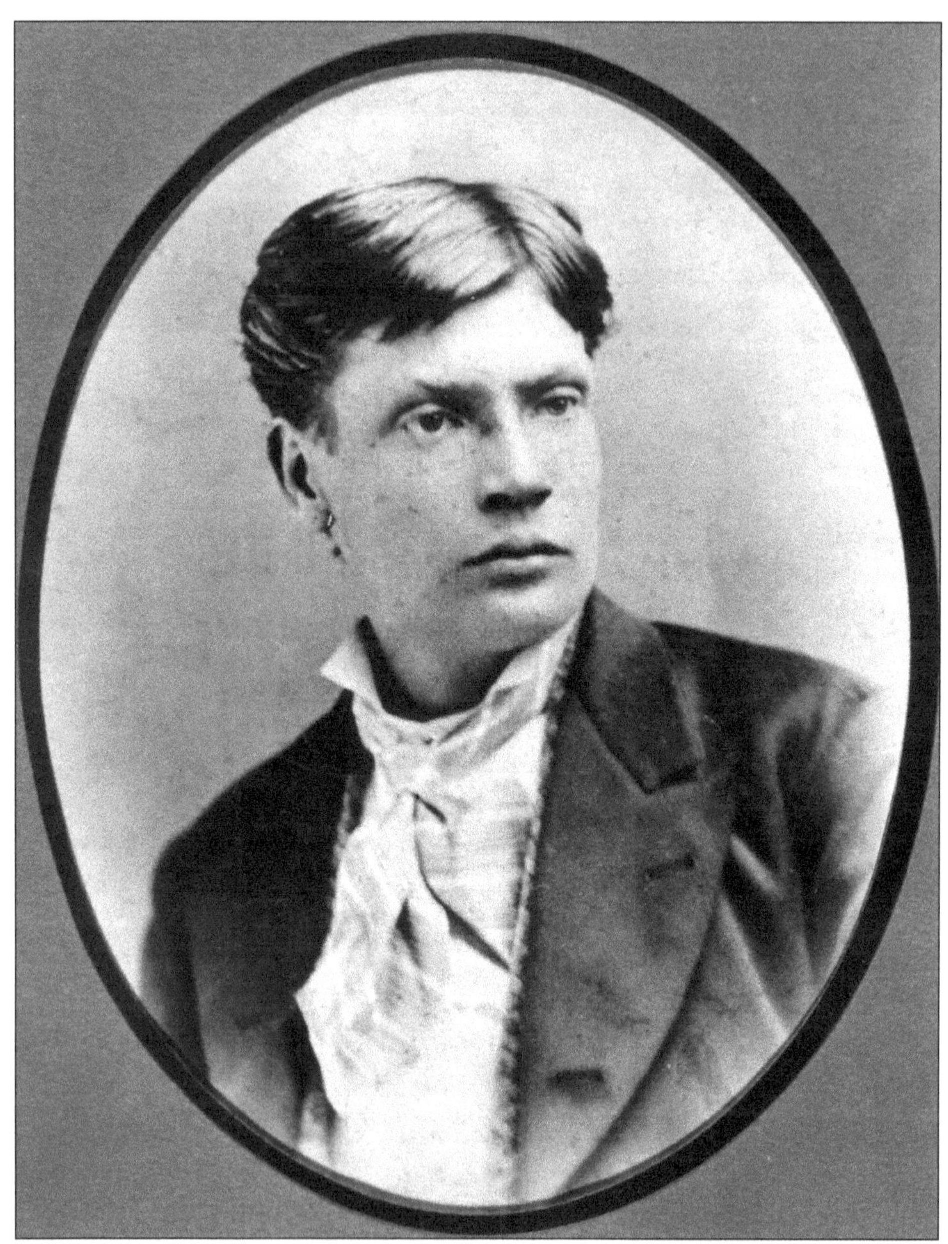

James Fallon was born in Columbia in 1857, the son of Owen and Ellen Fallon who had built and managed the Fallon Hotel. James was a self-taught artist who was responsible for many works in Columbia, including the murals of St. Anne's Church. He also did pen and ink drawings, illustrations, and sign painting. As a member of the Independent Coronet Band of Columbia, James played in various social events including St. Patrick's Day celebrations. In the early 1880s, when his father and mother died, James took over full management of the Fallon Hotel. He made several major improvements, increasing his debts until he eventually lost the hotel. Returning to his artistic endeavors, he married a much younger woman, Rose Siebert, with whom he had a daughter named Ellen. The marriage ended in divorce and Rose got custody of Ellen. James, who served as justice of the peace for several years, was reelected in November 1910 but died suddenly at the age of 51.

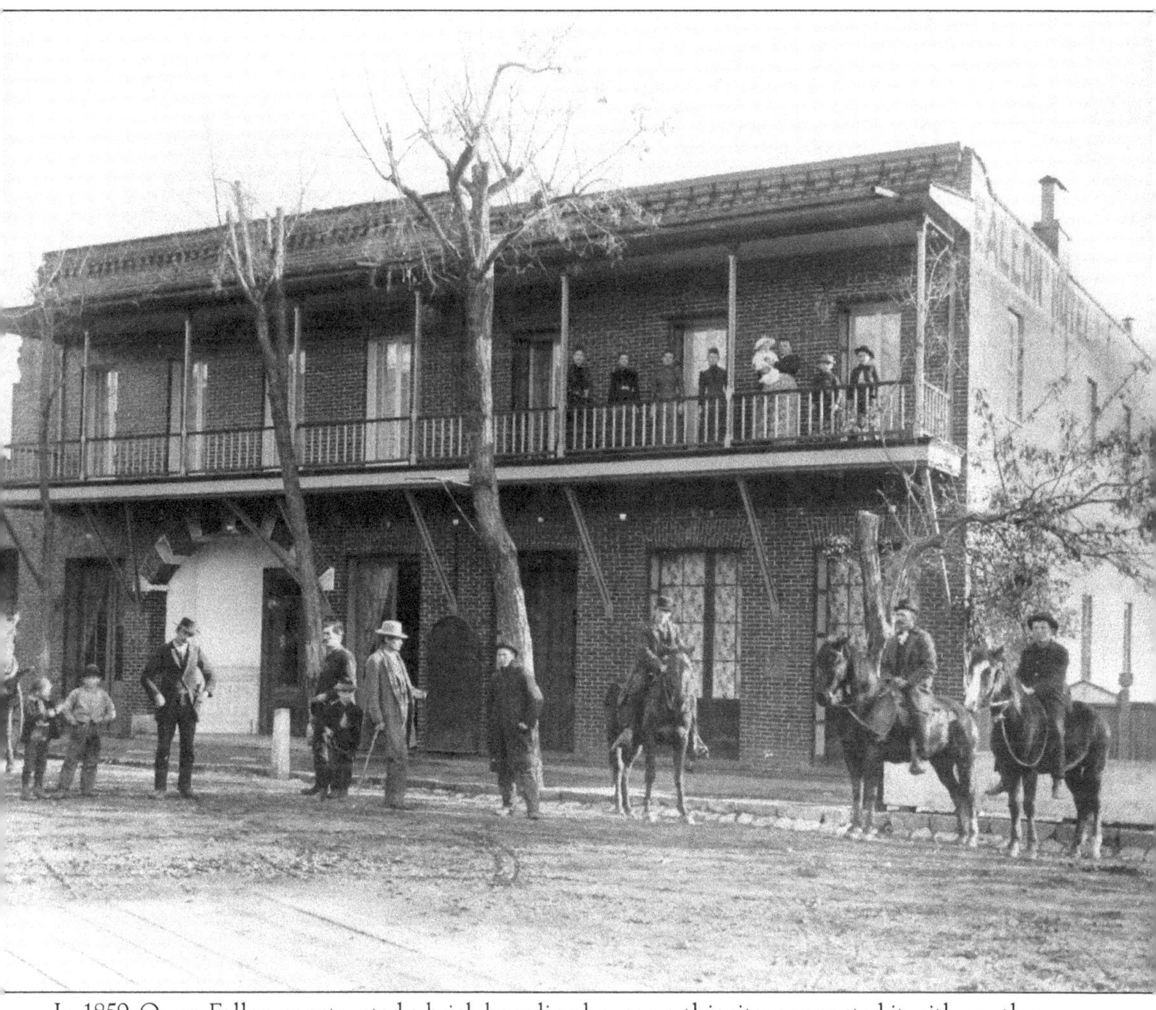

In 1859, Owen Fallon constructed a brick boarding house on this site, connected it with another brick building located directly to the east, turned the second floor into a ballroom, and opened the Fallon Hotel. In 1885, with his parents dead, James Fallon took over the hotel. He made many improvements such as adding a bar, a theater, a large stage, a billiard room, and a dance floor. In 1887, James deeded the property to Rose Gallagher, who sold it to Tom Conlin. From about 1890 until 1944, it was owned by several different people and was known by many different names: Kress Hotel, Columbia Hotel and Opera House, Smith Hotel, and Columbia Inn. Robert Burns, the president of the College (now University) of the Pacific, and his wife owned the building in 1947 when the California State Parks system bought the property. The theater was used by University of the Pacific theatrical students for summer performances. In 1986, the entire structure was restored and reopened as the Fallon Hotel and is now operated by the Columbia City Hotel Corporation.

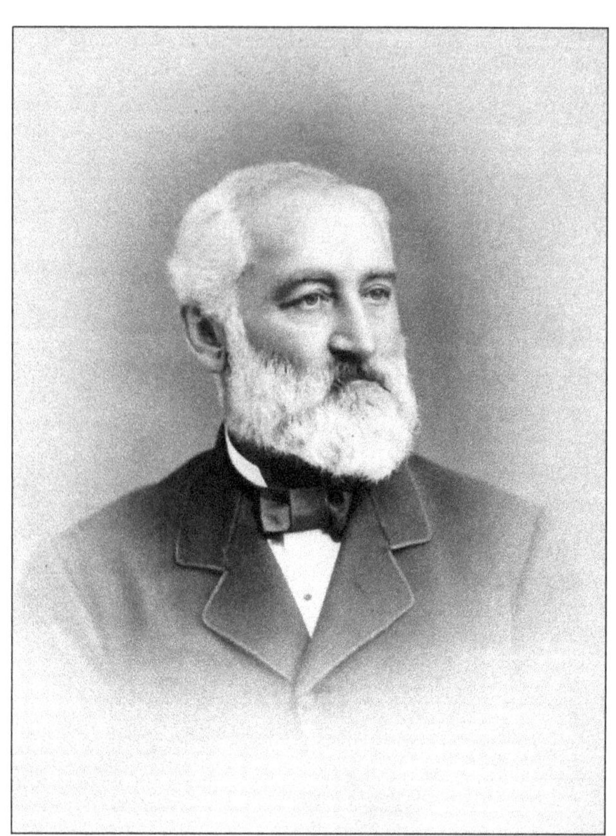

Anton Bixel was born in Germany in about 1823 and emigrated to America in 1849 with his older brother Joseph. Anton came to California in 1851 and settled in Columbia in early 1854, where he established a brewery north of town in Matelot Gulch on Italian Bar Road.

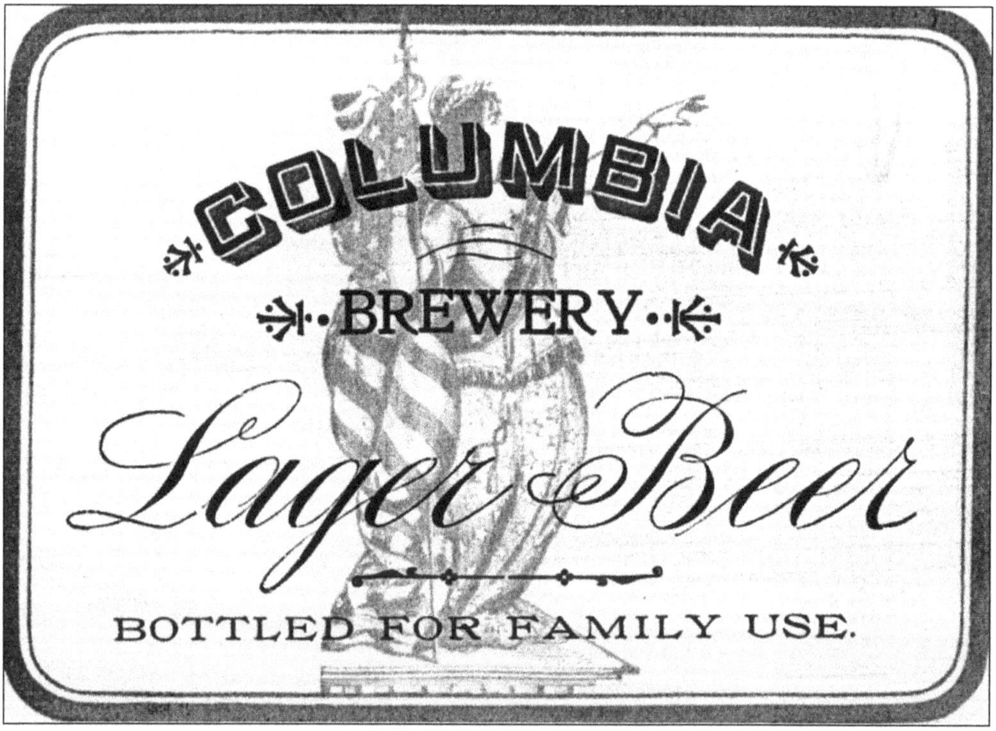

COLUMBIA
BREWERY
Lager Beer
BOTTLED FOR FAMILY USE.

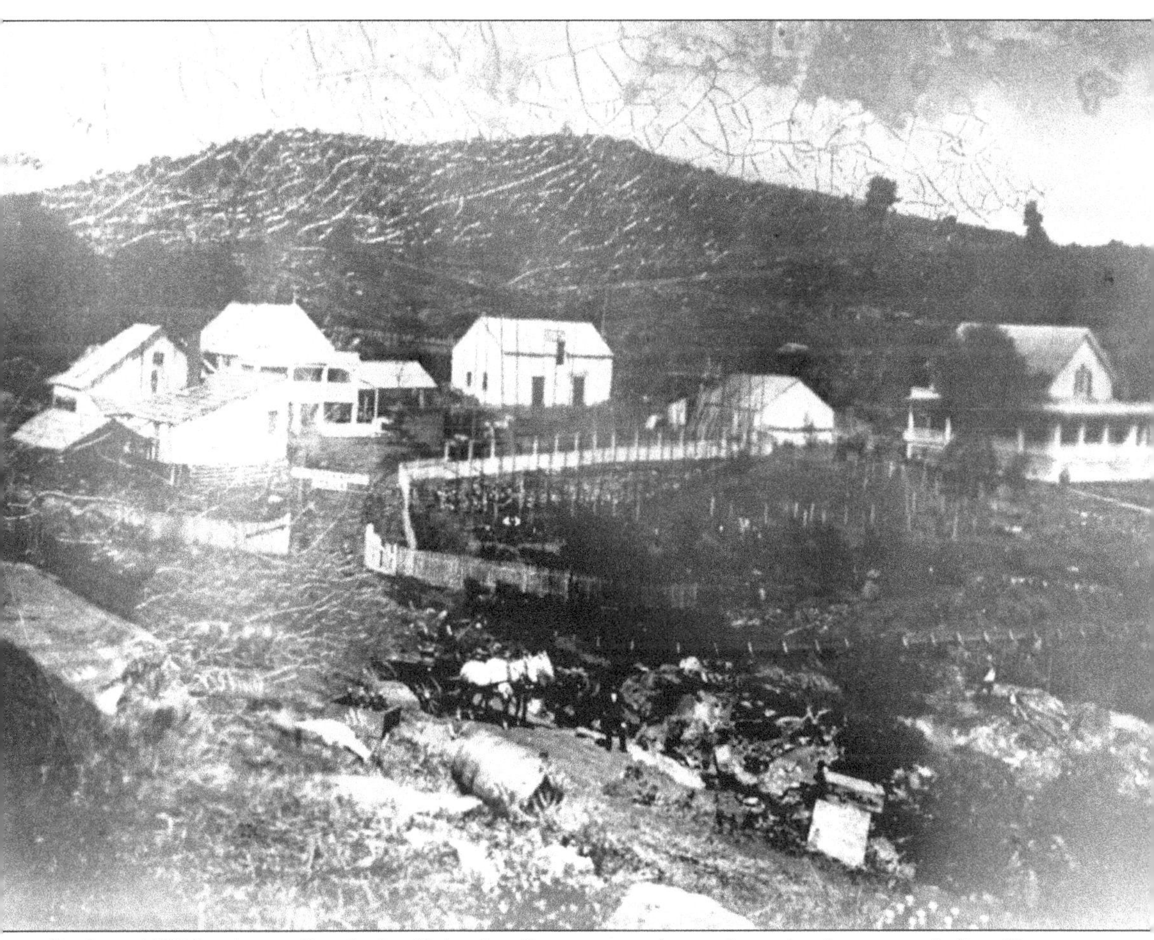

Built in 1854 by Anton Bixel, the Columbia Brewery was located north of town on Italian Bar Road. Anton sold his interest in the brewery to his brother Joseph in 1856. Joseph expanded the brewery, and added a beautiful home in 1860. The Bixel grounds were the scene of many picnics and parties over the years. Fire took down most of the brewery in 1883, but Joseph rebuilt immediately. He is buried in the Columbia Masonic Cemetery. Joseph's son Paul ran the business for several years, and when he died in 1889, his wife, Mary, took over and ran it until her death in 1897, when it was taken over by Paul's brother-in-law, Amel Nelson. After his death, it was inherited by Amel's daughter Ethel. The brewery ran down and the metal was donated to the war effort in World War II. In 1944, while Ethel Nelson was burning trash, the fire got away from her. Her residence burned and was never rebuilt.

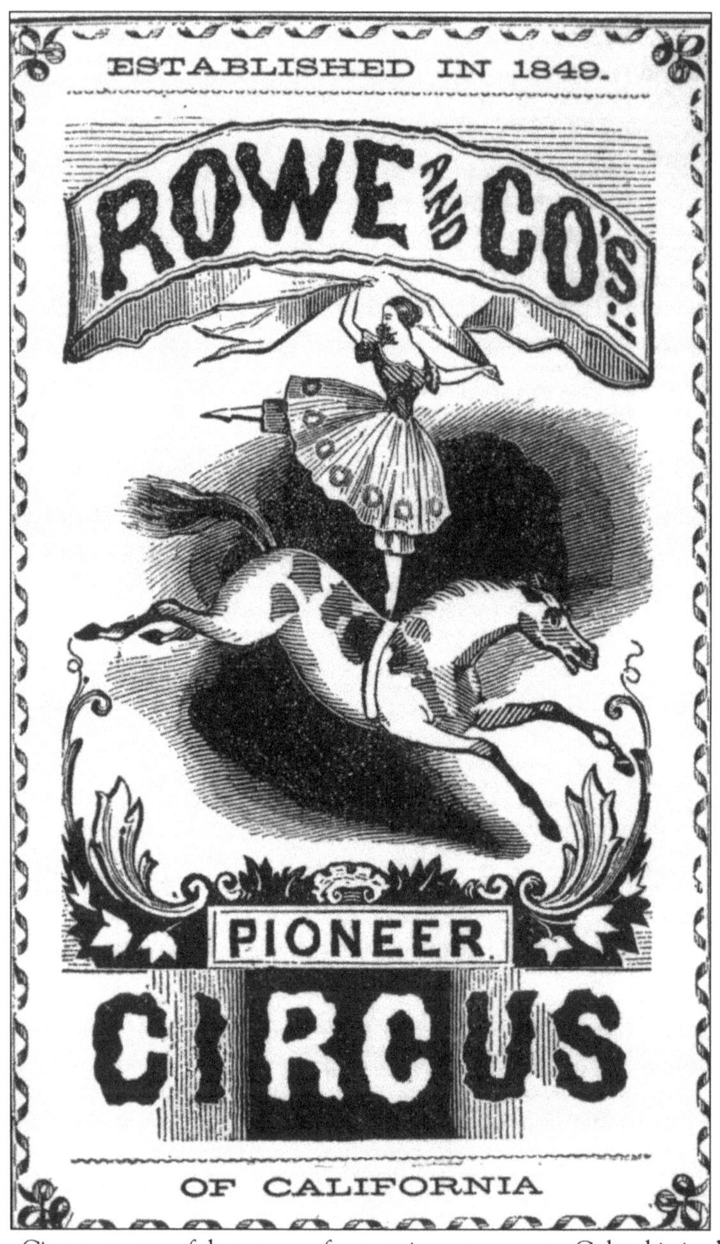

Rowe's Pioneer Circus was one of the groups of entertainers to come to Columbia in the 1850s. The main acts were centered on equestrian events that included a female performer who enchanted the audience with her grace and beauty. Other performers rode in pyramids on multiple horses. Joseph Rowe, owner of the circus and himself a superb horseman, performed graceful, exciting feats while riding on one or more horses. Other circuses that came to Columbia included the Wilson and Zoyara Circus, the National Circus, and Lee and Marshall's Circus. After the fire of 1854 destroyed most of the town and damaged equipment belonging to the Columbia Hook and Ladder Company, Lee and Marshall's Circus performed in a benefit to help replace the damaged fire equipment. Among the many other entertainers enjoyed by residents were Elisa Biscaccianti, an opera star known as "The American Thrush" who gave three performances in Columbia, and the Backus Minstrels who gave a concert at the Columbia Exchange in June 1854.

Printed and sold by Wm. B. Cooke & Co., Law Stationers,
No. 158 Montgomery Street. San Francisco.

Warrant.

In the Justice's Court of the Second **Township,**

IN AND FOR THE

County of Tuolumne

The People of the State of California,

To the Sheriff or any Constable of the County of Tuolumne

Information, upon oath, having been this day laid before me, by I. B. Ford that the crime of murder has been committed, and accusing George Hildreth thereof, you are therefore commanded forthwith, to arrest the above named George Hildreth and bring him before me, at my Court, or in case of my absence or inability to act, before the nearest or most accessible magistrate in this County.

Dated at my office, this 21st day of November A. D., 1859

[signature]

Justice of the Peace of said Township.

In November 1859, Deputy George A. Hildreth was on his way to Yankee Hill to serve some papers when he stopped at a saloon for a drink. He got into a fight with George W. Chase, shots were fired, and Chase was killed. Rumors began to circulate that Hildreth had gotten away with murder. The city marshal charged Hildreth with willfully and unlawfully killing Chase. At his trial, Louisa Passemore said that Hildreth used abusive, vulgar, and threatening language with Chase, and that Hildreth drew a pistol hidden in his sleeve and fired it at Chase. She added that Chase returned fire. Other witnesses disagreed and said that Chase started the fight, fired first, and that Hildreth acted in self-defense. Passemore finally admitted she had lied. She then testified that Chase drew his pistol first. When Hildreth had been Columbia city marshal, he had arrested Chase, and Chase had threatened Hildreth many times since then. Two days before the shooting, Chase was heard to say that he would kill Hildreth if he ever crossed his path. Hildreth was exonerated.

Printed and sold by Wm. B. Cooke & Co., Importing and Jobbing Stationers, 624 Montgomery Street, Montgomery Block, San Francisco.

State of California.

In the Justice's Court Second Township,

IN AND FOR THE

COUNTY OF Tuolumne

The people of the State of California to

J. A. Smith ×
J. B. Douglass ×
G. Millard
A. S. Hildreth ×
Abner Potts
Saml Elten ×

R. Downer

GREETING:

We command you, and each of you, that all and singular business and excuses being laid aside, you and each of you be and appear before the undersigned, one of the Justices of the Peace of the said Township, in the said County, on the 6th day of August A. D. 1864 at 10 o'clock A M., then and there to testify in a certain action now pending before said Justice, wherein The People are Plaintiffs, and George Kowgun is Defendant, on the part of Deft

and for a failure to attend, you will be deemed guilty of a contempt of Court, and liable to pay all loss and damage sustained thereby to the party aggrieved.

Given under my hand this 6th day of Aug A. D. 1864

C. C. White JUSTICE OF THE PEACE OF SAID TOWNSHIP.

George Kow Gun, a prosperous Chinese Columbia merchant, was ordered to appear in the Columbia Justice Court on August 6, 1864, to answer the charge that he murdered Tuck Lem. He was found not guilty of the charge.

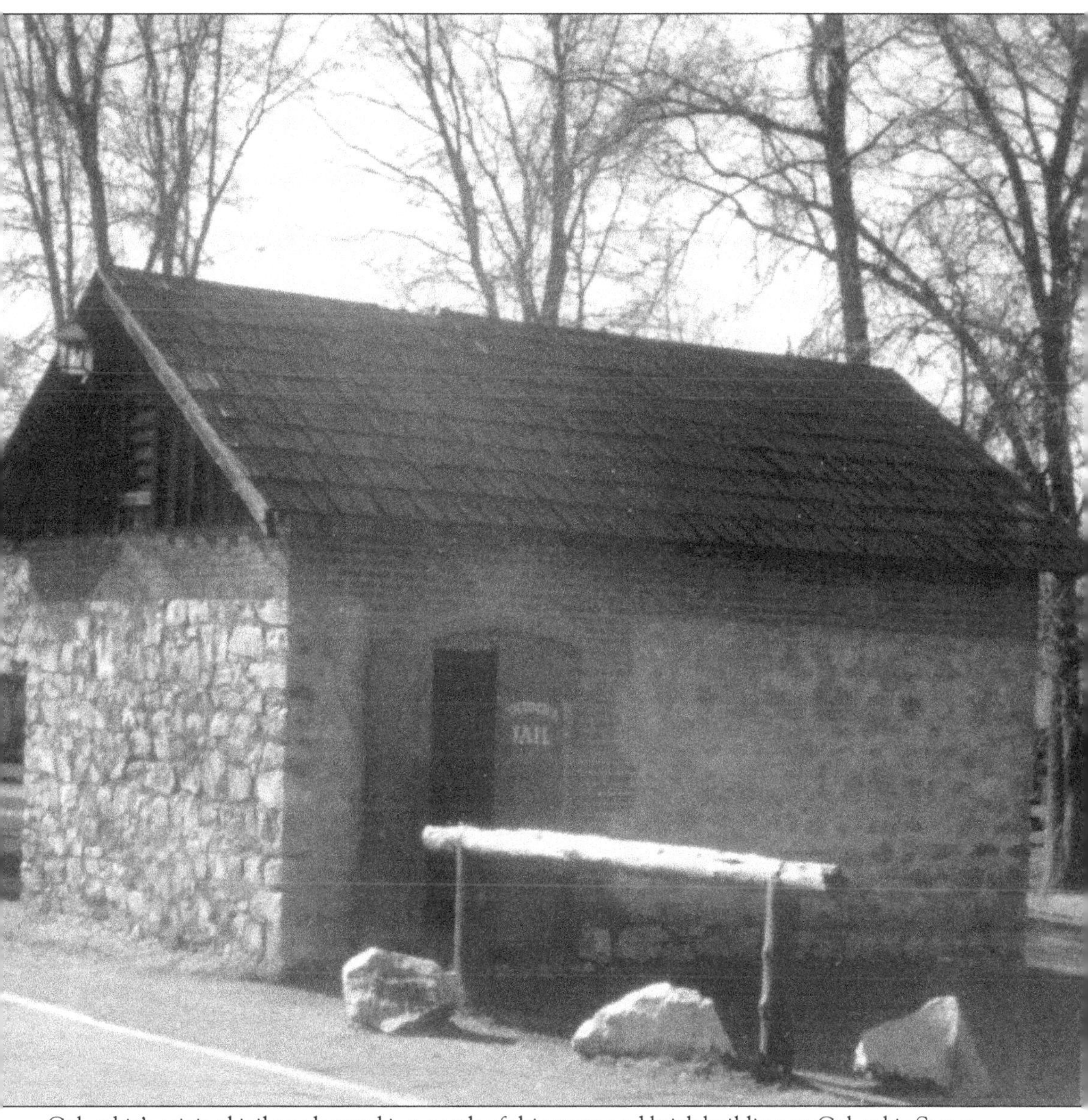

Columbia's original jail was located just north of this stone and brick building on Columbia Street. This building was used to store black powder, but served as the town jail from the 1890s through the 1930s. It has two jail cells with wooden doors and a hinged pass-through window for food. There are no other windows in the building.

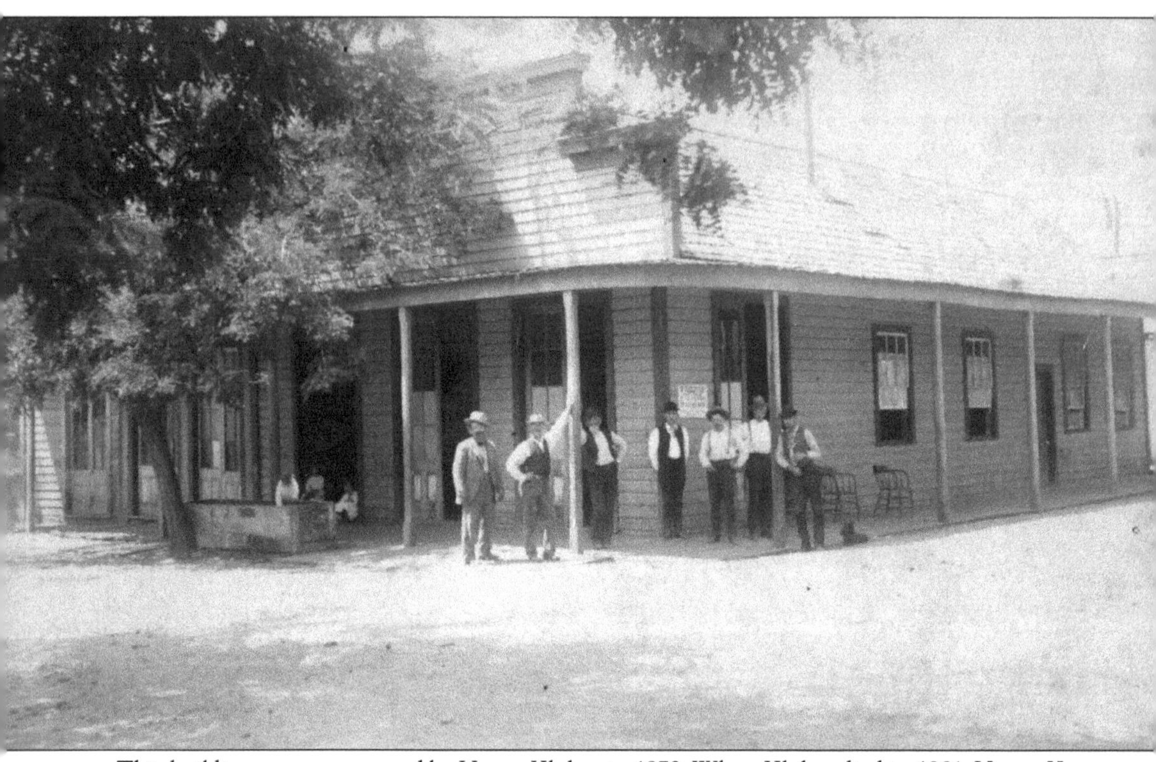

This building was constructed by Henry Kluber in 1879. When Kluber died in 1881, Henry Kruse purchased the building and owned it through 1890. A fire that started in the premises destroyed the building in 1920. It was subsequently rebuilt by Angelo Nadotti and is now the Columbia House Restaurant. Here several Columbia residents can be seen in what was then the Kruse saloon and, from left to right, include Louis Page, Charlie Grant, Joe Johnson, Bill Sweeny, Ed Murphy, Henry Kruse, and Will McKenzie. In the doorway are two sisters, Norma and Carrie. Henry J. Kruse, son of the owner, is playing in the water trough.

Five

FIRE!

Columbia's first buildings were constructed of boards and canvas and crowded together, while cooking and lighting utilized open flames—an obvious recipe for disaster.

With foresight, Col. Thomas Cazneau helped to organize the Columbia Hook and Ladder Company. Members carried pikes and ladders to tear down walls, clear fuel, and cut off flames. In April 1853, a committee was organized to hire night watchmen, procure taxes for funding the fire company, and develop the fire prevention ordinances in town.

On July 10, 1854, a fire ignited in an empty store at the southern end of Columbia and raced through the dry wood and canvas buildings. Not until the flames reached the edge of town, where houses were spaced farther apart, was the fire company able to stop the fire. In town, one building survived and eight others under construction were left relatively undamaged. What was the building material used in the surviving structures? Brick.

On March 31, 1856, John Leary set about organizing a hose company for the town. Water was to be supplied from the domestic pipes of the New England Water Company, and soon the Columbia Hose Company was erecting a frame building on Fulton Street for their hose cart.

On August 25, 1857, a fire started in the Chinese section of town north of Jackson Street and again raced through the business section of town, consuming the many wooden structures rebuilt after the fire of 1854. Many citizens had learned from the previous fire and had rebuilt using brick, but the new buildings' walls were too thin, and their super-heated status ignited the contents in neighboring stores.

The hose company was valiant in its efforts to fight the fire, as were the hook-and-ladder men, but the water failed. Sewell Knapp reportedly used barrels of vinegar applied by bucket brigade to extinguish flames in his store, but H. N. Brown wasn't so lucky. Even though the fire had passed his store, Brown raced there nonetheless, knowing there was black powder stored in the basement. As he opened one of the doors, the building exploded, collapsing two walls and killing him and four others. One man was caught under the iron door as it was blown from its hinges into the street. The quickly advancing fire was finally halted on Broadway by using water from the flumes of the Tuolumne County Water Company.

Most buildings after the 1857 fire would be rebuilt of brick. Columbia's citizens were tired of being burned out, but it would take women to finally set things right. They would raise the capital to purchase the town's pumping engines.

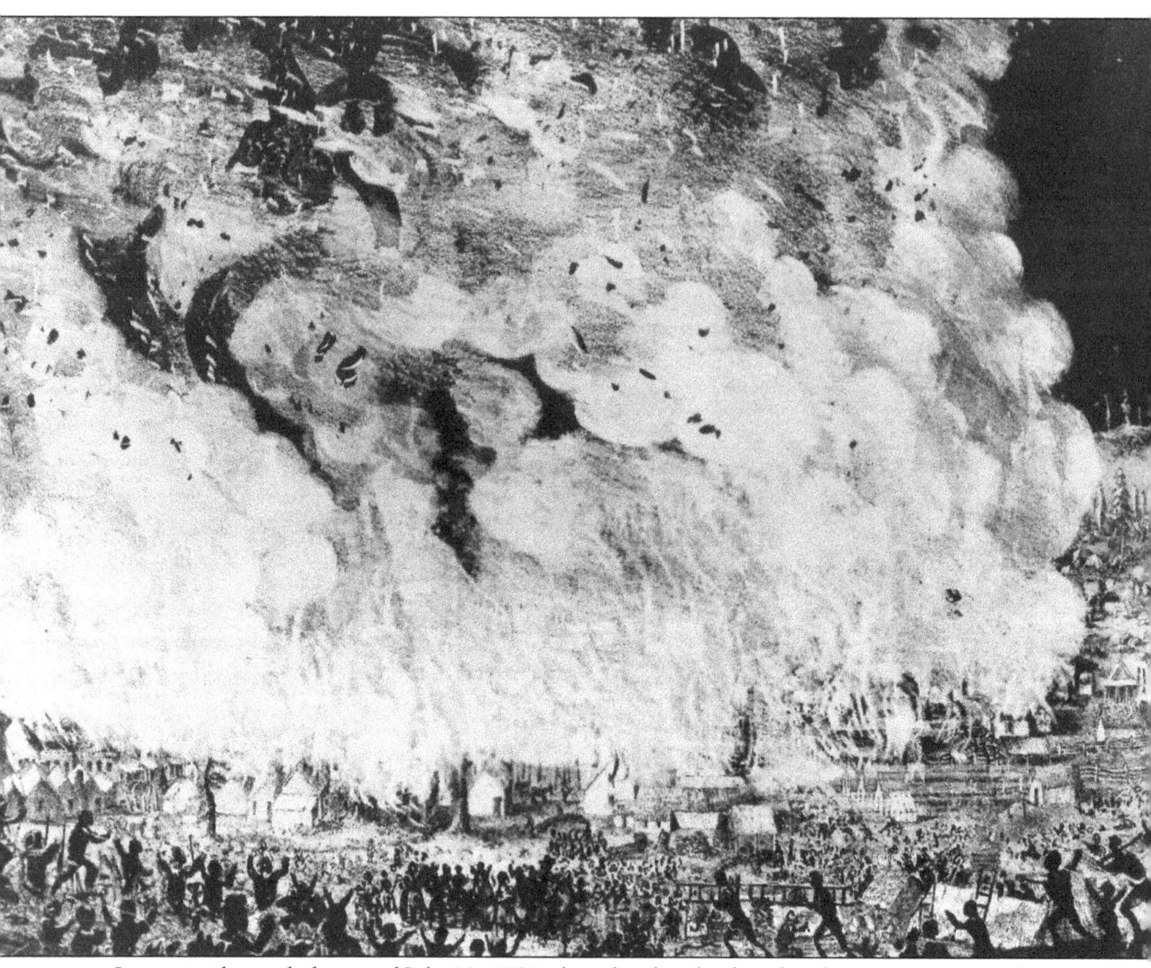

It was in the early hours of July 10, 1854, that the drawbacks of early construction techniques finally caught up with the booming city of Columbia, when canvas, wood, and other easily ignitable materials quickly fed a hungry fire that eventually destroyed the commercial district. Then, as now, summers in the California gold country are dry and hot, and together the weather and flammable building materials used to construct most of the town, created a recipe for disaster. When the smoke cleared and citizens were able to venture back into town, only one commercial building remained: the Donnell & Parsons Building, the only finished brick building in town. In the aftermath of this fire, the appearance of the town would change dramatically. Even before the ashes cooled, kilns were built and brick buildings began to rise in place of many of the burned wooden structures.

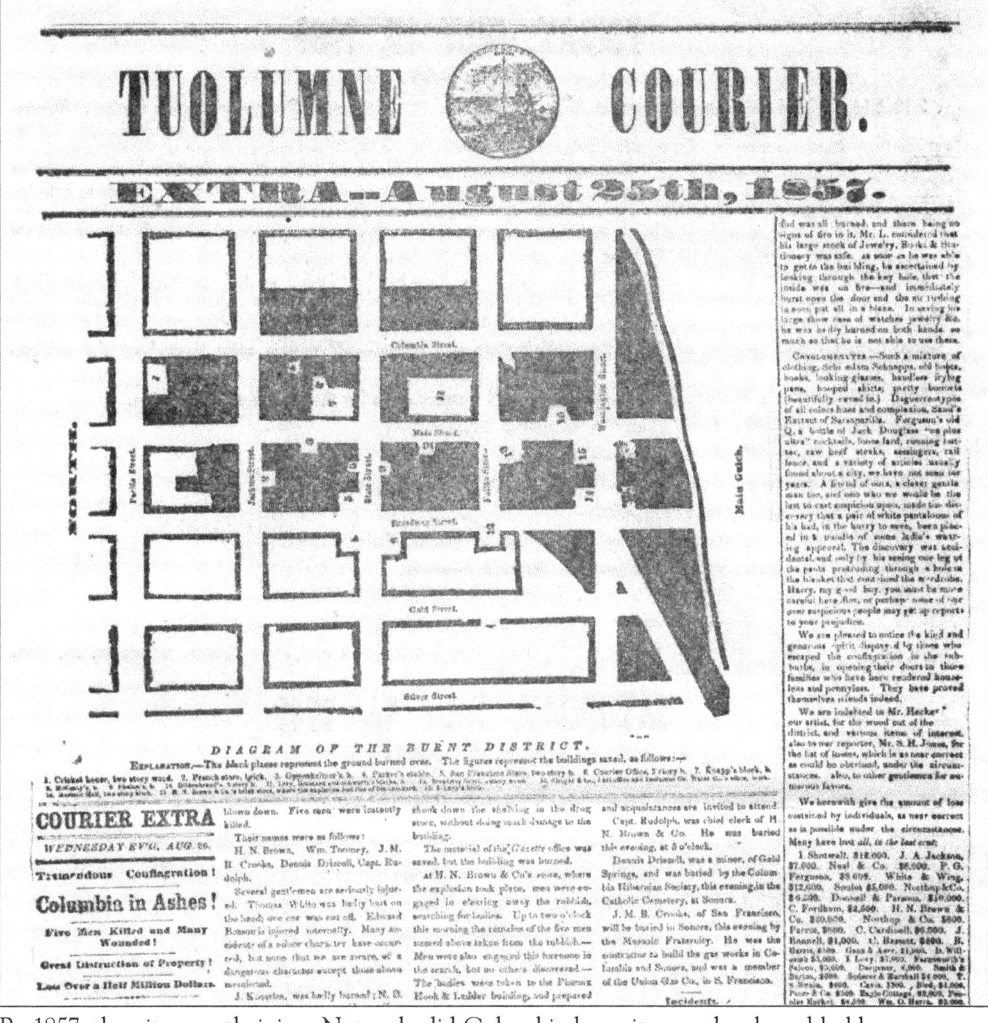

TUOLUMNE COURIER.

EXTRA—August 25th, 1857.

DIAGRAM OF THE BURNT DISTRICT.

EXPLANATION.—The black places represent the ground burned over. The figures represent the buildings saved, as follows:—

COURIER EXTRA

WEDNESDAY EVG. AUG. 26.

Tremendous Conflagration!

Columbia in Ashes!

Five Men Killed and Many Wounded!

Great Destruction of Property!

Loss Over a Half Million Dollars.

[illegible] blown down. Five men were instantly killed.

Their names were as follows:

H. N. Brown, Wm. Toomey, J. M. B. Crooks, Dennis Driscoll, Capt. Rudolph.

Several gentlemen are seriously injured. Thomas White was badly hurt on the head; one ear was cut off. Edward Bosson is injured internally. Many accidents of a minor character have occurred, but none that we are aware, of a dangerous character except those above mentioned.

J. Knowles, was badly burned; N. D. [illegible] shook down the shelving in the drug store, without doing much damage to the building.

The material of the Gazette office was saved, but the building was burned.

At H. N. Brown & Co's store, where the explosion took place, men were engaged in clearing away the rubbish, searching for bodies. Up to two o'clock this morning the remains of the five men named above taken from the rubbish.—Men were also engaged this forenoon in the search, but no others discovered.—The bodies were taken to the Phoenix Hook & Ladder building, and prepared [illegible] and acquaintances are invited to attend.

Capt. Rudolph, was chief clerk of H. N. Brown & Co. He was buried this evening, at 5 o'clock.

Dennis Driscoll, was a miner, of Gold Springs, and was buried by the Columbia Hibernian Society, this evening, in the Catholic Cemetery, at Sonora.

J. M. B. Crooks, of San Francisco, will be buried in Sonora, this evening by the Masonic Fraternity. He was the contractor to build the gas works in Columbia and Sonora, and was a member of the Union Gas Co., in S. Francisco.

Incidents.

[illegible] was all burned, and there being no signs of fire in it, Mr. L. considered that his large stock of Jewelry, Books & Stationery was safe. As soon as he was able to get to the building, he ascertained by looking through the key hole, that the inside was on fire—and immediately burst open the door and the air rushing in soon put all in a blaze. In saving his large show case of watches jewelry &c. he was badly burned on both hands so much so that he is not able to use them.

CHALOUPEAUTTES.—Such a mixture of clothing, Schiedam Schnapps, old boots, books, looking glasses, handless frying pans, hooped skirts, pretty bonnets (beautifully caved in.) Daguerreotypes of all colors hues and complexion, Sand's Extract of Sarsaparilla, Ferguson's old Q. a bottle of Jack Douglass "ne plus ultra" cocktails, loose lard, running butter, raw beef steaks, sausages, rail fence, and a variety of articles usually found about a city, we have not seen for years. A friend of ours, a clever gentleman too, and one who we would be the last to cast suspicion upon, made the discovery that a pair of white pantaloons of his had, in the hurry to save, been placed in a bundle of some ladie's wearing apparel. The discovery was accidental, and only by his seeing one leg of the pants protruding through a hole in the blanket that contained the wardrobe. Harry, my good boy, you must be more careful here after, or perhaps some of our over suspicious people may get up reports to your prejudice.

We are pleased to notice the kind and generous spirit displayed by those who escaped the conflagration in the suburbs, in opening their doors to those families who have been rendered houseless and pennyless. They have proved themselves friends indeed.

We are indebted to Mr. Hecker our artist, for the wood cut of the district, and various items of interest, also to our reporter, Mr. S. H. Jones, for the list of losses, which is as near correct as could be obtained, under the circumstances, also, to other gentlemen for numerous favors.

We herewith give the amount of lose sustained by individuals, as near correct as is possible under the circumstances. Many have lost all, to the last cent.

I. Shotwell, $12,000, J. A. Jackson, $7,000, Neal & Co. $6,000, P. G. Ferguson, $8,000, White & Wing, $12,000, Soulot $5,000, Northup & Co. $6,500, Donnell & Parsons, $10,000, C. Fordham, $2,500, H. N. Brown & Co. $30,000, Northup & Co. $600, Parrot, $600, C. Cardinell, $6,000, J. Bonnell, $1,000, C. Bassett, $400, B. Harris, [illegible] Gans & Auer, $1,[illegible] [illegible] $1,000, I. Levy, $1,000, Farnsworth's Saloon, $5,000, [illegible] Smith & Barton, $800, Soderer & Marshall $4,000, T. [illegible] $400, Cava, $300, Bied, $1,000, Page & Co. $300, Eagle Cottage, $3,800, Peoples Market, $4,500, Wm. O. Harris, $3,000.

By 1857, the city was thriving. Not only did Columbia have its own hook and ladder company, but it also had a hose company, organized after the 1854 fire. Both forces were fairly successful against a number of small fires, but in the evening of August 25, 1857, a fire broke out in what was later claimed to be the Chinese section of town. Again, fire raced through wooden buildings and again the fire companies responded, but the water system failed, rendering the hose company powerless. As the fire gained momentum, thin, eight-inch common brick walls transferred heat from the burning contents of one building to its neighbor so that the fire moved through town brick building to brick building from within. Fire companies from Sonora eventually arrived to help and together they were able to stop the fire at the south end of town with water from the Tuolumne Water Company flumes. The town began to rebuild yet again the following day, but something needed to change.

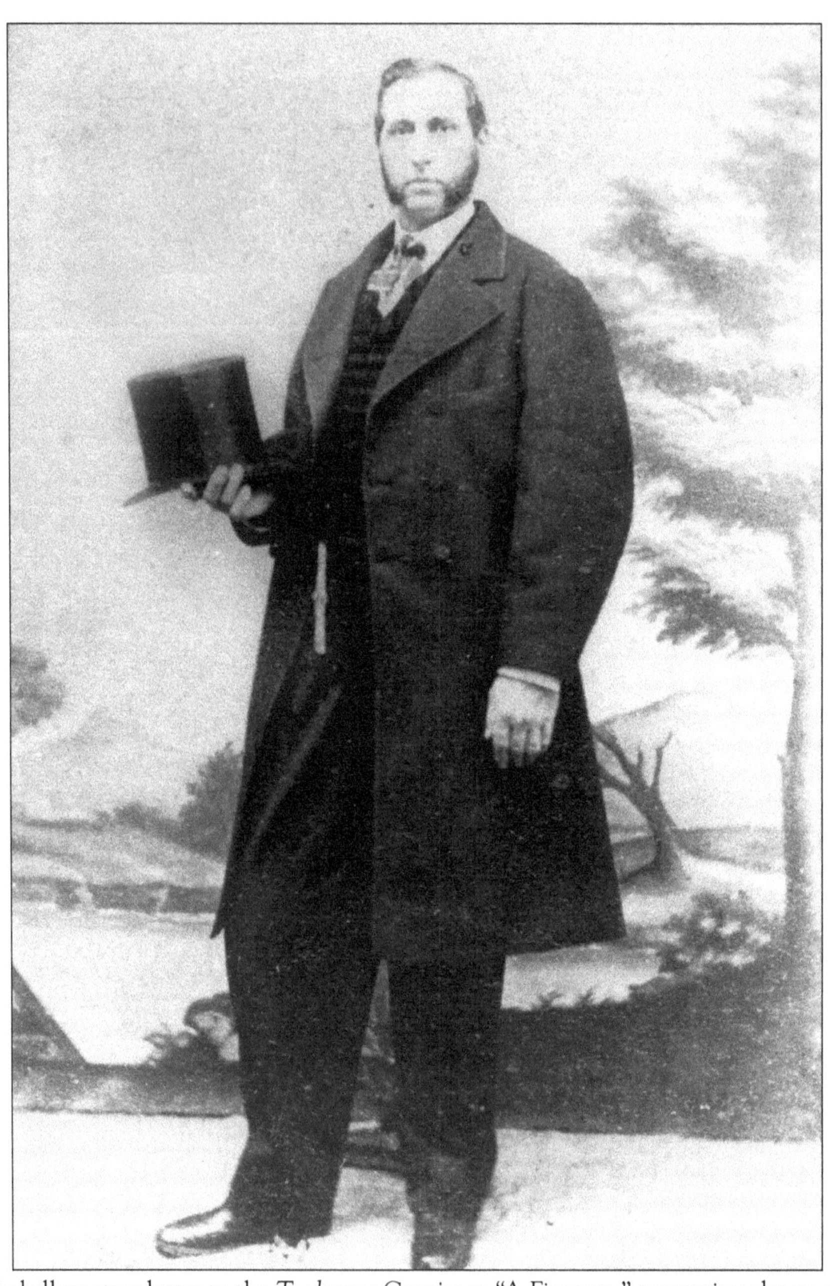

John Haskell wrote a letter to the *Tuolumne Courier* as "A Fireman," suggesting the purchase of pumping engines for the town. Haskell was very much in favor of two engines because one engine could pump from a water supply and send the water to the second, increasing the distance that hose could be utilized. Prior to this, the city council had considered the idea of building a new reservoir with new pipes, at the estimated cost of $12,000. Haskell pointed out that, in fact, two engines and houses for each could be had for around $6,500, far less than the anticipated cost of a new water system. It was an easy sell and a man was appointed to examine an engine reportedly for sale in San Francisco. The engine was found to be satisfactory, and a request for money was sent back to Columbia. Merchants in town were suddenly engaged in heated discussion about how to tax themselves for this new level of protection, with no agreement being reached.

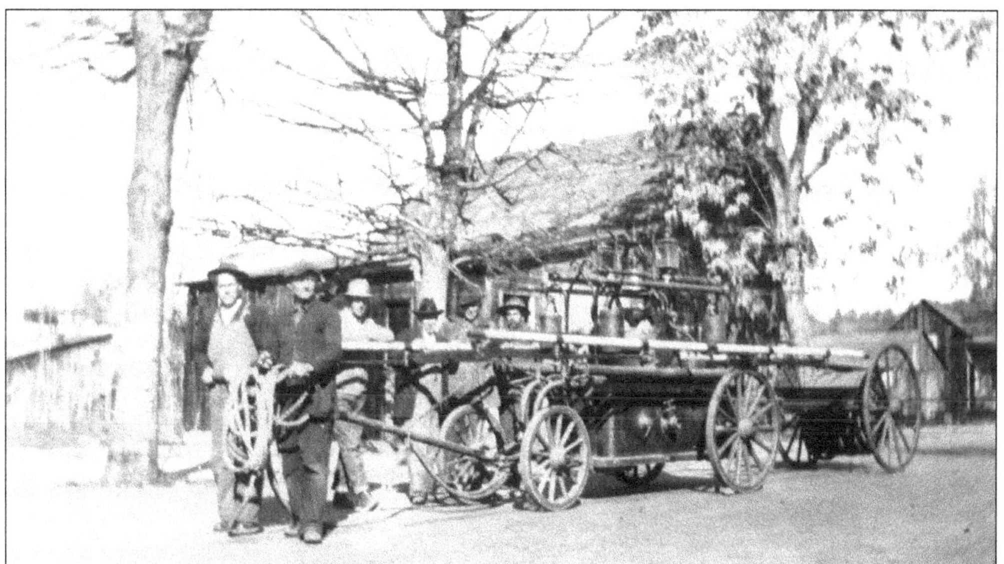

"Papeete" was built in Boston by the Hunneman Company, a renowned builder of pumping engines. She could be had for a mere $1,800, but the money was an issue with the merchants of Columbia. A few women, growing upset at the balking merchants, organized themselves, held a fund-raising "Engine Fair," and raised nearly $2,000 within a week, much to the consternation of the men. The money was promptly sent and the engine purchased.

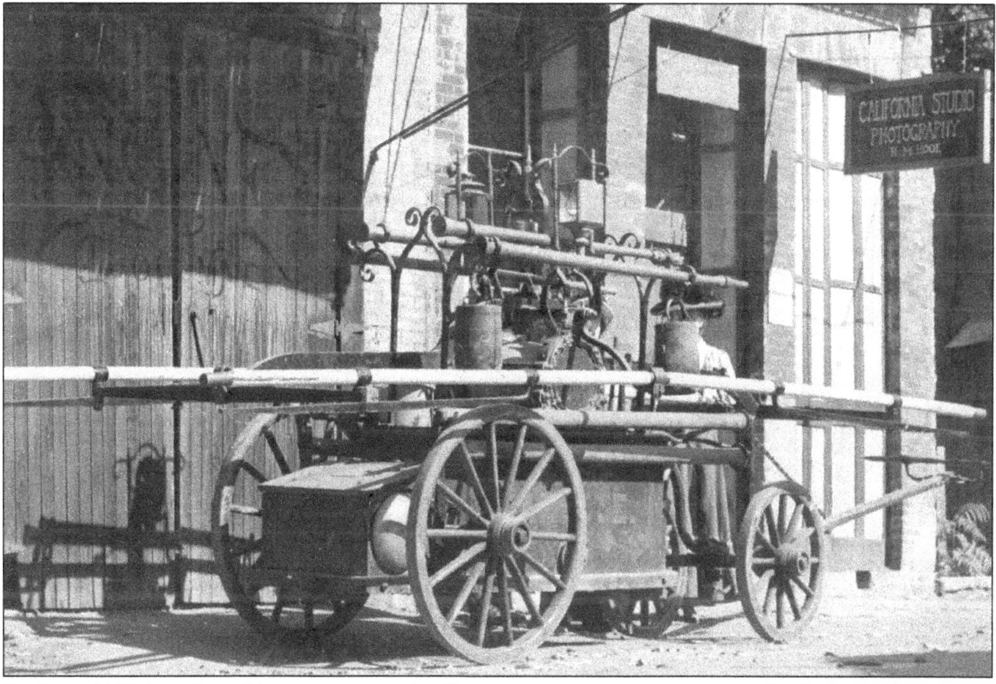

Built in 1852 for a Brooklyn company, the Papeete pumping engine was rebuilt in 1854 as a very ornate affair intended for the island of Tahiti. Instead it ended up in San Francisco in 1859. Because women had raised money to purchase the machine, concerns were raised about the scantily clad sea goddesses on the sides. Screens, fitted over the paintings, provided modesty as the engine was pulled into town late in 1859 with much fanfare.

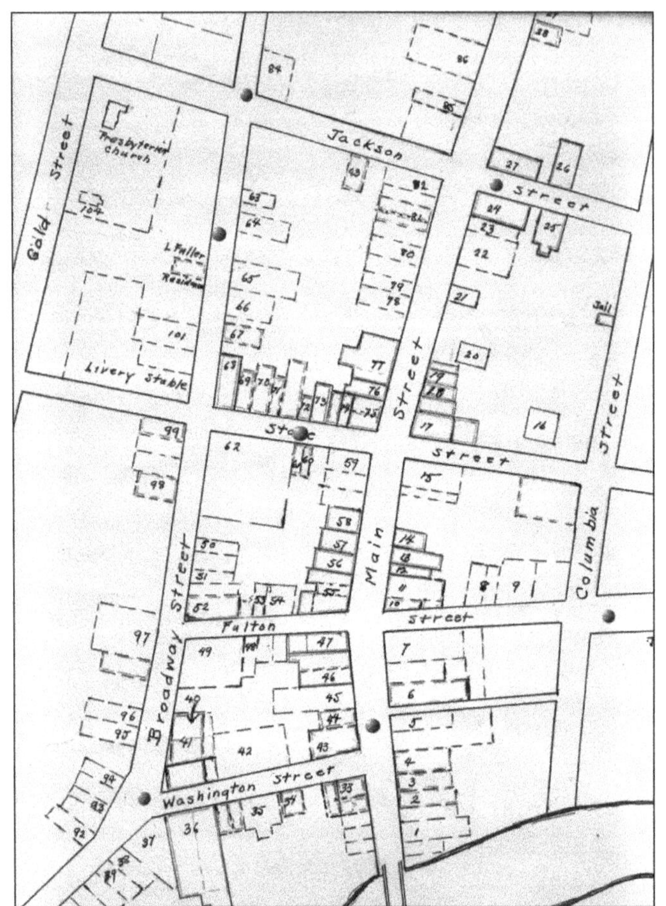

The next issue in terms of fire fighting was obtaining a reliable water supply. In fact, reliable water had been Columbia's biggest problem in terms of mining and fighting fire. In response, the city council decided to build a series of cisterns throughout town. Cisterns, or underground tanks, would always be full and ready for service in time of need. Two engines could easily provide water to all parts of town with one engine pumping from the cistern to the other fighting the fire. The cistern shown here is located on Jackson Street in front of the Mercantile. A hard suction hose was placed into the hole and the engine would draft directly from the tank below, either fighting fire or supplying the other engine.

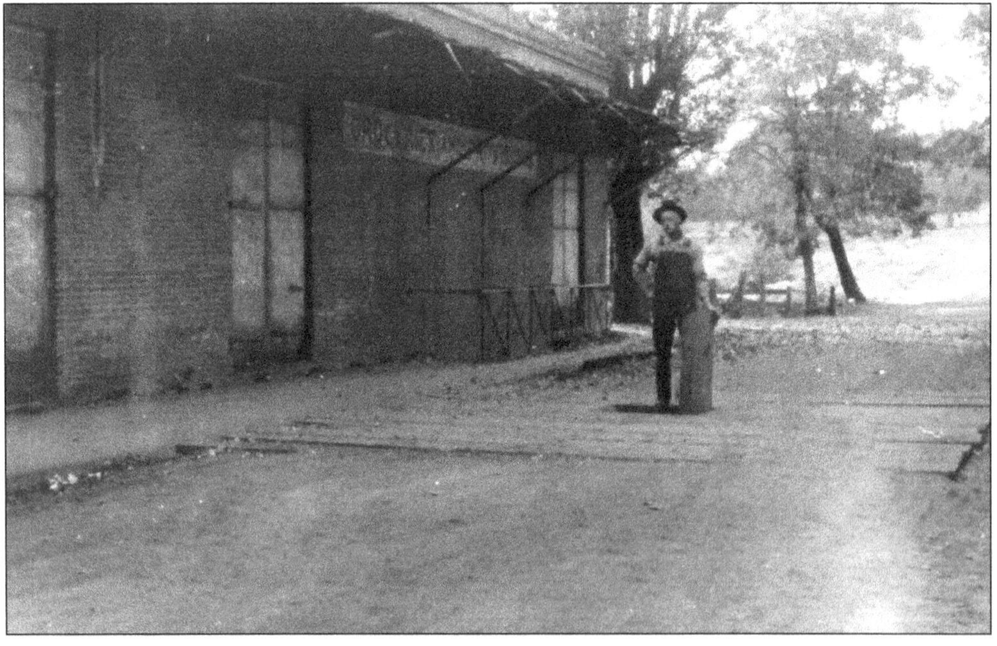

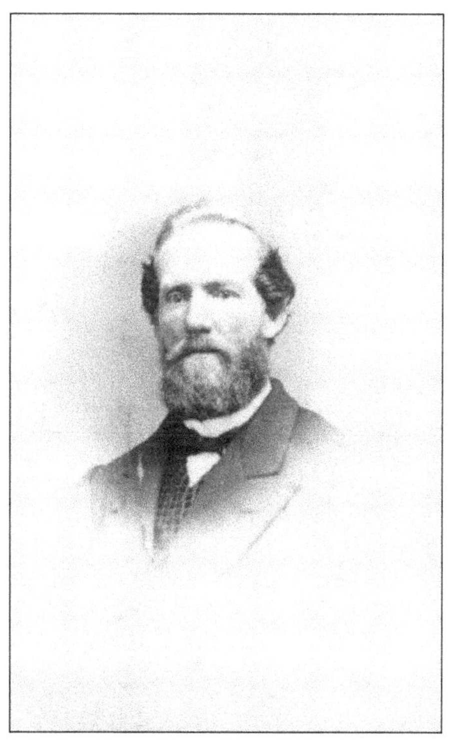

In 1860, James McClean, the first chief of Engine Company Two, went to San Francisco to purchase "Monumental." Built by the Wm. Toboss Company of New York, she weighed 5,000 pounds. She was so heavy, in fact, that during the response to a fire in 1861, Udo Von Keller slipped while grabbing the rope to assist moving the engine and was crushed beneath the wheels. Her size proved unsuited to the hills of San Francisco and she was sold for $2,500, about a third of the original cost. The funds for her purchase were again raised by the ladies of the town. Engine Company Two elected to remain an independent organization, not joining the city fire department until 1868. Major fires would ravage the town in 1860, 1861, 1865, 1866, 1885, and 1920, but due to the efforts of the two companies, the town would never again be a total loss.

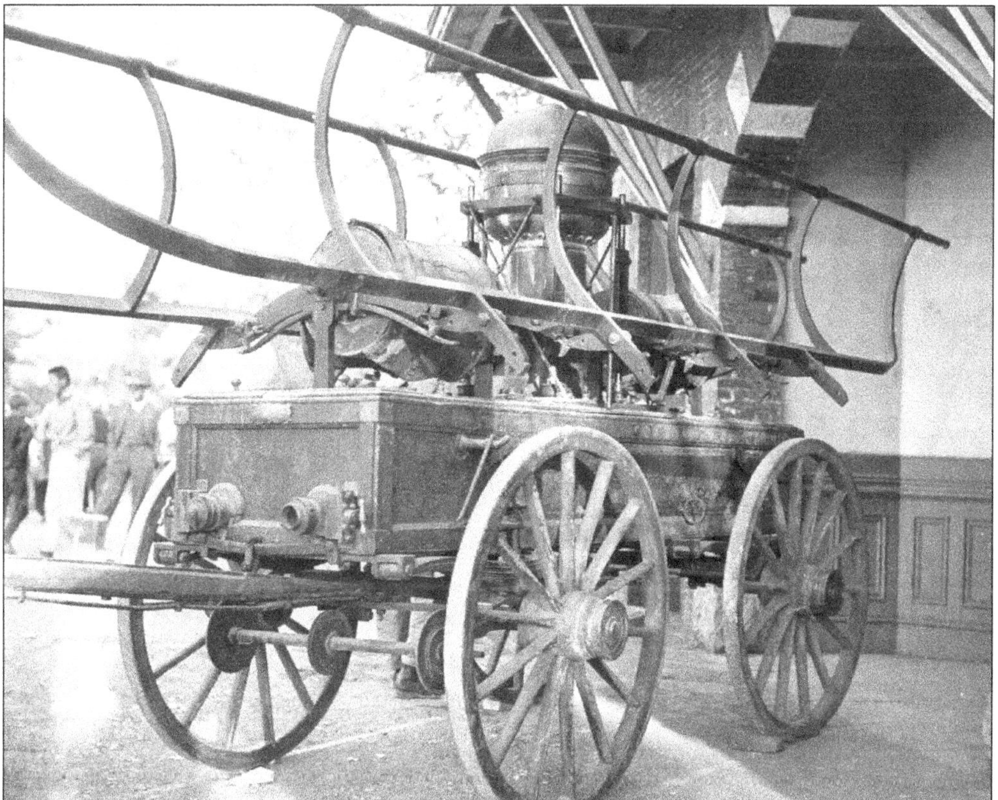

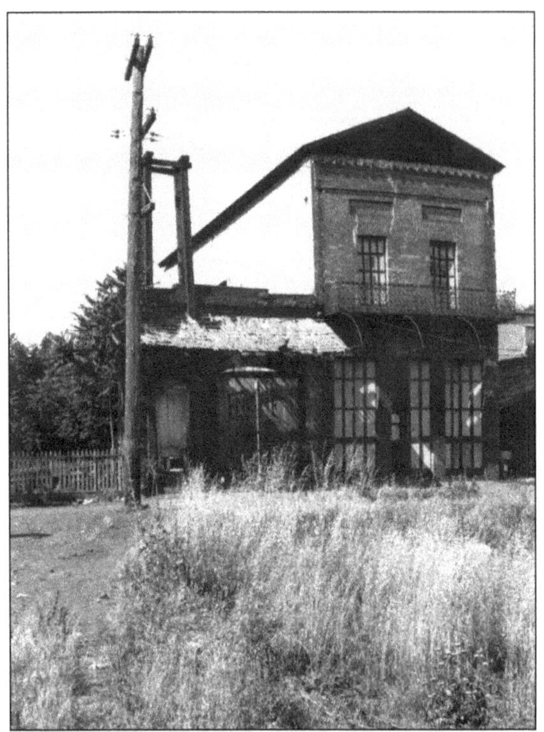

Firehouse taxes were approved by vote in 1860. Papeete was housed in this building on State Street, a remodeled store that was purchased by the city. Engine Company Two, not having joined the city fire department, had difficulty in obtaining funds from the city for a house. Eventually an agreement was struck, and the city bought a house and leased the building on the east side of Main Street to Engine Company Two.

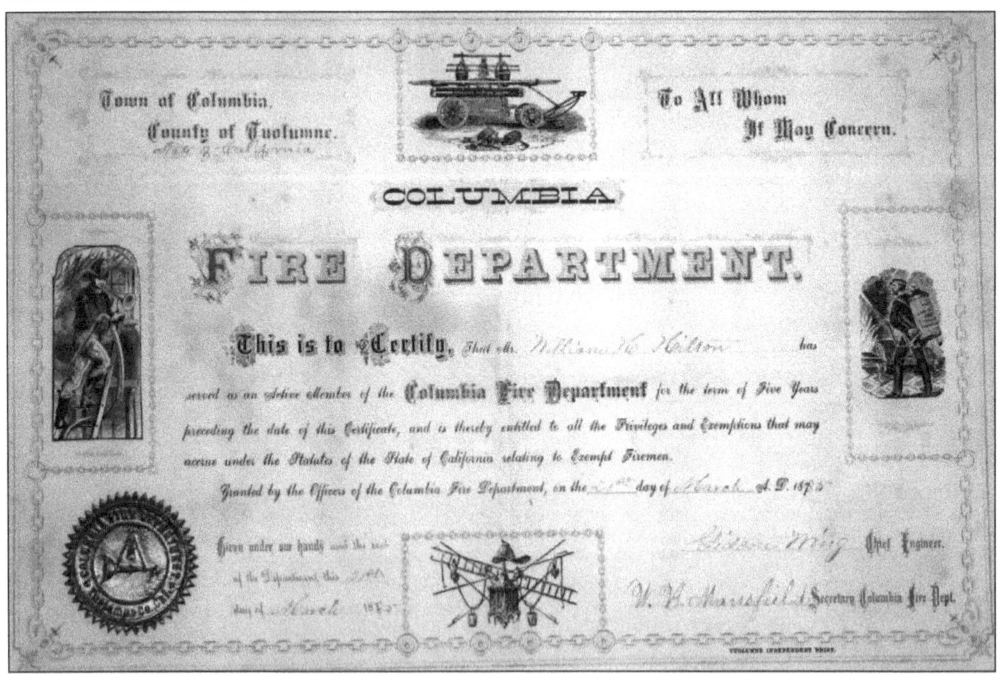

Town of Columbia,
County of Tuolumne.
[illegible]

To All Whom
It May Concern.

COLUMBIA

FIRE DEPARTMENT.

This is to Certify, That Mr. William H. Hilton has served as an Active Member of the Columbia Fire Department for the term of Five Years preceding the date of this Certificate, and is thereby entitled to all the Privileges and Exemptions that may accrue under the Statutes of the State of California relating to Exempt Firemen.

Granted by the Officers of the Columbia Fire Department, on the [illegible] day of March A. D. 187[illegible]

Given under our hands and the seal of the Department, this [illegible] day of March 187[illegible]

[illegible] Chief Engineer.

W. H. Mansfield Secretary Columbia Fire Dept.

Service in the fire department and their respective companies was highly regarded by members. Friendly rivalry was the impetus for contests of skill and daring. Men were recognized for service to their companies and the town. Membership in a company was no different than any other fraternal organization with members proudly displaying certificates such as this, and they never missed a chance to parade around town in full dress.

In 1885, Antone Siebert, a baker in town, was elected to the chief's position with Engine Company Two. The company had a roster of 40 men, but times were getting tough and the membership, along with the population of the town, was declining.

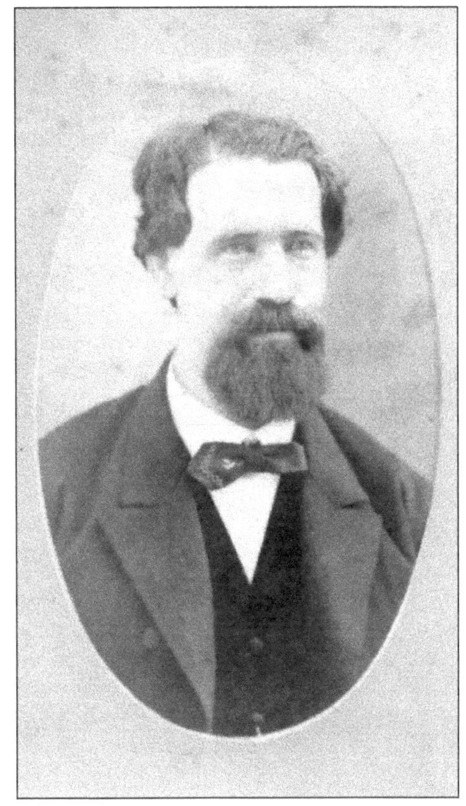

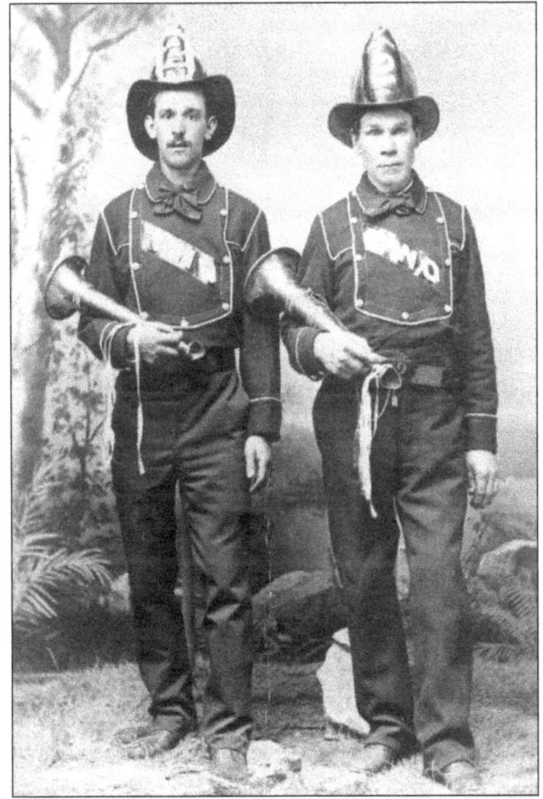

Pride in their service to the community continued to run high, as evidenced by Frank Caveron and John Conlin who posed for this portrait in the late 1800s wearing the uniform and helmet of Engine Company Two. They are holding speaking trumpets, used to give commands at the scene of a fire.

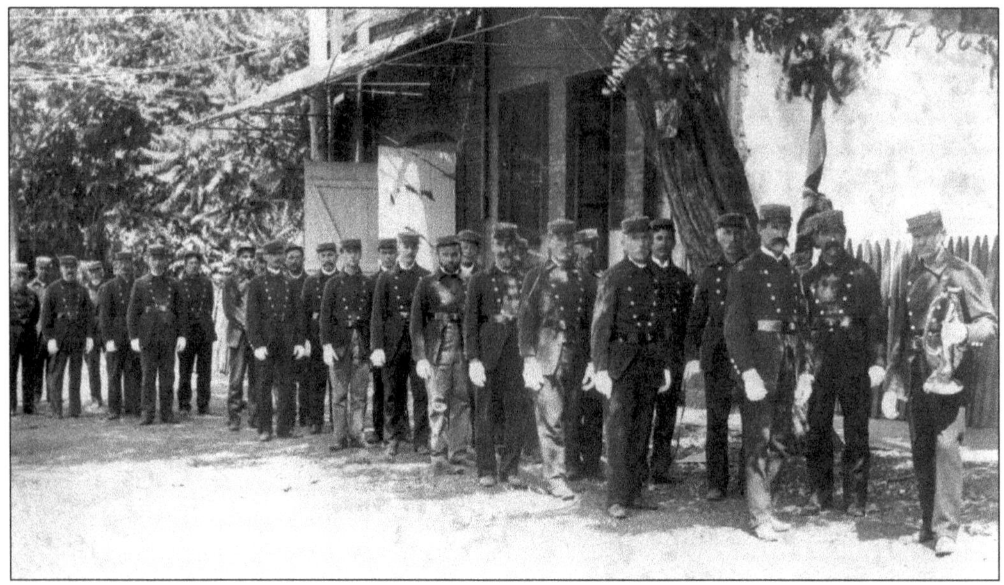

On July 4, 1903, Columbia Engine Company One was still going strong and proud. Pictured here on the shaded street in front of their State Street house, members of Papeete's company are resplendent in their dress uniforms. It took approximately 30 members to effectively use the hand-pumped engine and fight a fire.

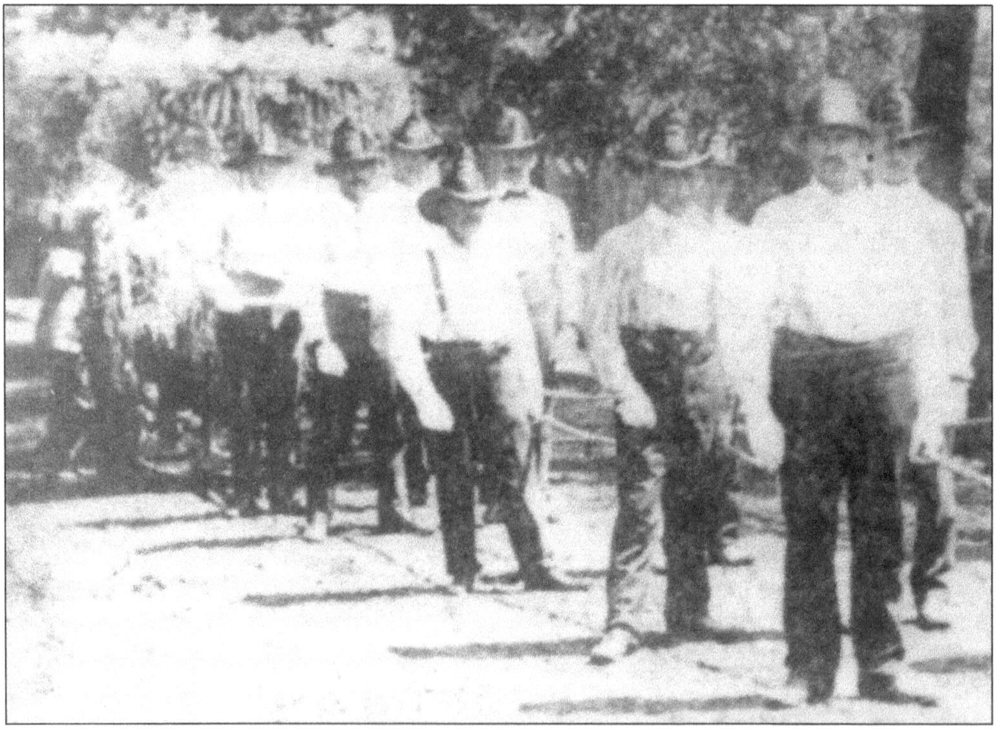

As Columbia's population declined, membership in both companies dwindled. With the Monumental being so large and cumbersome, it was often left behind when the alarm sounded. Engine Company Two often responded with only its hose cart. Here on July 4, 1903, members of Engine Company Two pose for a parade with their gaily decorated hose cart.

Lyman C. Tibbets, a popular druggist who worked out of the old bank building and lived across the street in the early 1900s, helped to reorganize the fire companies in 1908, when the shortage of men became severe. When the companies were combined, the State Street house was sold and all the equipment was moved to Main Street.

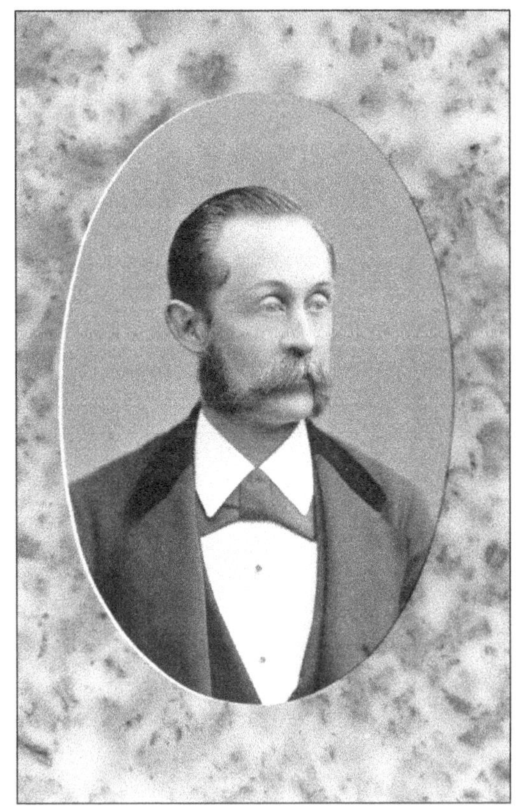

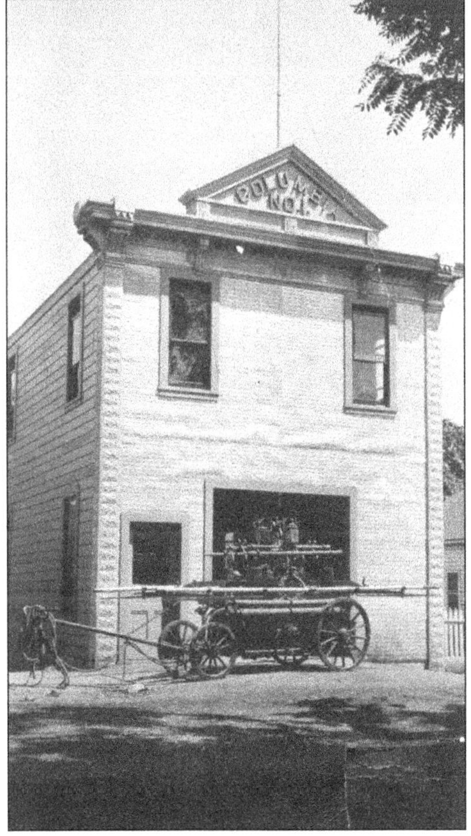

This new firehouse on Main Street was constructed in 1911 to house both engines and the department. The foundation was built with bricks from the torn down rear portion of the old Engine Company One house on State Street. Tin siding, popular at the time, gave the building a look of brick. Papeete is shown in front of the brand new structure.

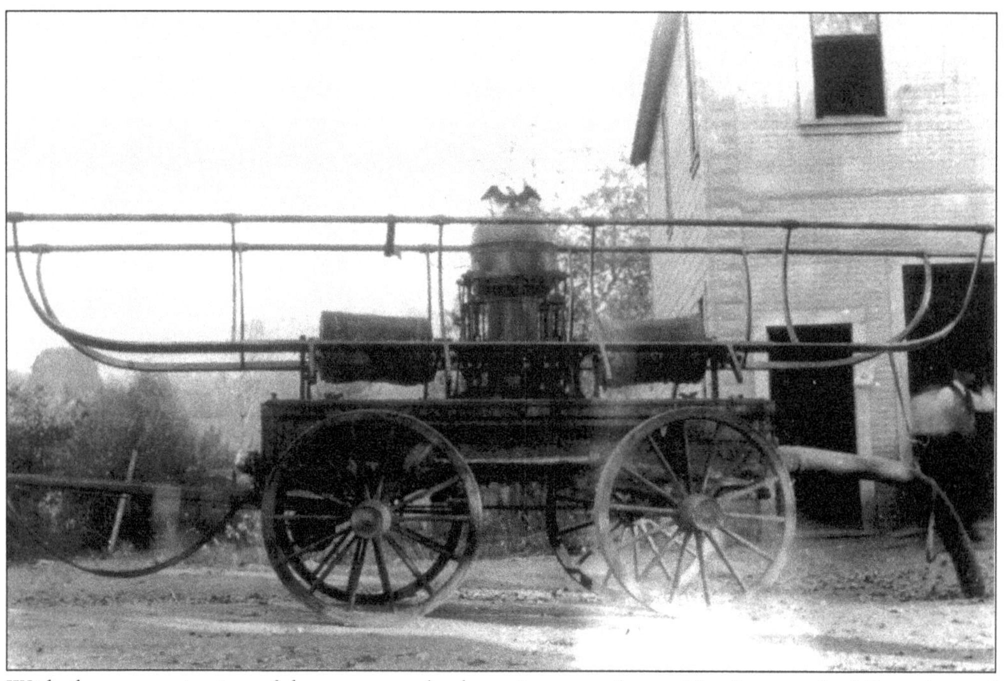

With the reorganization of the company, both engines were housed in the same building pictured here. Monumental, however, was used very little. Although more powerful than the smaller Papeete, Monumental was much more cumbersome and difficult to work. In fact, it was used only once more in firefighting efforts in 1920; it continues to be stored in the "new" firehouse on Main Street today.

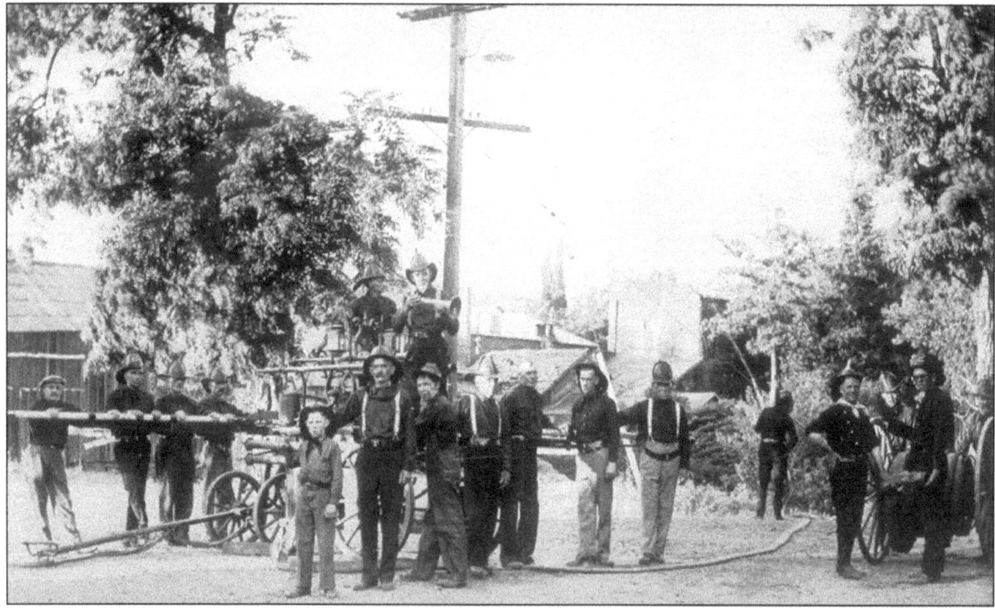

Utilizing the engines was an involved process. Between 15 and 20 men were needed to effectively pump the "brakes" (or arms) to make the machine work. Another group of men were tasked with laying out the hose and fighting the fire. Overall, about 30 men were needed by each company to fight fire. Here Papeete is used to display the various aspects of a hand pumping operation.

Hand-pumping engines could deliver a sizable stream of water and were very simple to maintain. Papeete, even after restoration in 1960, can still manage to shoot a stream nearly 200 feet when operated properly. She is often used in demonstrations during Fourth of July celebrations. Here the cistern in front of the Tuolumne Engine Company house is used for a demonstration of her capabilities.

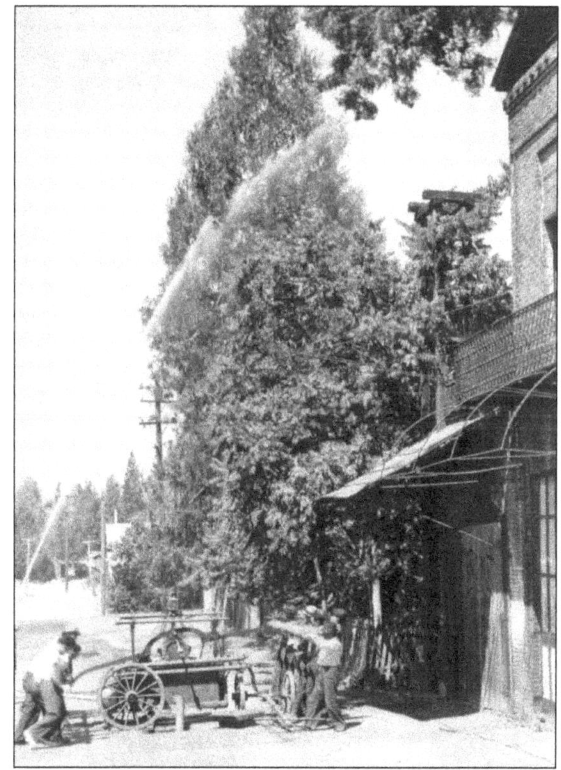

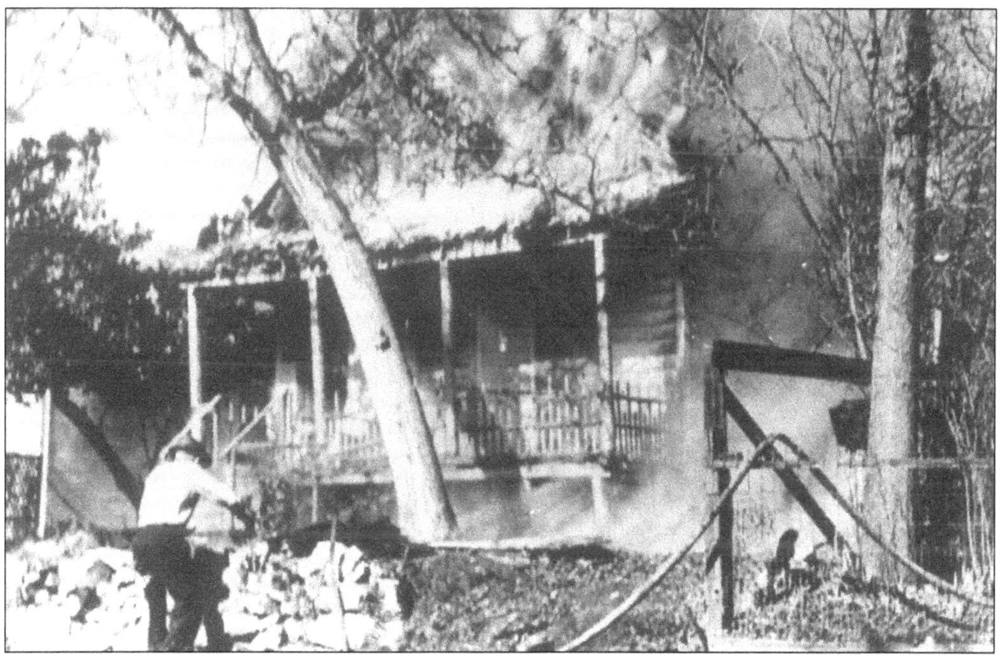

Even in the early 1900s, fire continued to plague the town. This house on Columbia Street near Jackson burns on April 30, 1920. This fire was the last big fire that burned more than one structure in town. Originating in the Kruse Saloon on Main and State, the fire sent embers into the air, igniting many frame structures throughout town.

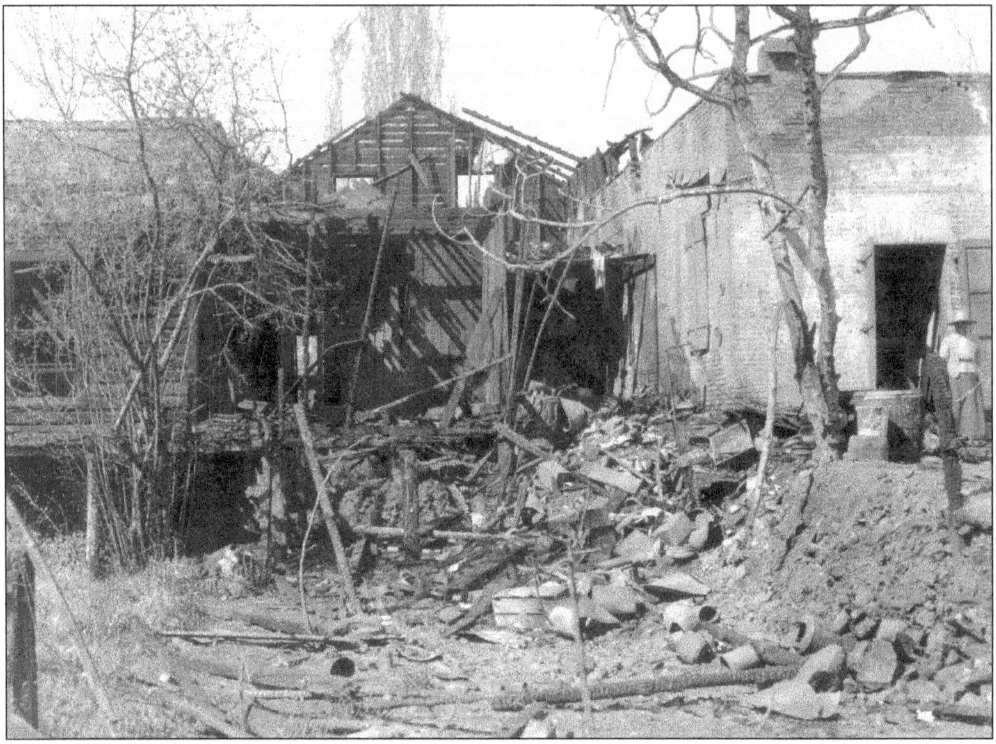

Mrs. Solari stands near the ruins of her home on Jackson Street after the 1920 fire. This would be the last major fire fought using hand-operated engines. Firemen were kept busy running all over town fighting the spot fires ignited by embers spread by the wind. The fire burned all day and firefighters had to take turns pumping the "brakes" to deliver water.

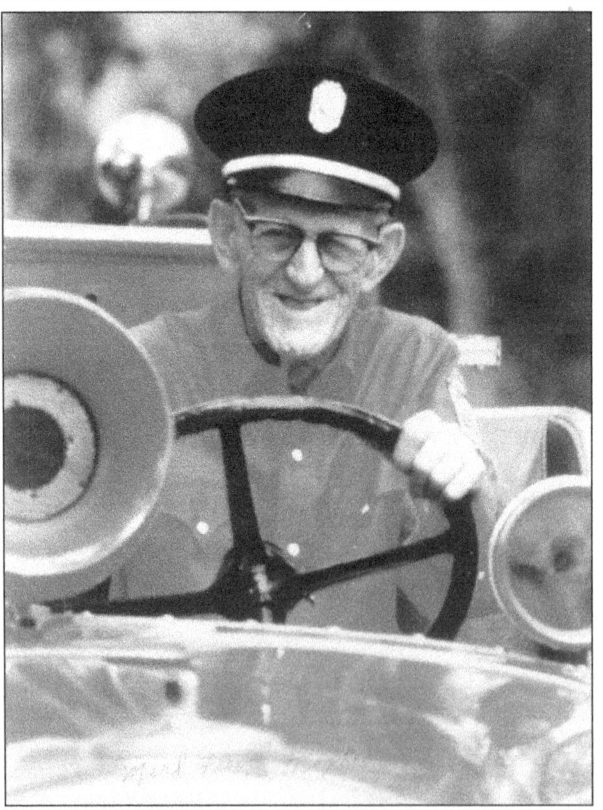

Merl "Fuzzy" Hughes was the last of the "old time" firemen. His first fire was the 1920 fire when he was just 14. He would eventually hold every position in the department. He helped to raise funds for a new 1931 Dodge fire engine, the first motorized equipment in town. A refurbished Model T Ford became a hose wagon at the same time, and the hand pumpers were retired.

Six

Reading, Writing, and Religion

As the town became more established, miners sent for their families and "civilizing" influences began.

Children needed an education and Mrs. Betsy Haley opened her private school in the summer of 1852. Other private schools, including church-run schools, followed. The first public school opened in January 1854 in a rented building. Townspeople, however, were soon demanding a permanent public school equal to, if not better than, those in other towns. In response, women of Columbia raised the necessary money through many community activities, and a two-story brick structure, on a hill northeast of town, was built in 1860.

Religion was very important. The Methodist Episcopal South Church held services as early as the fall of 1851 and built a wooden church in the summer of 1852. In 1855, the property was sold to the Presbyterian congregation, who had been organized in Columbia since 1854.

The Methodist Episcopal North Church was established in 1852 and a structure built in 1853. Although Catholic priests from Sonora gave services in Columbia, the first Catholic church was not built until 1854, which within a few years was replaced by St. Anne's, still standing on Kennebec Hill. With no synagogue nearby, early Jewish citizens used part of the first Odd Fellows Hall as a place of worship. Chinese constructed temples for their houses of worship.

Newspapers soon met the call for news of home. *The Columbia Star* produced its only issue on October 25, 1851. Columbia's second newspaper, *the Columbia Gazette*, was more successful and continued publishing for several years as did many other newspapers.

Columbia, like other communities, suffered a high death rate. Mining accidents and violence accounted for some deaths but many were from diseases, especially consumption (tuberculosis). Too often children were victims of diseases such as scarlet fever or diphtheria. When a rich gold strike was discovered next to Columbia's first cemetery on Gold Hill, miners washed out some graves and knocked over tombstones. In 1855, the Columbia cemetery was moved next to the Masonic and Odd Fellows graveyard located behind the schoolhouse. The tombstones tell the story of early Columbia and the fate of those who lived there.

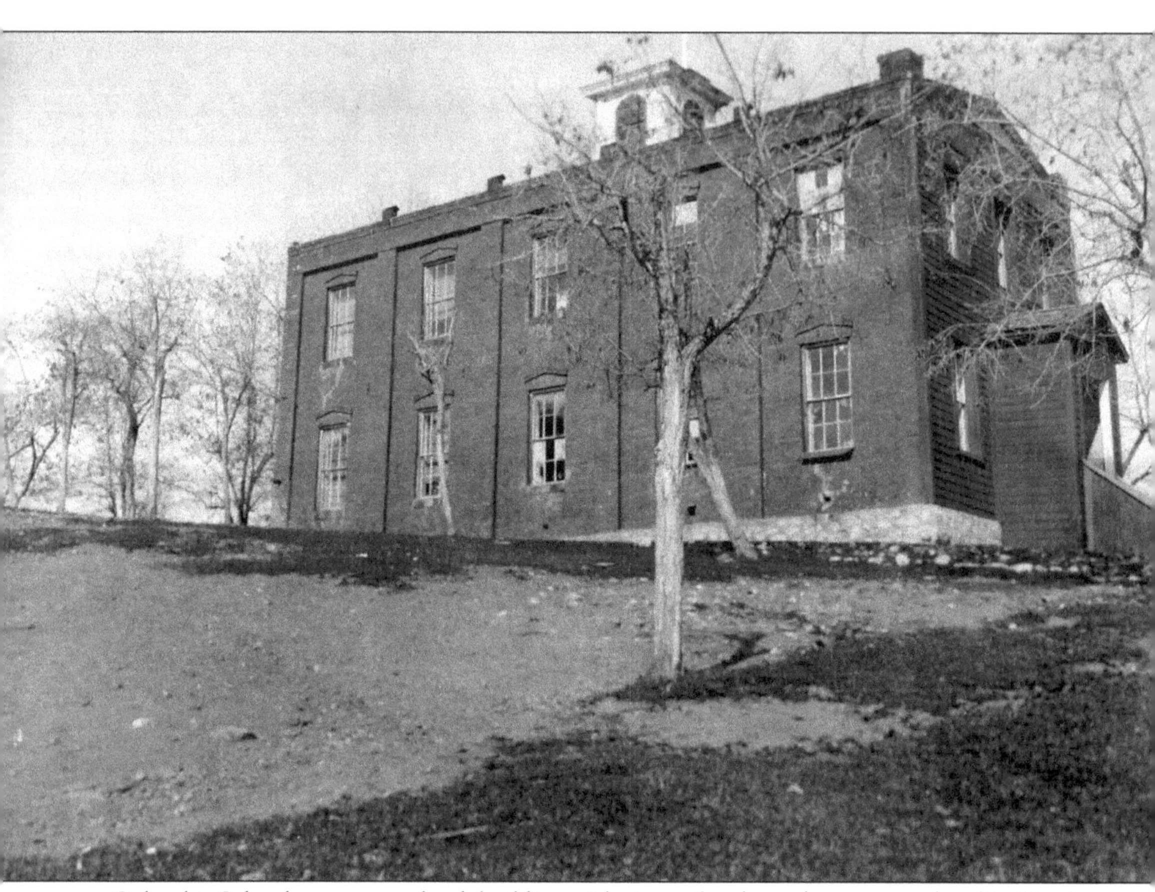

Columbia School, a two-story brick building with tin roof and cupola, was completed in October 1860 and dedicated in November, providing Columbia with a public school large enough for the many children in the area. The schoolhouse was built of locally made bricks, which were very porous. In some old photographs, the school appears to be made of wood, the result of attaching wood over the bricks to protect them from moisture. The first class began March 18, 1861, in a school without furnishings. The students sat on the floor. When public funds ran out, the school closed July 31, 1861. The ladies of the town raised money with a "grand calico party" and purchased furnishings and equipment so that the school could reopen September 9, 1861. First through sixth grades were taught downstairs, and the seventh and eighth grades were on the second floor.

Anna Marie Carr Dealy opened a private school in rented quarters and later taught in her home. George P. Morgan, son of George Morgan, was a student. Dealy was described as a "cultured lady of the East" who wore a black dress with white collar and cuffs and sat in her rocking chair on a raised platform keeping an eagle eye on the brood in front of her.

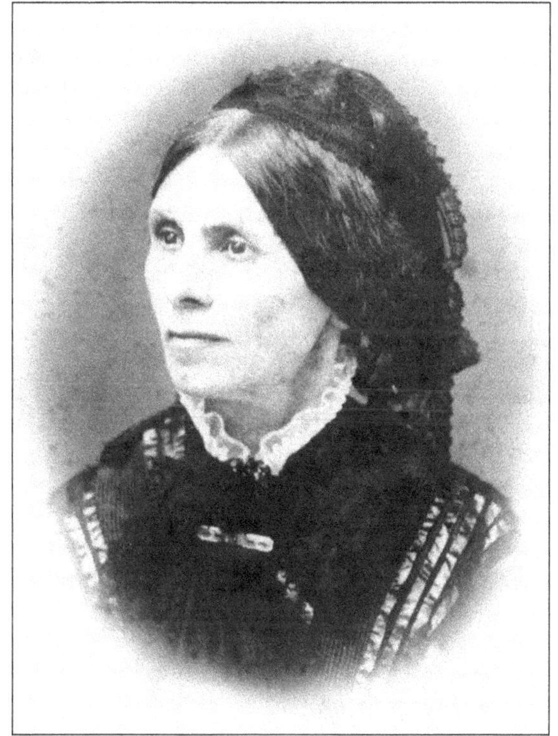

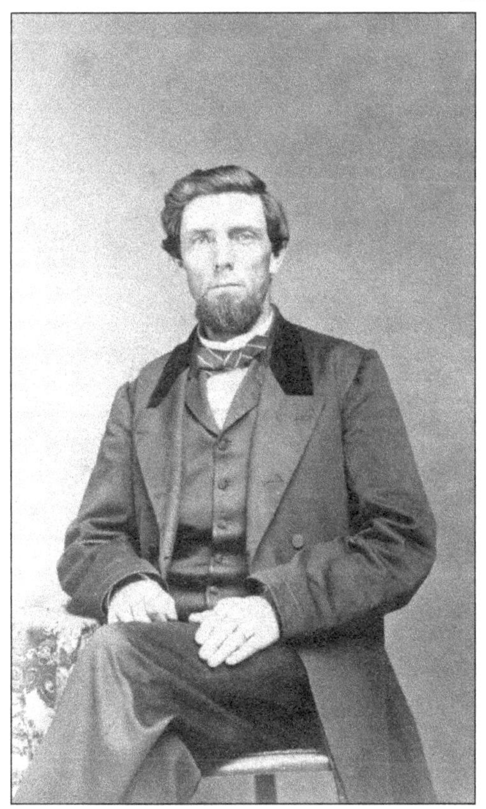

John Graham opened a private school in early 1859, but closed it in May in anticipation of presiding at the new Columbia school. When he wasn't hired, Graham taught in Springfield at a private school and later at the Springfield public school. He became a Columbia school trustee in 1861, a teacher at Columbia school in 1862 and 1863, and was appointed superintendent of schools in 1864 and 1865.

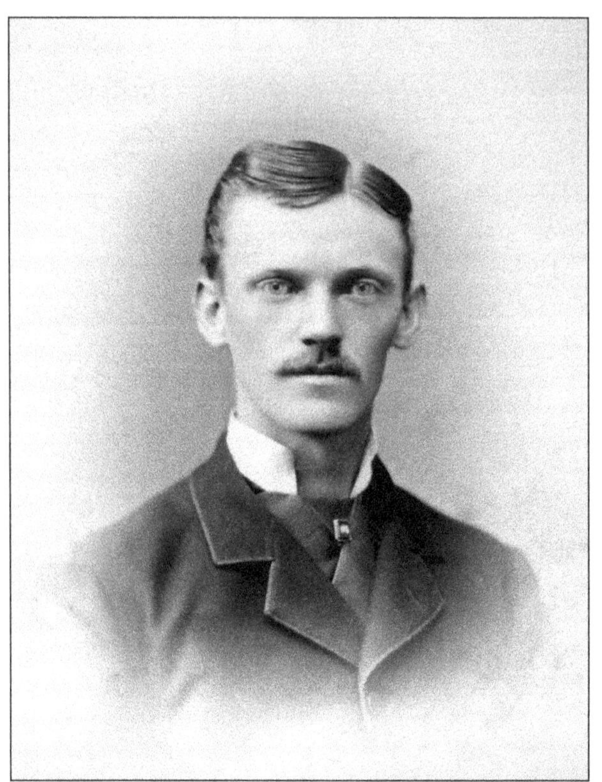

George P. Morgan, son of George and Margaret Morgan, was born in Columbia's City Hotel. Graduating from San Jose Normal School, he progressed from being a Columbia teacher and principal to superintendent of schools. He served in education for a total of 56 years. Many of his students claimed his initials G. P. stood for gunpowder, referring to his short temper.

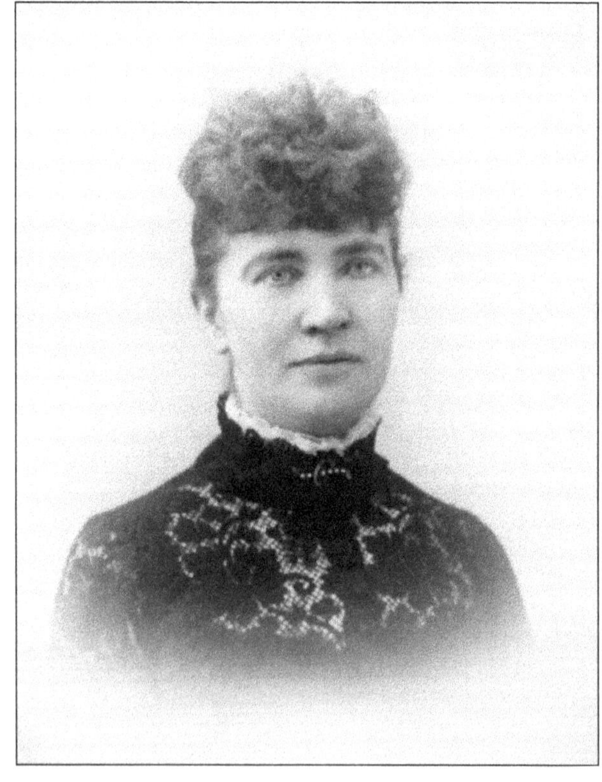

Rose Morgan, daughter of George and Margaret Morgan and sister of George P., became assistant principal at the Columbia school in 1871. In 1874, Rose attended the San Jose Normal School to complete her education. Returning to Columbia in 1876, Rose was one of the first four women elected superintendent of schools in California. She later moved to San Francisco where she taught for many years.

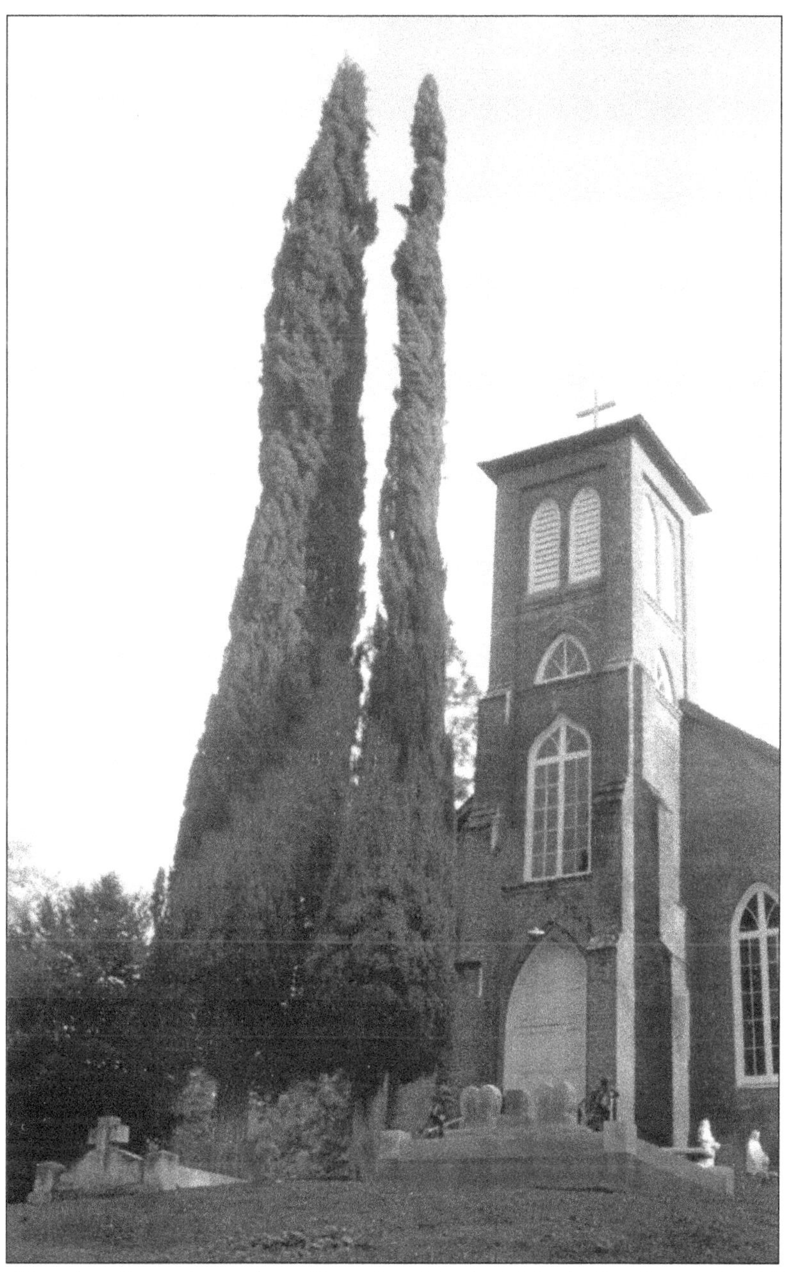

St. Anne's Church still stands watch on Kennebec Hill. In 1850, the families on Gold Hill, mostly from Ireland and Italy, erected the first Catholic church, a small structure of rough logs and covered with canvas. A campaign was launched to raise funds for a "real" church. Five partners on Kennebec Hill donated the land, and late in 1855, construction of the brick church began. The doors opened in March 1856, although it was not completed and dedicated until November 2, 1856. The 1,600-pound silver alloy bell, cast in Troy, New York, was shipped around the Horn and installed in the church steeple in the spring of 1858. The miners had given another $1,500 for its purchase. Condemned in 1911, St. Anne's was restored in 1926. In 1974, the little church was again condemned because of safety codes. This time, donations were made by tourists, other churches, and local people to further restore the structure.

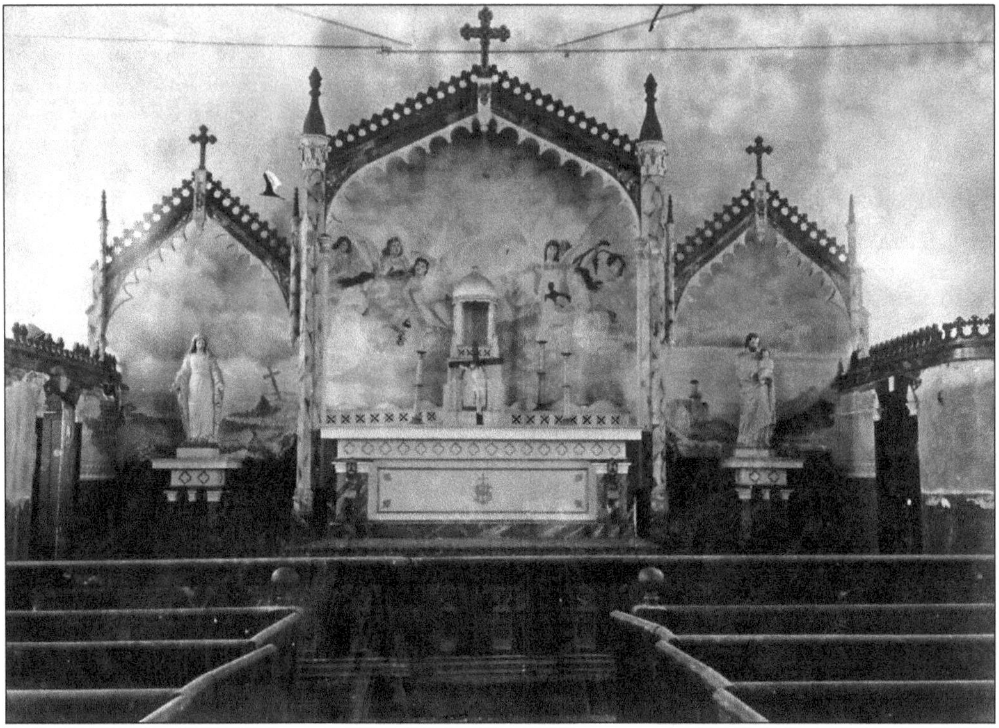

St. Anne's beautiful celestial scene behind the altar was painted by James Fallon, son of Owen Fallon, owner of the Fallon Hotel.

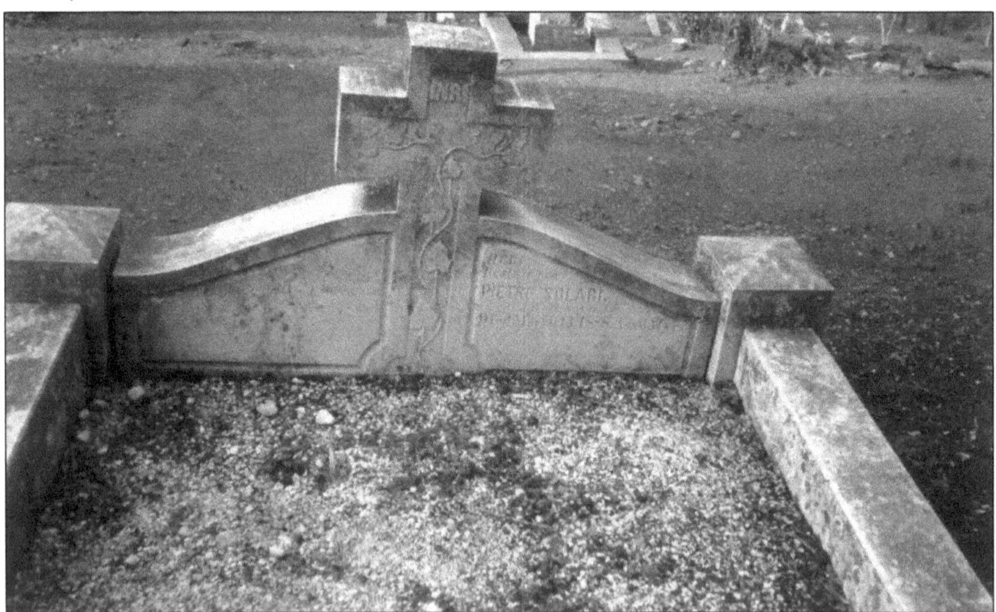

Pietro Solari's final resting place is seen here. Coming from Genoa, Italy, in the 1850s, he returned to Italy to marry Rosa Lagomarsino. After returning to California, the couple eventually settled in Columbia in 1883 and opened a mercantile on Jackson Street. Pietro died suddenly in 1888, and Rosa had him buried at St. Anne's. His large marble headstone is in an enclosed plot with two cypress trees.

Irish-born Fr. Daniel Slattery was the first priest assigned to Columbia and arrived in 1856. He began at once to start a building fund for a new Catholic church at Columbia as the parish had outgrown the small building on Gold Street. The local miners, many being Irish or Italian, gave generously. With Father Slattery's help, they did get their little gothic-style church on Kennebec Hill.

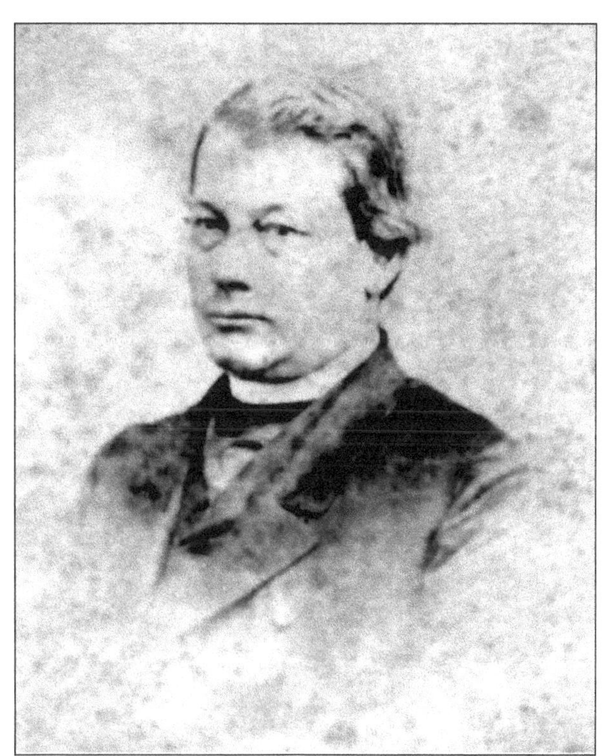

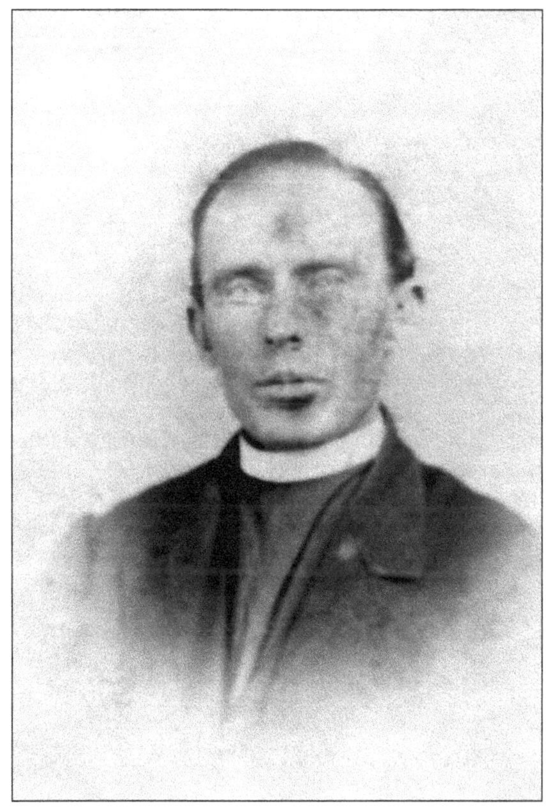

Fr. Terrance J. Smith, shown here in a traditional clerical collar, was appointed to St. Anne's Church by Archbishop Allemany O. P. of San Francisco and arrived in Columbia in the summer of 1862. Although suffering from tuberculosis, he was an energetic young man and established Columbia's first parochial school.

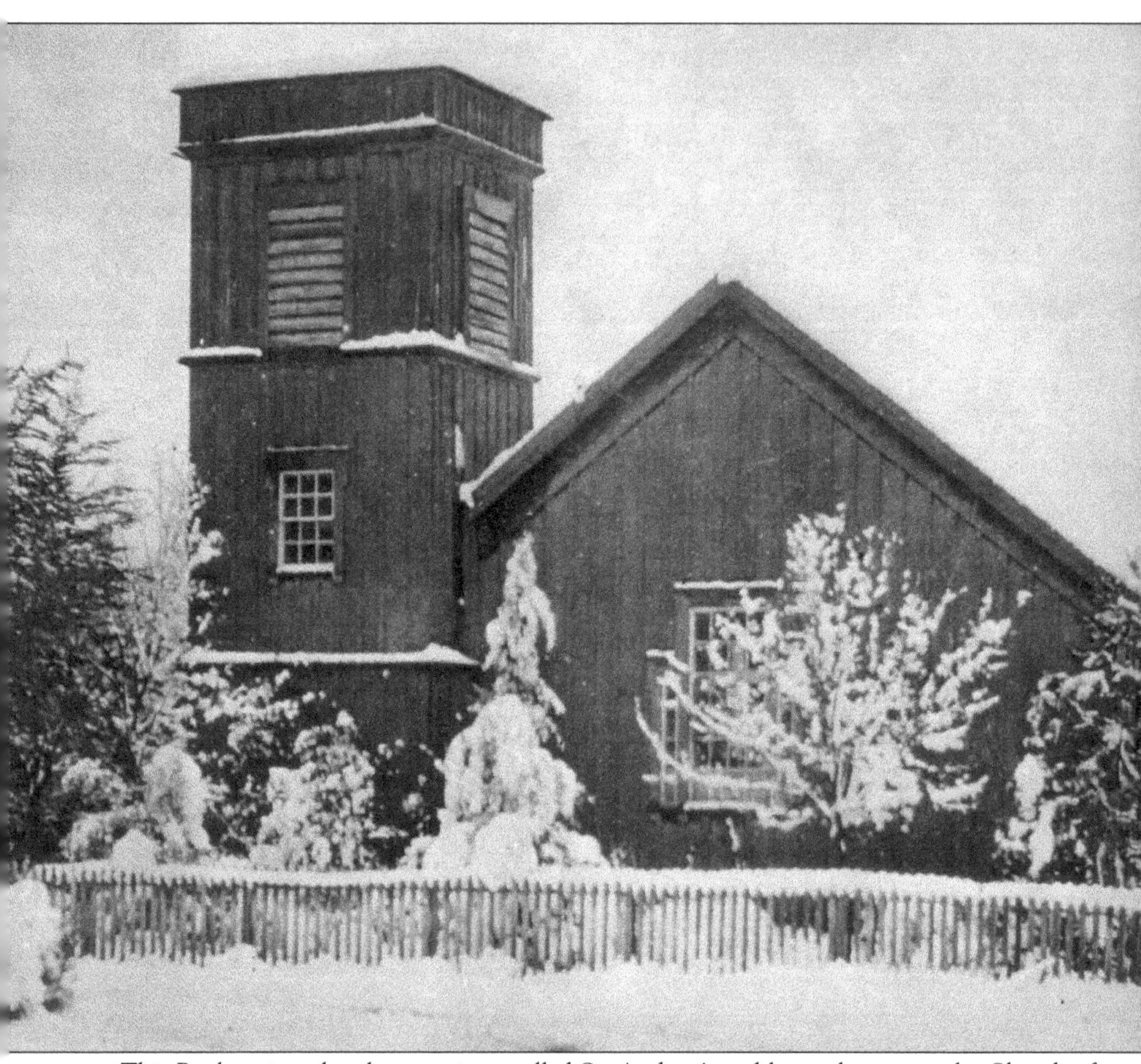

This Presbyterian church, sometimes called St. Andrew's and better known as the Church of the 49ers, is a replica of the earlier church built in 1864. Columbia's first Presbyterian church was organized by Rev. John Henry Brodt in 1854, with only 19 members. Services were held in both the Methodist Episcopal Church South and Methodist Episcopal Church North, until they purchased the two-story Methodist South frame church. This church was torn down in 1864 and replaced with a larger one, the original of the structure that stands there today. On June 22, 1950, the residents of Columbia were awakened by the sound of sirens and the bright glare of fire in the sky. The Church of the 49ers was burning. There was no way to save the old wooden church that had served Columbia for so many years. Through the efforts of many, a replica of the original historical Church of the 49ers was dedicated less than five years later.

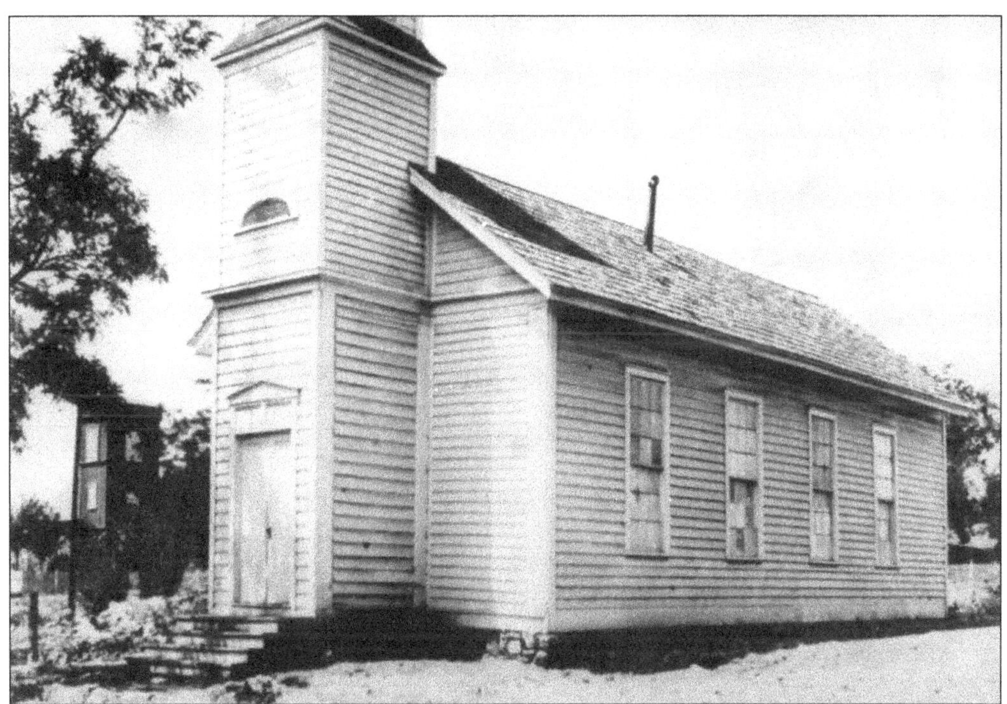

The Methodist Episcopal Church South of Columbia is thought to have been established by Rev. Joseph S. Malone in the spring of 1852, and the church building erected by June 19, 1852, on the corner of Jackson and Gold Streets. In early 1855, the church joined with the Methodist Episcopal Church North.

In 1854, the Independent Order of Odd Fellows, a benevolent fraternal organization, built their first hall in Columbia at the corner of Broadway and Jackson Streets. To meet the needs of the town's Jewish merchants and families, a room in the hall was rented to them as their place of worship. The hall, destroyed by the 1857 fire, relocated at State and Broadway Streets.

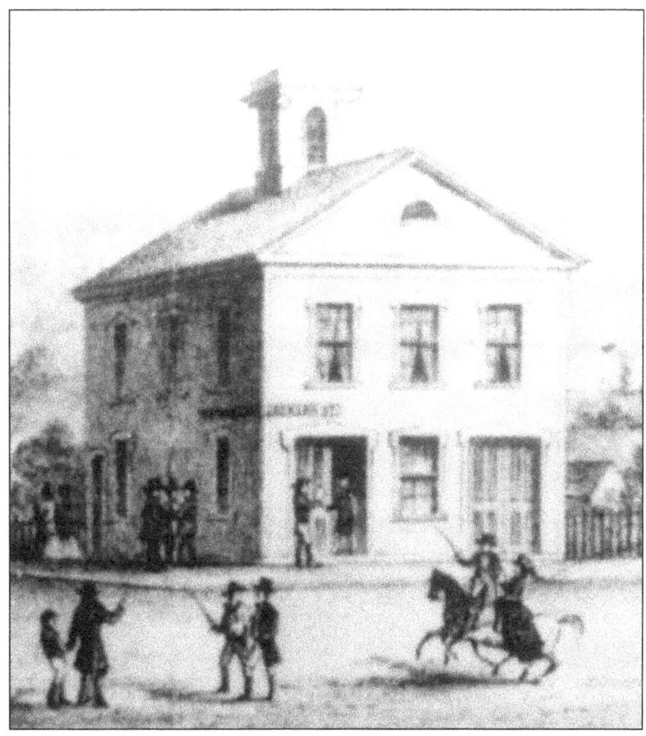

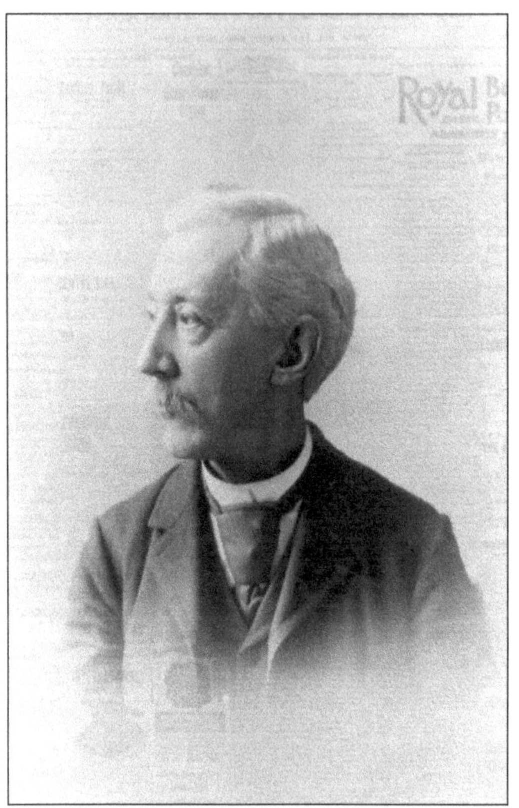

In 1830, John Duchow was born in Salem, Massachusetts. At the age of 14, he apprenticed to the *Salem Gazette*. In April 1852, Duchow sailed for California where he joined Edward Boden, a friend and fellow apprentice from Salem. In Columbia, Duchow continued his long career in journalism. As founder of the *Tuolumne Independent*, he worked almost continuously in Tuolumne County for 46 years.

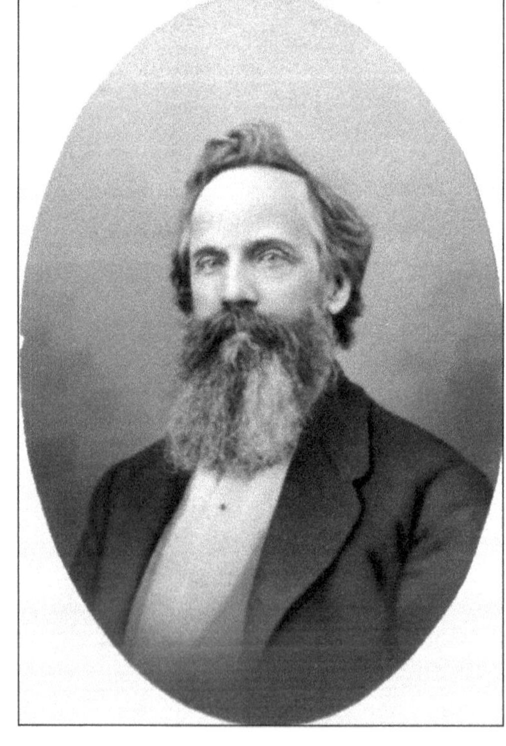

Gen. Jonas Winchester came to California in 1849. He was once owner and editor of the *Golden Rule*, a publication of the Odd Fellowship. Trained as a journalist, he was also involved in quartz mining, although he lost money in his many ventures. He was also a member of the Society of California Pioneers and a member of the Tuolumne County Pioneer Association.

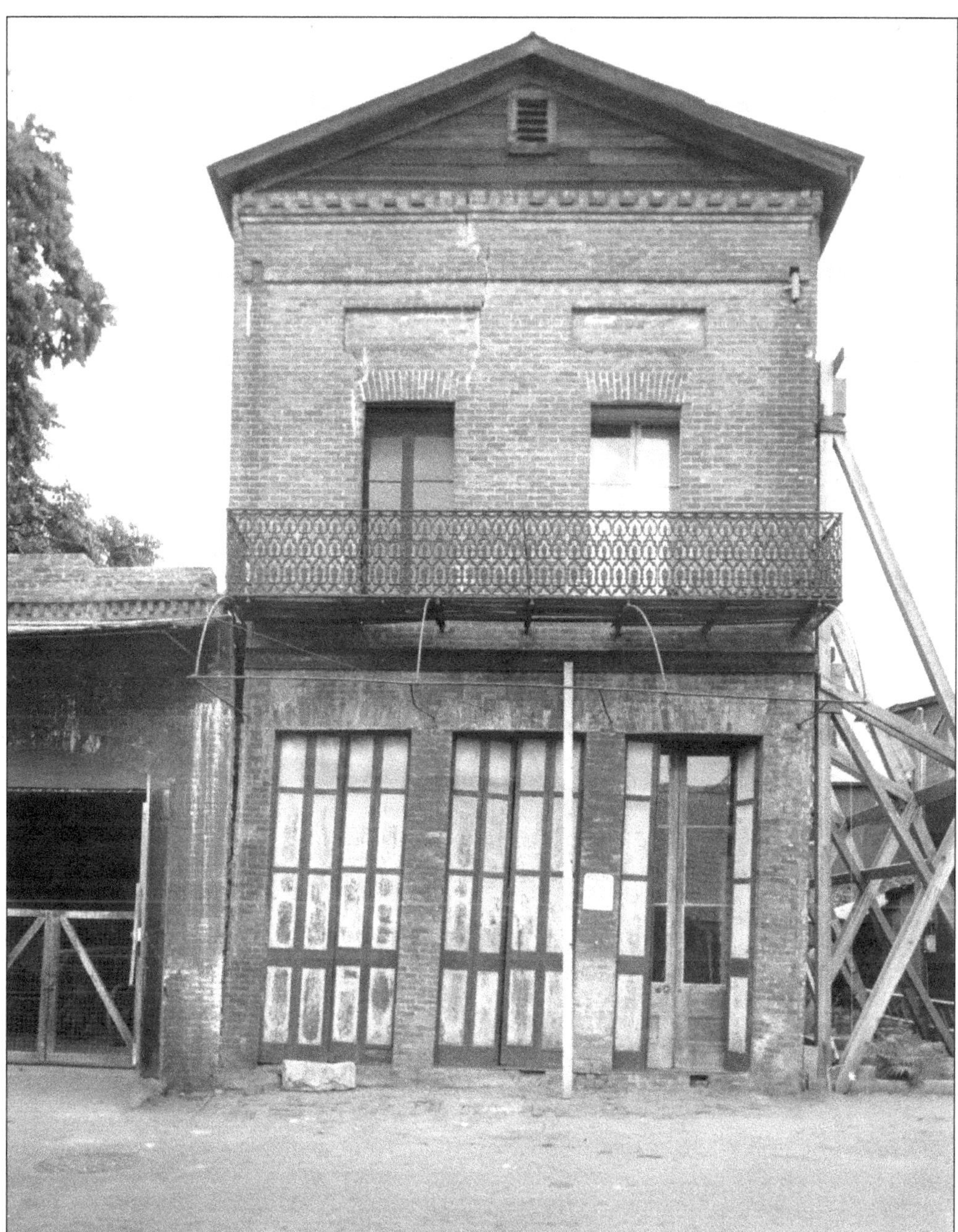

Sometimes called the Duchow or the Drug Store Building, this restored two-story brick building was constructed in July 1856. Previously a wooden building, it was owned by Dr. James McChesney, who established a drug store there. The west part of the lot was occupied by Drs. Oxley and Campbell. In July 1854, this building was destroyed by fire and was replaced with a canvas structure. In 1856, the lower floor was occupied by Dr. Parsons, a dentist, and the upper floor by a print shop and the office of the *Weekly Columbian*, published by J. W. Oliver. That newspaper was moved out in 1856 and was later purchased by John Duchow. In 1866, Duchow purchased this building, returned the press and equipment to the second floor, and rented it to W. O. Dinsmore who published the *Columbia Citizen*.

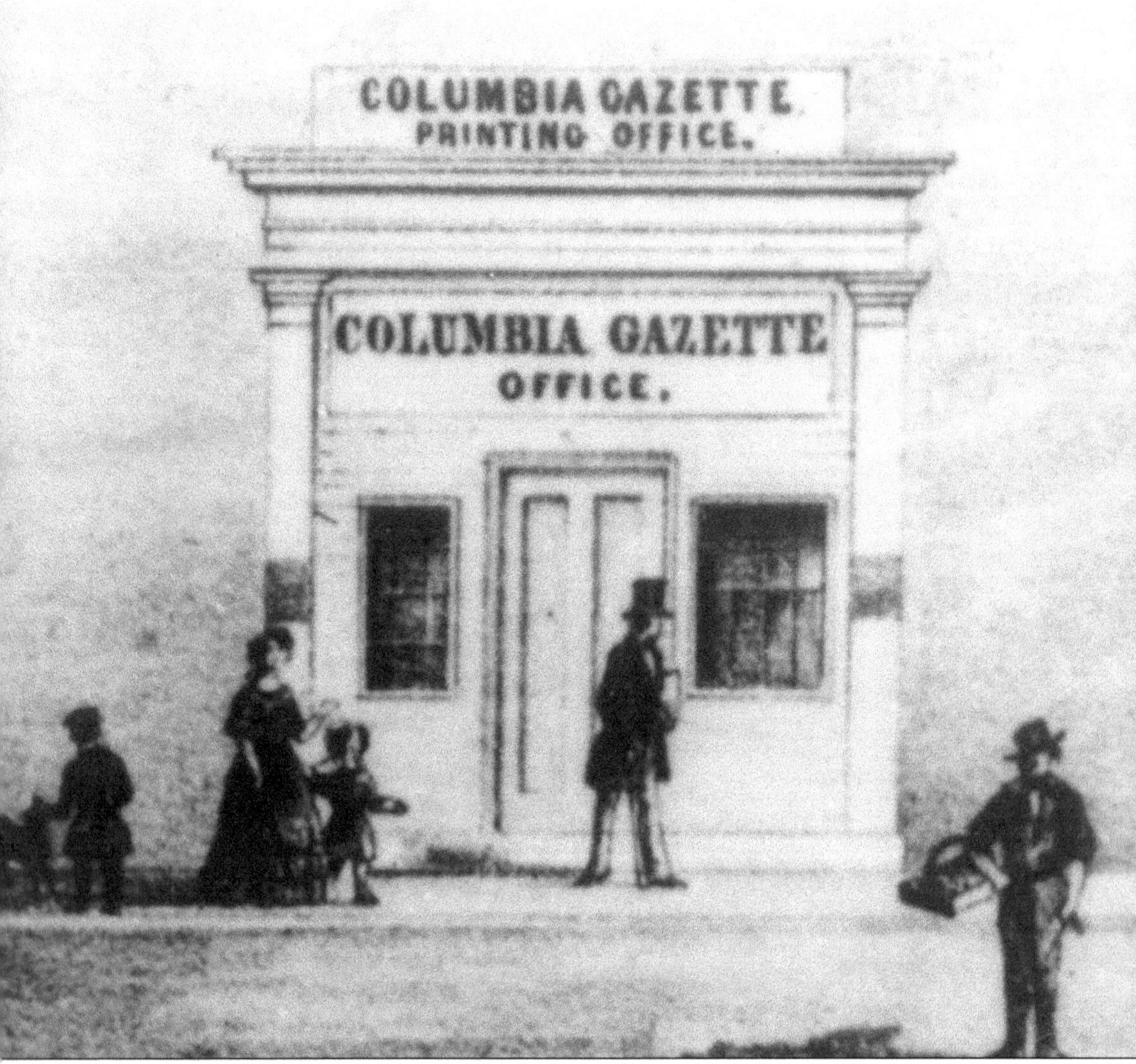

There are no known photographs of the original *Gazette* building, but this 1856 lithograph by Towle and Leavitt shows a drawing of the *Gazette*'s facade. The original wood structure was constructed between 1852 and 1853. Col. Thomas Falconer first published the *Columbia Gazette* on September 23, 1852, in an office on Main Street, but on March 5, 1853, moved his office to the *Gazette* building. In November 1853, John Duchow and Tyron Milton Yancey moved into the building, which was destroyed in the 1854 fire. After the *Gazette* was rebuilt, John Duchow and R. J. Steele moved in. On November 10, 1855, the first issue of the *Columbia Gazette and Southern Miners Advertiser* was printed. This building has housed many businesses, including W. C. Parker's stationery and book store, Gilbert Beach's Broadway Bakery and Temperance House, which Beach moved to the location, and the offices of Smith, Morse, and Company, lumber merchants. The *Gazette* building met its end in the disastrous fire in August 1857.

This simple archway leads to the final resting place of Columbia's pioneers. In this hallowed ground are three cemeteries, the Masonic, Odd Fellows, and the public cemetery, which includes two veteran's sections. To the left is the Masonic Cemetery, encircled with a picket fence, and the Odd Fellows, beyond it to the north and west. Both were established in 1855. In 1857, the public cemetery moved to Reservoir Hill next to the lodge cemeteries.

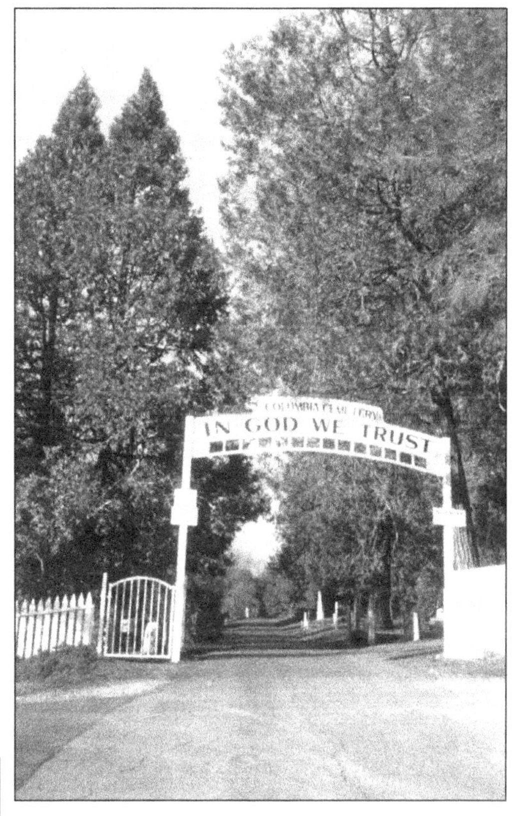

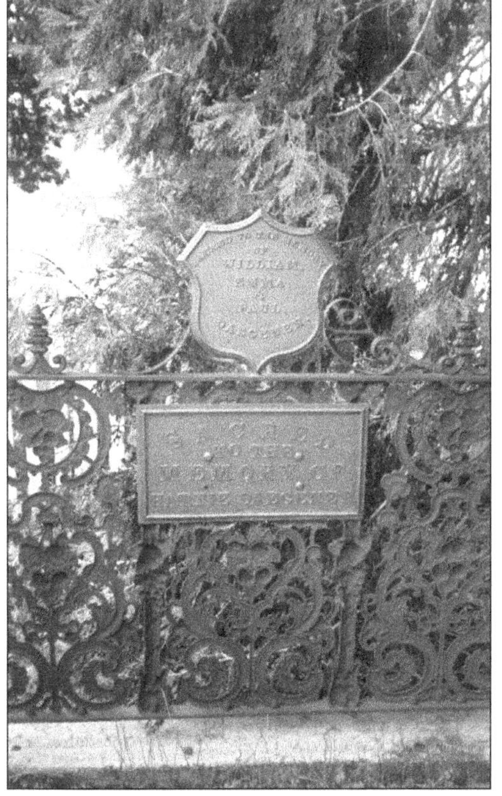

William Daegener, the first Wells Fargo agent, and his wife, Maria Schultz, had four children when tragedy struck during an epidemic of scarlet fever in December 1862. William, age four; Emma, age two; and Paul, eleven months, died of the fever between December 31, 1862, and January 6, 1863. Their plot, encircled with a decorative iron fence, also holds their sister Hattie who died in 1870.

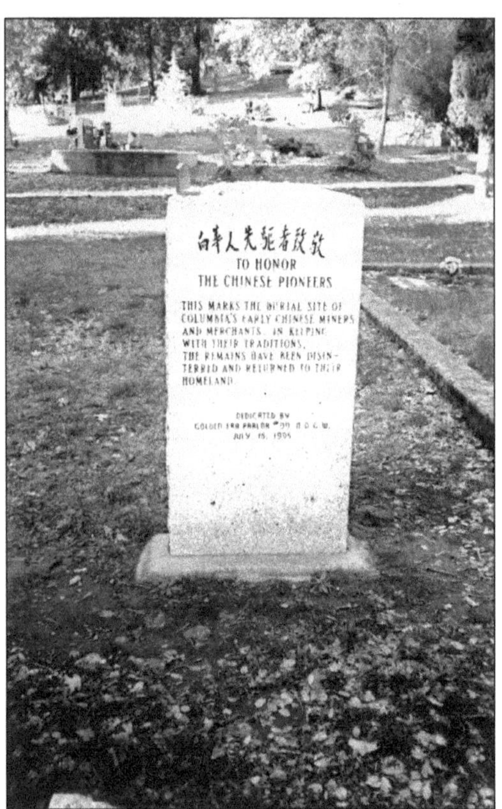

Columbia had many Chinese residents. Blamed for the 1857 fire, they were forced to move north of town, only being allowed to return when the population began declining during the town's economic downturn. Although subject to much prejudice, the Chinese were allowed burial in the public cemetery in what was called the Chinese plot. After several years, a bone cleaner would come from China and clean and prepare their bones for the return to China to be buried with their ancestors. Although no original markers remain, a monument dedicated to the Chinese people of Columbia is located a few hundred feet inside this gate.

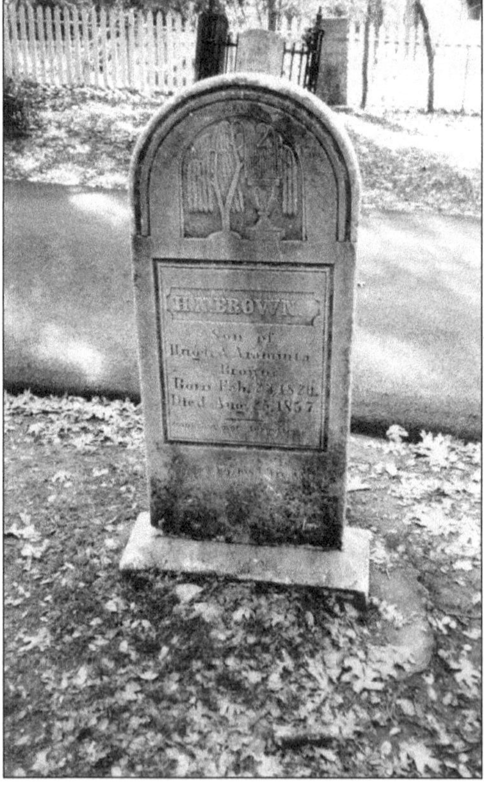

Columbia's devastating 1857 fire is said to have burned for 48 hours. Some described it as a "war zone" as the fire reached stores that carried large amounts of black power used by the miners, causing them to explode. H. N. Brown had a general store on south Main Street and was one of five men killed in such an explosion. His gravestone reads "Erected by friends."

Seven

We Gather Together

The miners and residents of Columbia formed clubs and associations from the earliest times. Some of these, such as the Masons and the Odd Fellows, were associations that were brought to California by the 49ers. Others, such as the Native Sons, were born in California. At least one, E Clampus Vitus, was started as a spoof on the serious lodges, orders, and benevolent societies.

Many joined these groups because they were miles from friends and family and were lonely. Italians, for instance, might join the Sons of Italy while the Irish found the Hibernian Benevolent Society to their liking. Others who were against "demon rum," or wanted people to think they were, might join the Dashaways or the Sons of Temperance.

Some of the organizations were for fun and entertainment. Bands, for example, were always a major part of life in Columbia. The Native Sons of the Golden West had its own band over the years. A local favorite for years, the Columbia Brass Band was playing as early as 1858, participating in local parades and celebrations.

Military organizations were also part of Columbia from its early days, a militia being necessary for the protection of the townspeople from increasing lawlessness. One of the first was the Columbia Fusileers commanded by Thomas N. Cazneau. Soon to follow was the Columbia Light Artillery in 1857. In 1861, during the Civil War, the Columbia City Horse Guards, the German Home Guards, the Tuolumne National Guard, and the Tuolumne Home Guard were formed, all of them composed of volunteers from Columbia and nearby towns. When there was no longer a need for a militia, the members were mustered out in 1868, and a grand ball was held in a farewell celebration.

And when it came time for celebrating, the folks of Columbia were not to be outdone. An article in the Stockton *Journal* dated July 13, 1852, reported that "the celebration in Columbia was by far the greatest demonstration yet made in Tuolumne County. It was participated in, from the first to the last, by from six to eight thousand persons." At the end of the day a grand ball was held at the Loring House where there were "thirty to forty American ladies present, of the first respectability, and a large representation of the beaus of Columbia, Sonora, and vicinity."

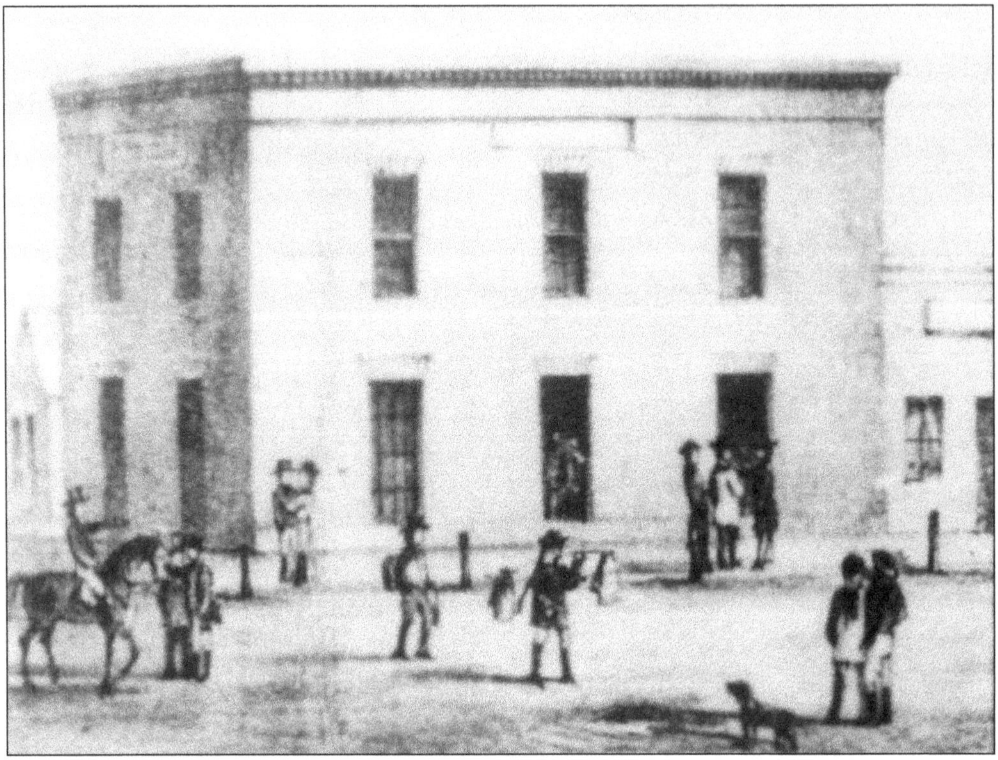

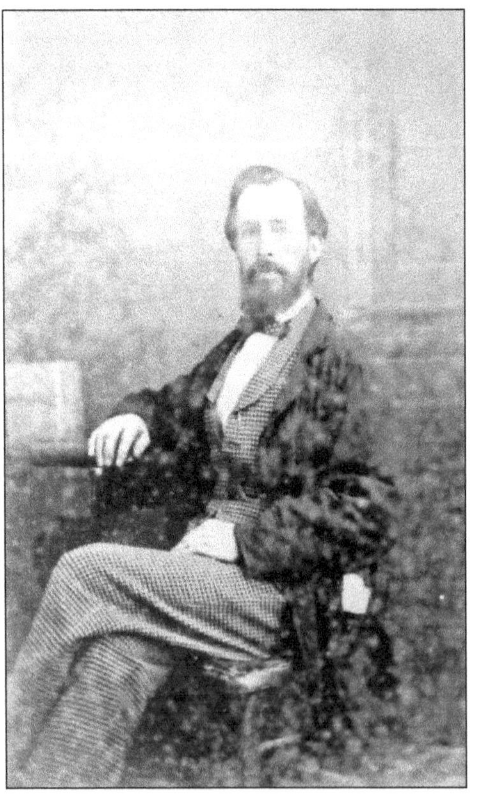

Columbia's Masonic Lodge No. 28 was founded in July 1852 and the first Masonic temple erected in 1854. Masonry, in simply terms, is a benevolent, charitable, educational, religious society that believes in brotherly love, philanthropy, and truth. Mr. Davies, seen here, was master of Columbia Lodge from 1860 to 1867. He then became grand master of California Masons, and upon his death was recognized by the Grand Lodge as the most outstanding Mason of his generation. Davies was a member of Tuolumne Engine Company One, city clerk, Columbia school trustee, a drummer in the Tuolumne Home Guard, and a brigadier general in the 3rd Brigade, California Militia Force, in 1864.

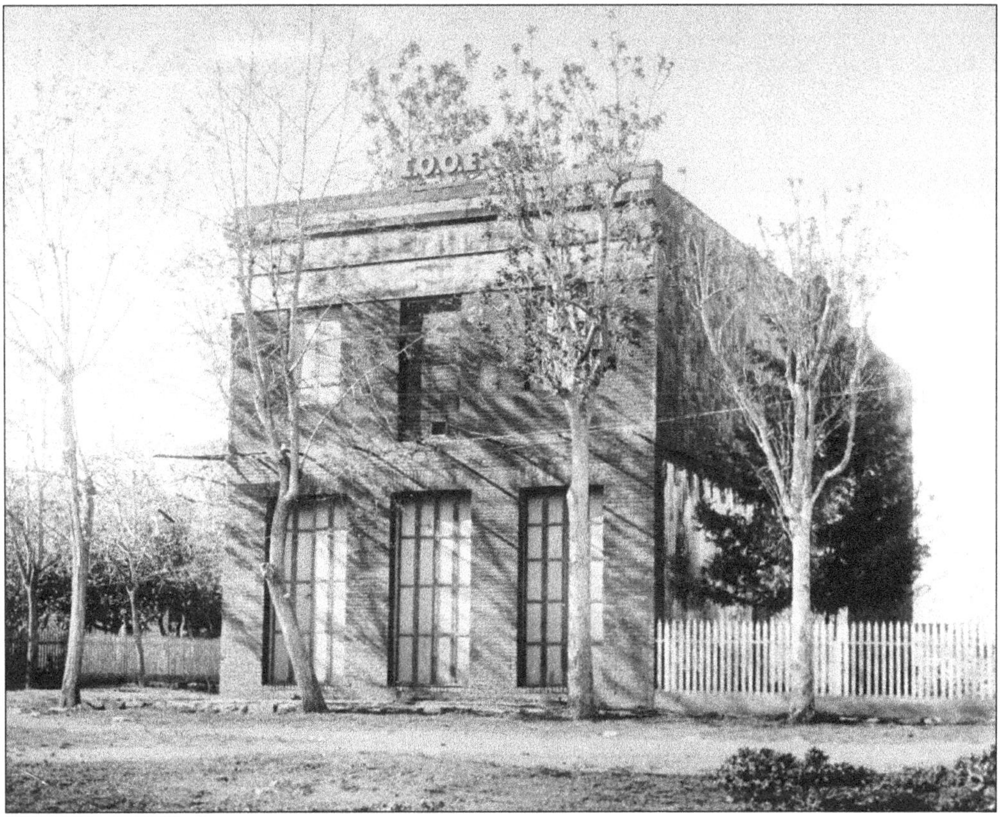

This building at State Street and Broadway was acquired by the Independent Order of Odd Fellows in 1868. The Odd Fellows were so named because in early England it was an "odd fellow" who belonged to an organization dedicated to helping those in need. The Odd Fellows were organized on this continent on April 26, 1819, in Baltimore, Maryland. The Ladies' Auxiliary off the Odd Fellows is known as the Rebekah Lodge.

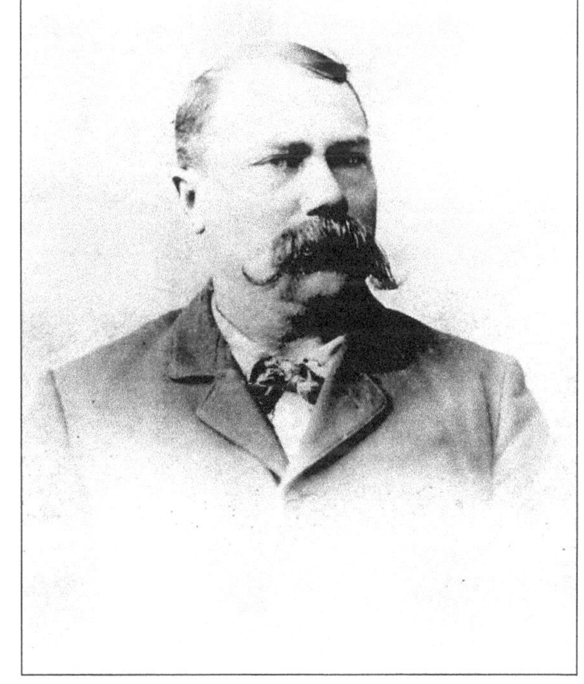

In 1864, Henry J. Dambacher was born in Massachusetts. A member of the Independent Order of Odd Fellows, he died in 1937 and is buried in the IOOF section of the Columbia Cemetery.

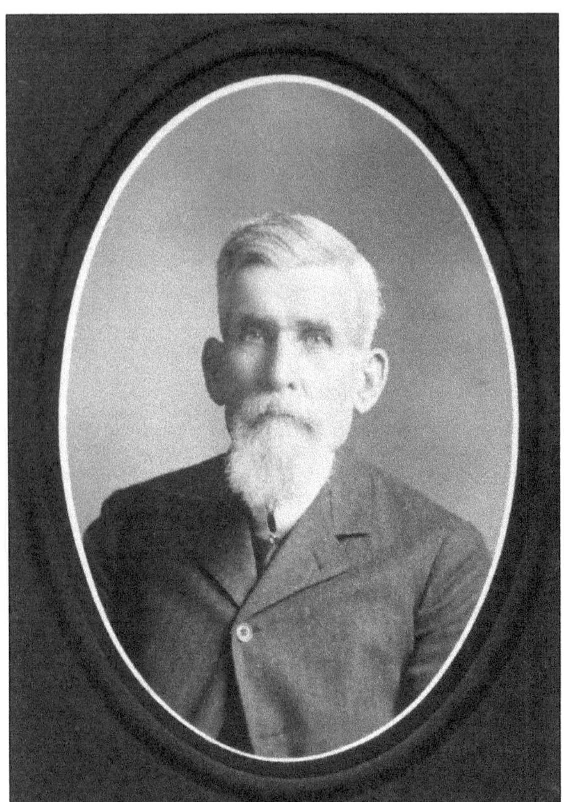

Thomas Birney was a member of the Hibernian Benevolent Society, which was dedicated to the welfare of Catholic Irish. The Columbia lodge was organized July 1857. Constable John Leary, a well-respected citizen, was president of this lodge at the time of his murder in November 1858.

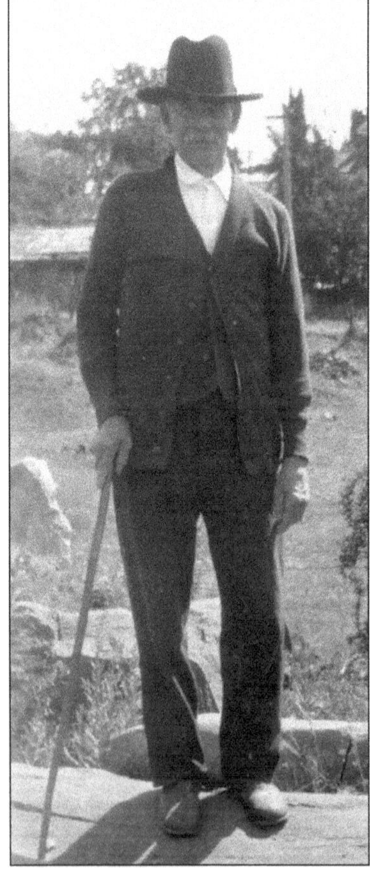

George Napoleon was a member of the Ancient Order of Foresters. The Foresters were known to exist in England as early as the mid-1700s, but its present form was established in 1834. It is a benevolent and fraternal organization that offers a range of insurance and savings plans designed to provide security and peace of mind for its members.

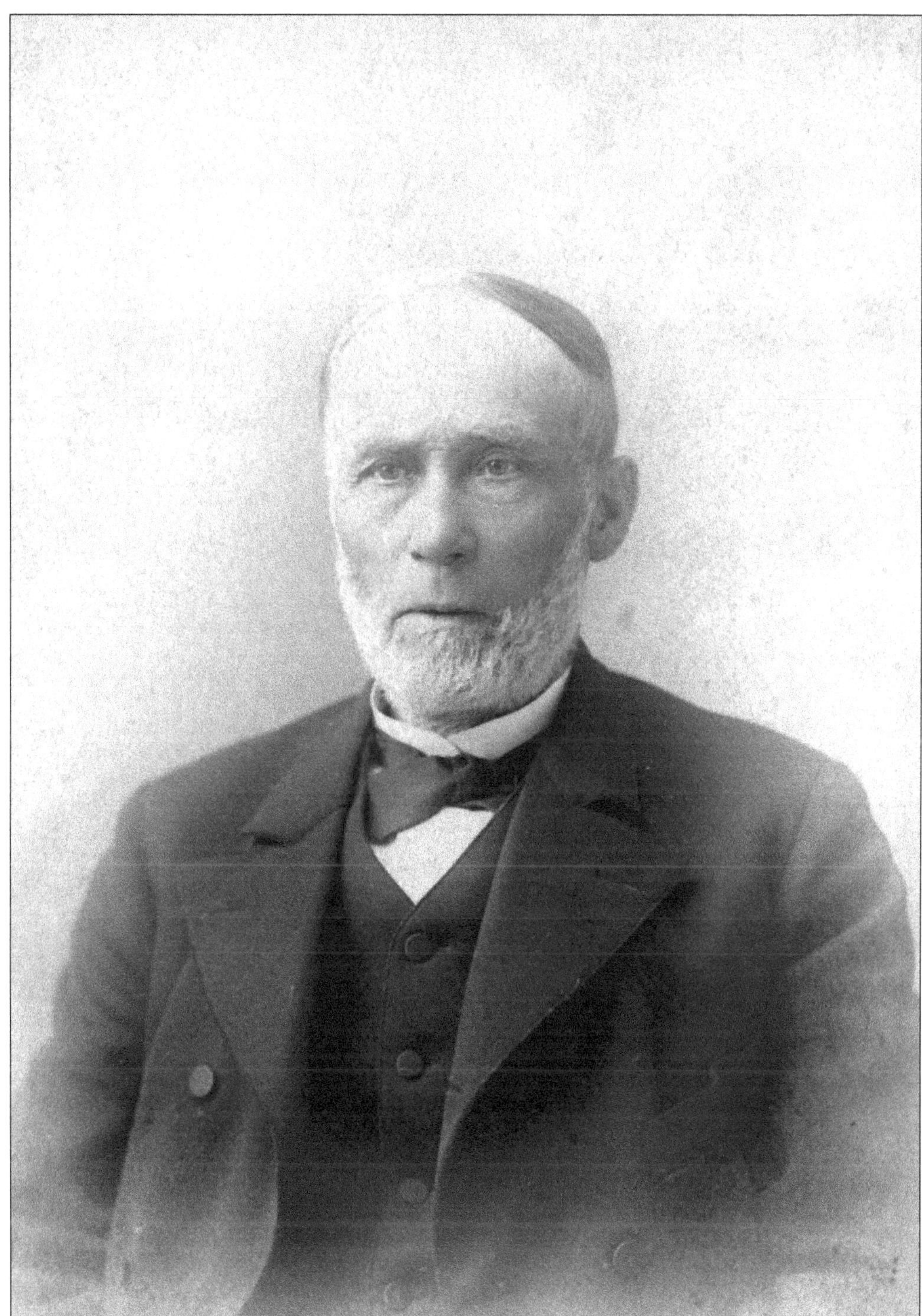

Sewell Knapp, a native of Maine, struck it rich at Moccasin Creek, where the Hetch Hetchy powerhouse now stands. He later established a mercantile business that became Columbia's most important supply center in the 1800s. His house can still be seen on Fulton Street. Knapp served in many public capacities in Columbia and was a member of the California Pioneer Society.

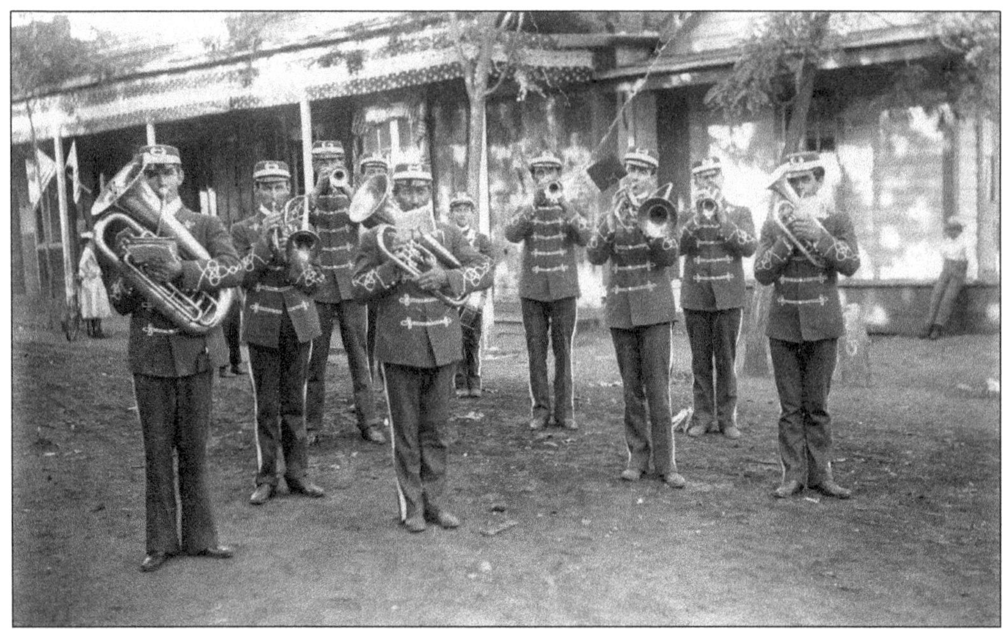

Bands were numerous in Columbia from the earliest days as music was a very important part of life. Many associations and societies had some sort of musical group if not their own bands. The Columbia Coronet Band still plays at celebrations.

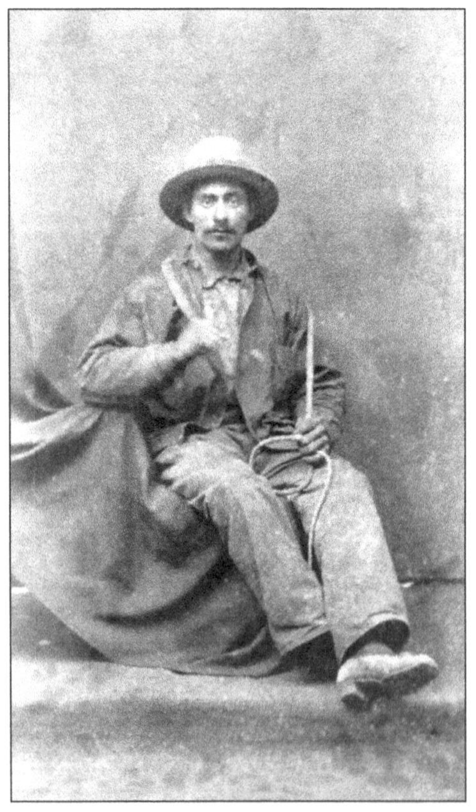

John Nash was a member of one of Columbia's early bands. Born in Columbia in 1852, he lived to be 100. He and his wife, Ellen, lived in one of the oldest homes in Columbia on Gold Street. He was an active member of the volunteer fire company until his death. While gardening next to his home one day he found a gold nugget.

This invitation to Miss McKenzie was for a military and civic ball given by the Columbia Corps of Fusiliers, March 15, 1855. John Leary and Col. Thomas N. Cazneau organized the Columbia Fusiliers in 1852. They were listed as a volunteer social military company. Cazneau built their first armory in 1852, but it was lost to fire in 1854. Leary built a second armory in 1854.

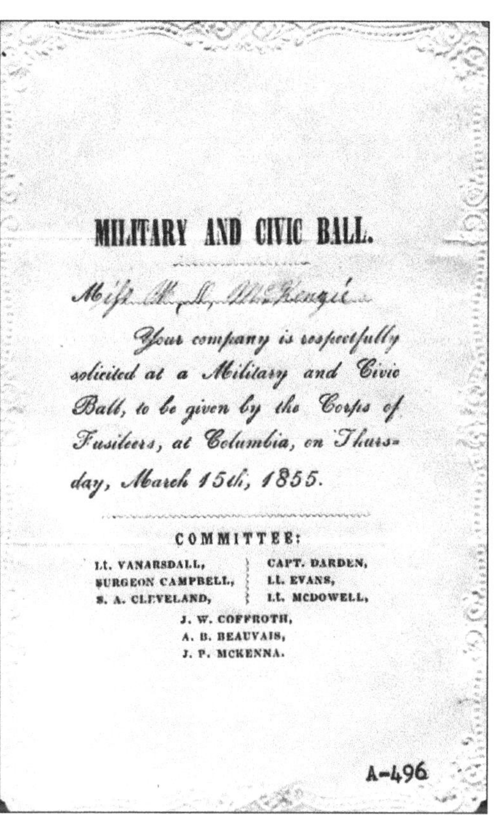

MILITARY AND CIVIC BALL.

Miss M. A. McKenzie

Your company is respectfully solicited at a Military and Civic Ball, to be given by the Corps of Fusileers, at Columbia, on Thursday, March 15th, 1855.

COMMITTEE:

Lt. VANARSDALL, CAPT. DARDEN,
SURGEON CAMPBELL, Lt. EVANS,
S. A. CLEVELAND, Lt. MCDOWELL,
J. W. COFFROTH,
A. B. BEAUVAIS,
J. P. MCKENNA.

A-496

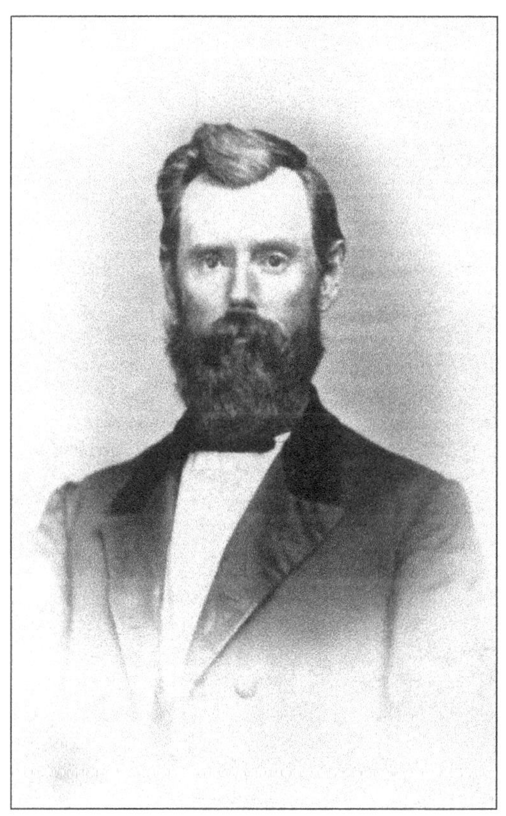

Dr. D. M. Baldwin was a member of the Tuolumne Home Guard. Organized in Columbia in 1861, the home guard's job was to restrain acts and expressions of disloyal people. Many towns and camps all over the area had home guard units.

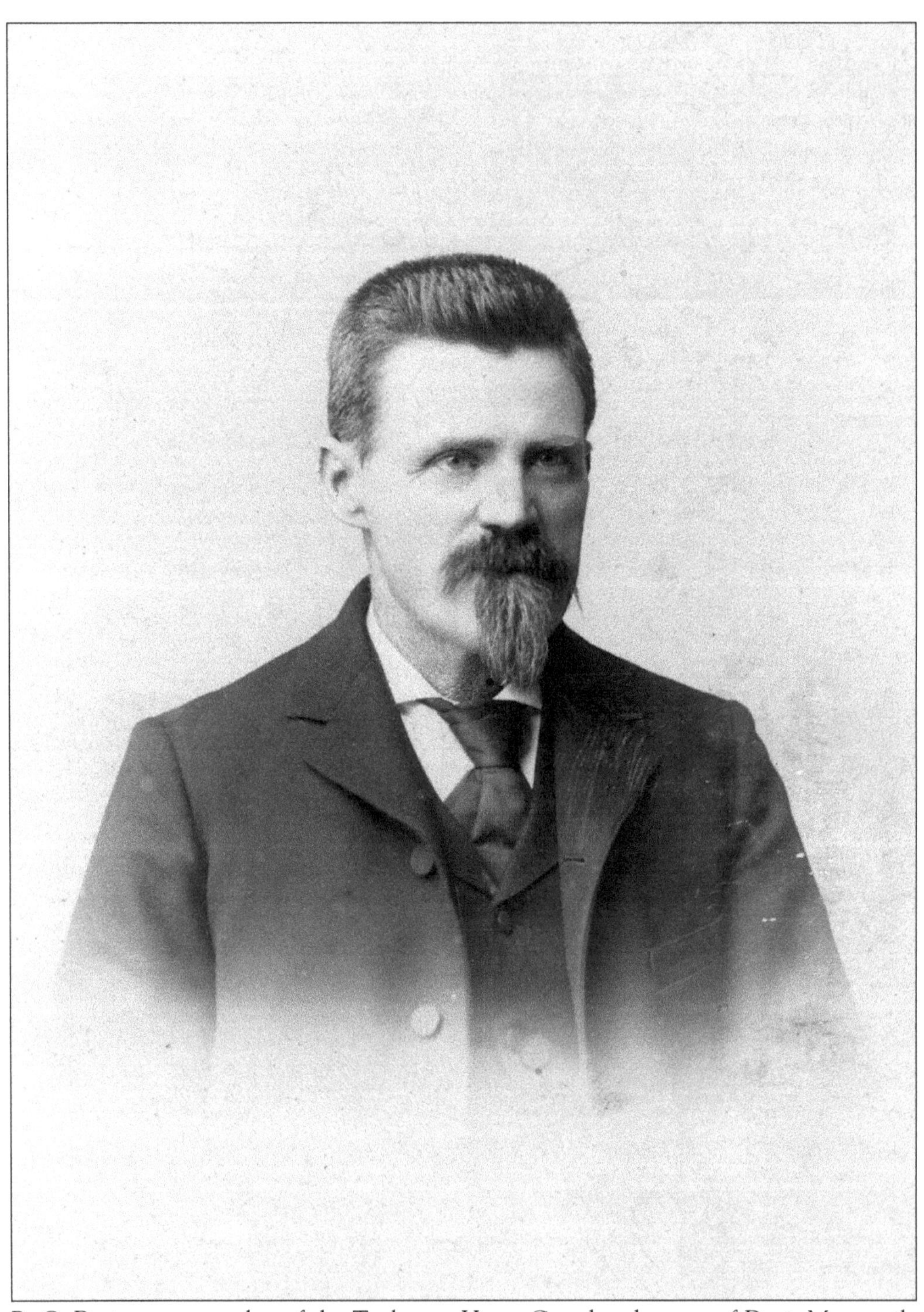

R. C. Davis was a member of the Tuolumne Home Guard and owner of Davis Mercantile (previously the Knapp Store) located in the building where the museum is today. In the late 1980s, descendents of Davis came to Columbia seeking permission to move his remains from the Bay Area to Columbia because Davis spent most of his life there and was happiest in Columbia.

Lt. John K. Hunter, a native of Indiana, was a member of the Tuolumne Home Guard of Columbia. Hunter was a senior lieutenant, 3rd Infantry Regiment, 3rd Brigade, California Militia Force in 1861 during the Civil War. He is buried in the Columbia Cemetery.

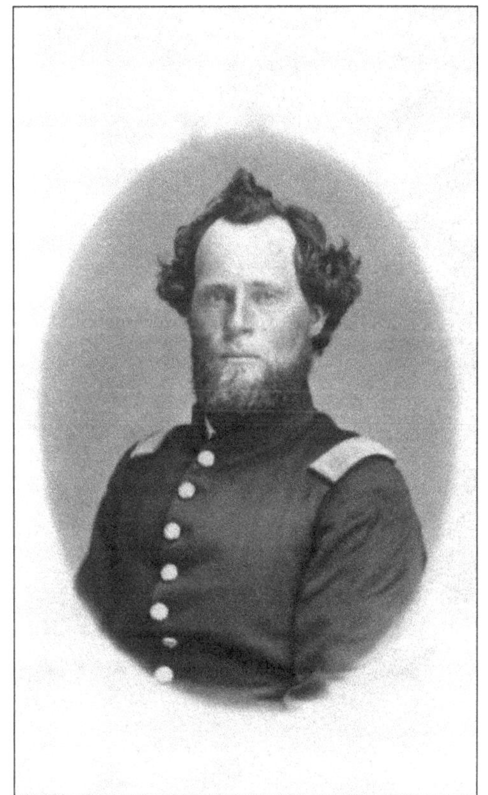

Shown here are Companies A and B of the 6th Infantry Regiment, California National Guard. James or Frank Vassallo of Columbia is seated third from left. Vassallo was a prominent businessman and large landholder in Columbia.

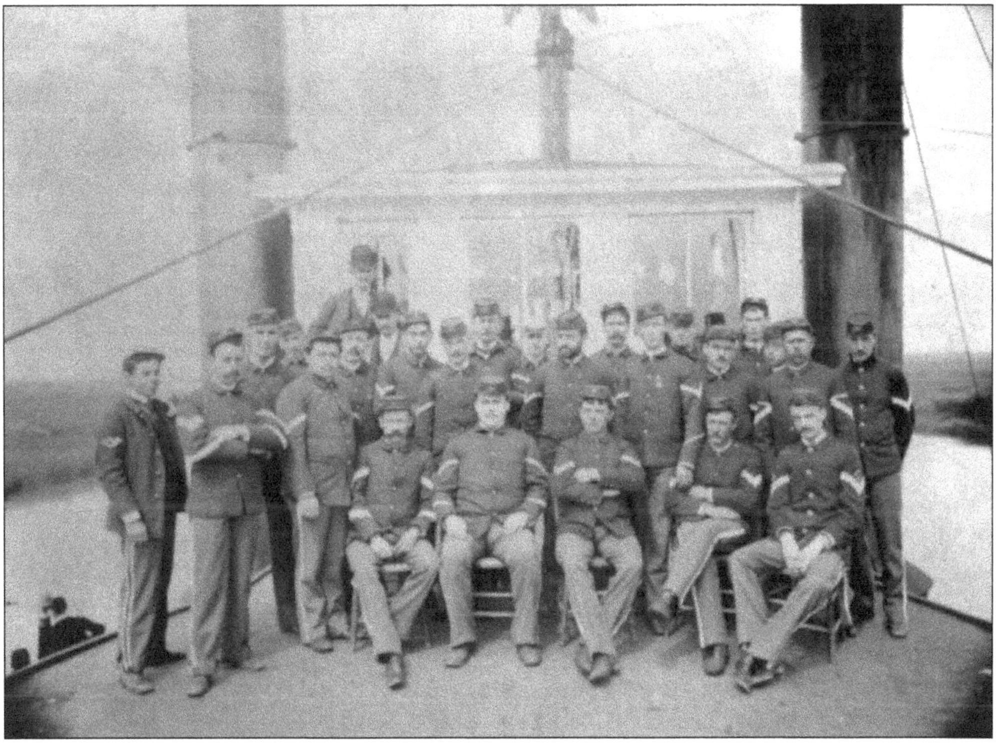

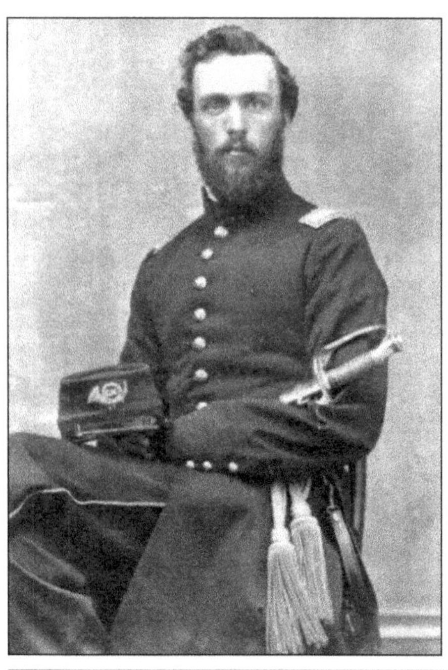

In 1861, C. C. Call was first assistant foreman on Tuolumne Engine Company One and a member of Company A, Tuolumne Home Guards.

This is the flag of the Tuolumne Rangers, many of whom were recruited from in and around Columbia. The women of Sonora made the flag for the Tuolumne Rangers, who served in the Civil War as a cavalry unit keeping order in two counties in northern California.

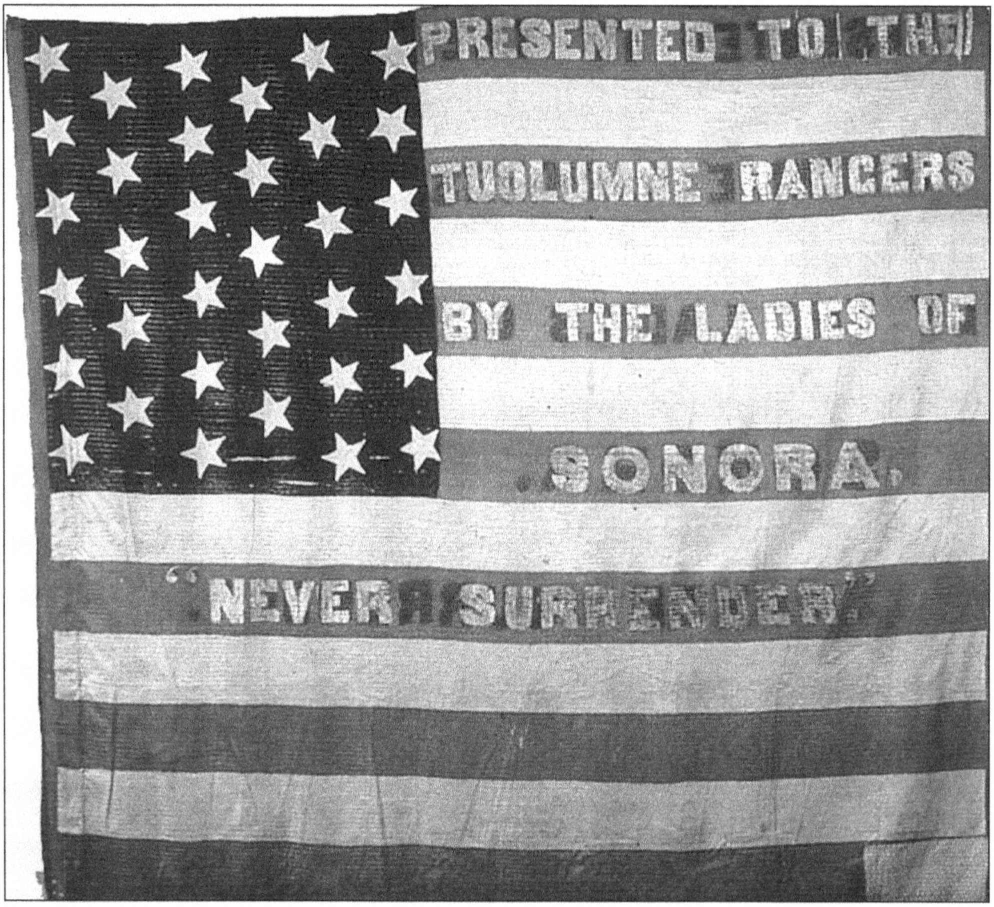

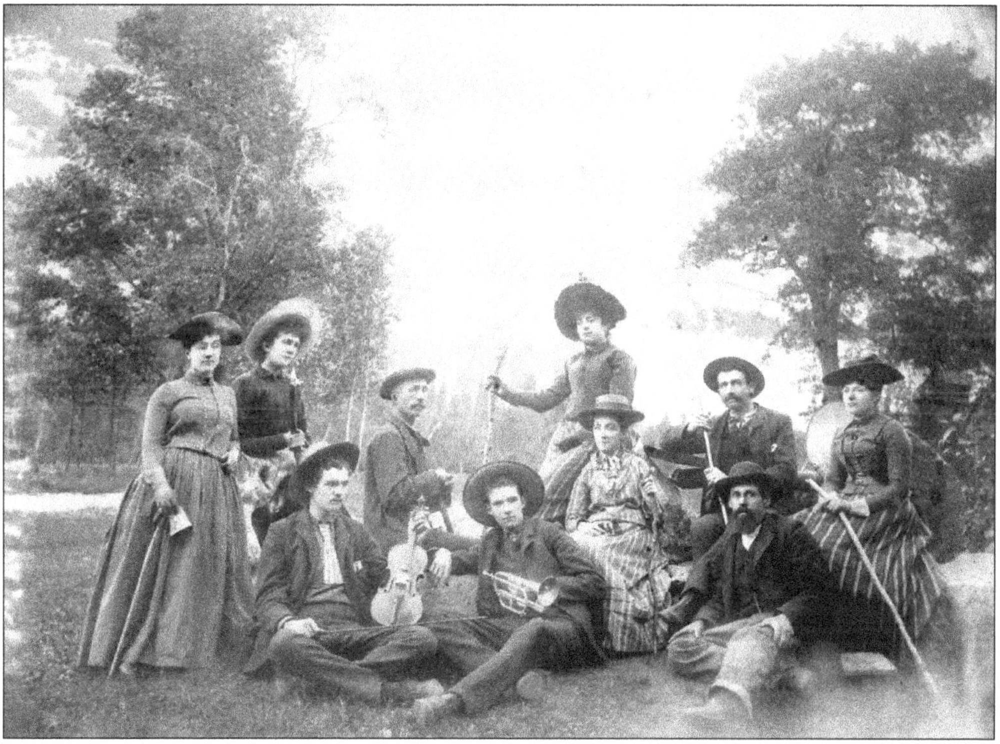

A group of Columbians celebrate the Fourth of July in Yosemite Valley.

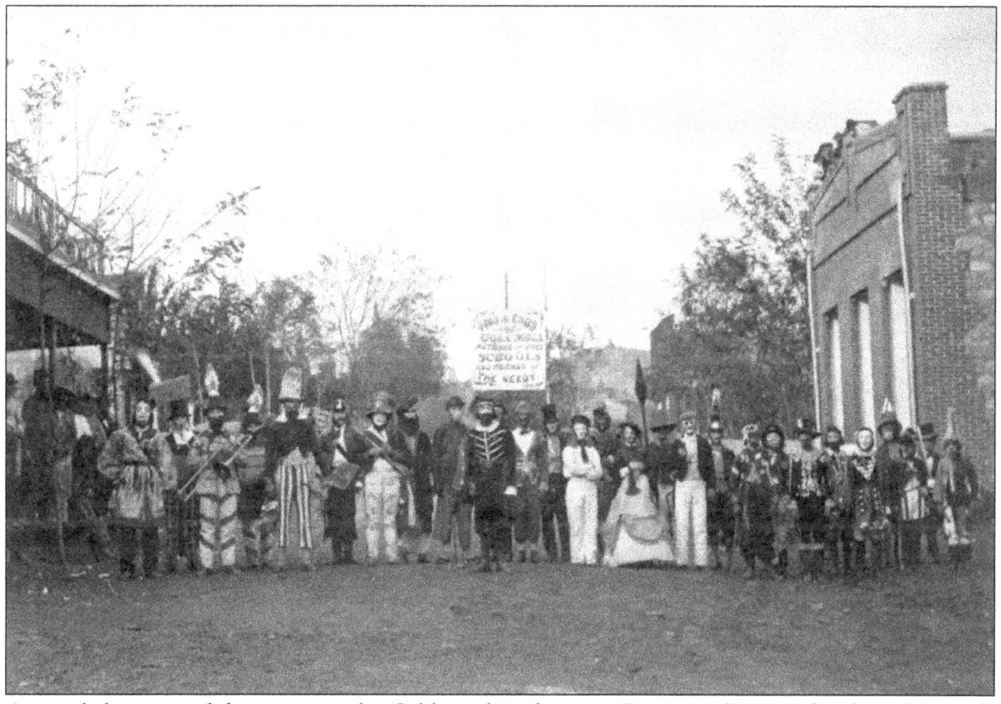

Around the turn of the century, the Odds and Ends were "Patrons of Free Schools and Friends of the Needy," according to their banner.

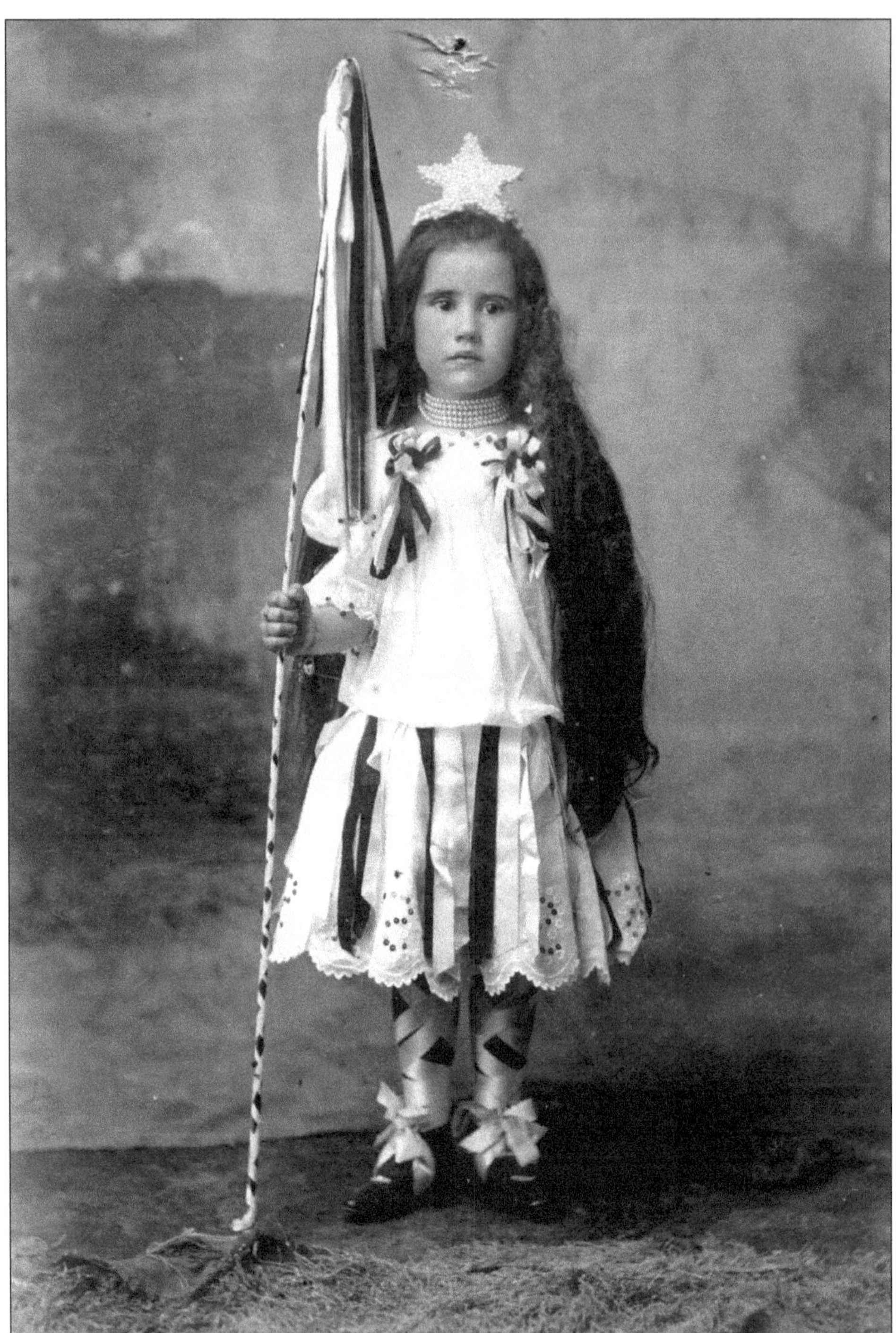

Elaine Pownall Mellor, shown here in a cute outfit, was the granddaughter of Dr. Joseph Pownall of the Tuolumne Water Company and lived in the water secretary's house on Pacific and Main Streets. Her father and grandfather were secretaries and trustees of the water company. She married Ted Mellor and together they ran a candy store in Columbia. She is buried in the Masonic cemetery with her sister and brother.

Eight

Life Goes On

By the 1860s, the heady days of prosperity were waning. The easily found gold was gone, miners were becoming employees, mining discoveries were occurring in other areas, and families were beginning to leave town. Then the dreadful winter of 1861–1862 arrived with rainstorms producing, according to local accounts, 102 inches of rain in 68 days. Bridges that provided access in and out of the county were destroyed, flumes and ditches were washed out, and the Central Valley was one huge lake. For a while, food and other supplies were unable to reach the county and near famine conditions existed. Two years following that flood, a severe drought struck in 1864. The school that opened in Columbia to such acclaim was having trouble staying open due to the loss of tax revenues.

The town was visibly in decline. Buildings stood vacant and real estate values were dropping. Town lots that had sold for $900 each were now worth half the price. Large hydraulic companies were moving into the main gulch, the mining area in the lower gulch expanded, and as buildings were torn down, mining companies moved into the downtown area.

The Haynes Ditch was built to supply water to the mining companies. The assessed valuation in Columbia fell from almost $1 million in the late 1850s to $150,000 in 1868. Then the *Columbia Citizen News*, the last newspaper in town, closed.

In 1876, town trustees gave up incorporation. The once booming town was now a sleepy little village making its living by supplying mining camps on the east slope of the Sierras and providing employees for the marble quarry, the water company, farming, and ranching. There was a minor resurgence of gold mining in the 1890s when the hard rock mining areas to the west and north of the town took off. The Densmore, Experimental, Hidden Treasure, Mountain Lily, and Von Trump mines, among others, opened and started producing gold.

In the 20th century, tourism, which had started in the late 1850s, was bringing more people to the small town. Moving pictures discovered the town as well. In an attempt to bring more attention to the town and encourage business opportunities, several celebrations were created in Columbia during the 1930s: "The Fiesta Days Celebration" in 1934, "The Days of Gold" in 1938, and annual Fourth of July Celebrations. Although there were hard times, Columbia was never completely abandoned.

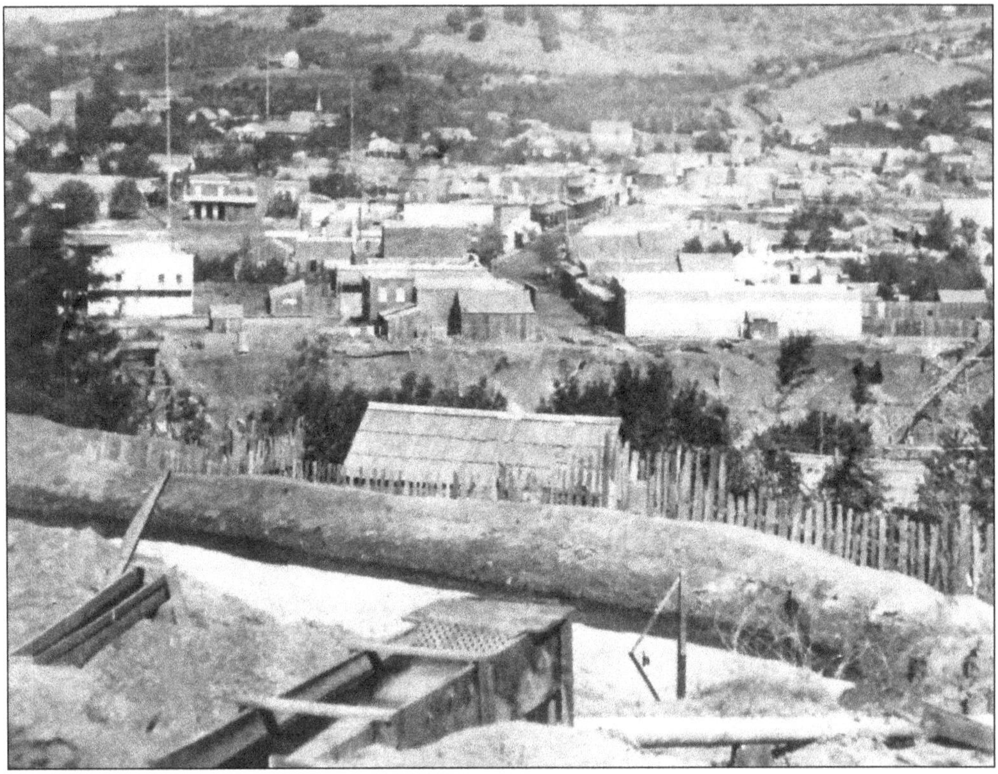

This photograph reveals signs that the boom times were over. The gap in the middle shows where the Main Street bridge, connecting the town and Kennebec Hill, had collapsed and not been rebuilt. Mining activity in the main gulch area is not apparent and the large waterwheels are gone. The tall poles were called liberty poles and were being installed in California prior to and during the Civil War.

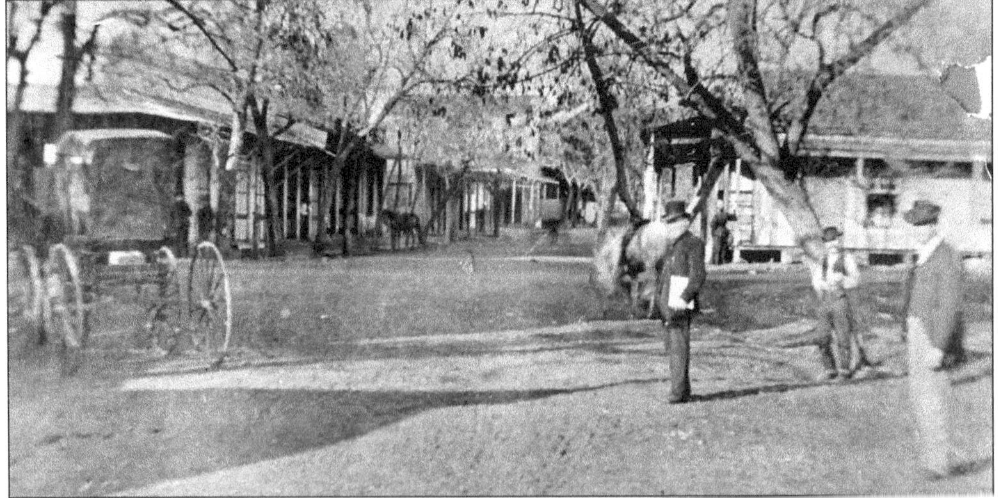

This view, looking north up Main Street from the intersection of Main and Fulton Streets, shows the Tibbitts house as the frame building on the right and the brick Stagedriver's Retreat Saloon on the left behind the carriage. The Brady Building has yet to be constructed, dating the photograph before 1899.

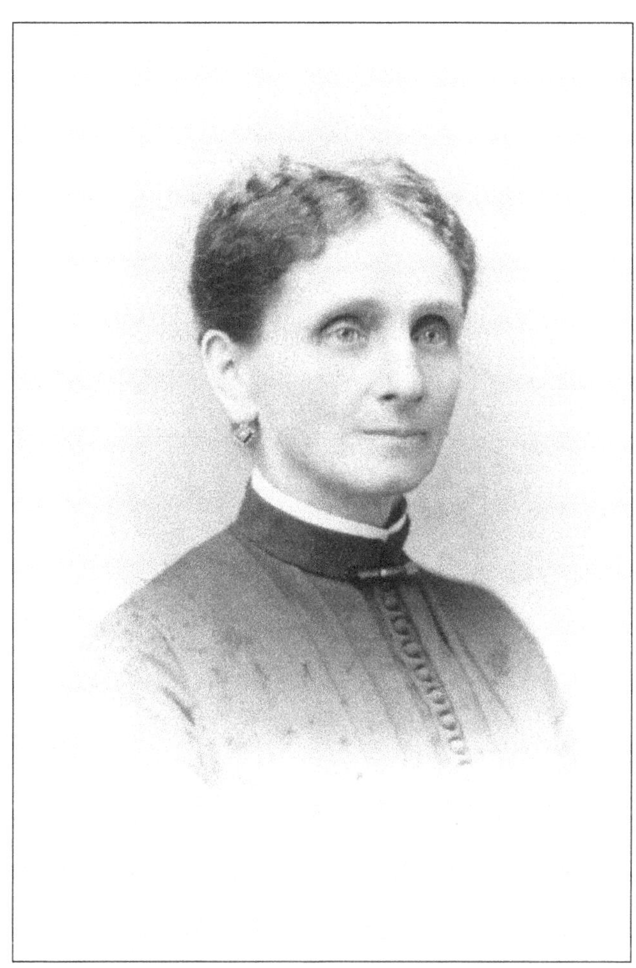

Rosien Rosasco Aste Wilson was born in Italy and moved to the United States with her first husband, James Aste. After his death, Rosien married James Wilson. The family moved to Columbia, where Wilson opened a shoe business in the brick building on Main Street. He was in the process of building a house on the lot next to his store in 1876 when he died. Mrs. Wilson not only saw to the completion of the house but took over the store, changing the business to "Boots, Shoes, Dry Goods and Gents' Furnishing Goods." Posing on the porch on May 8, 1893, 15 years after the house was finished, from left to right, are Louisa Seibert, Mrs. Rosasco, Miss Seibert, Rose Wilson, Annie Wilson, Katie Seibert, and William Sevening.

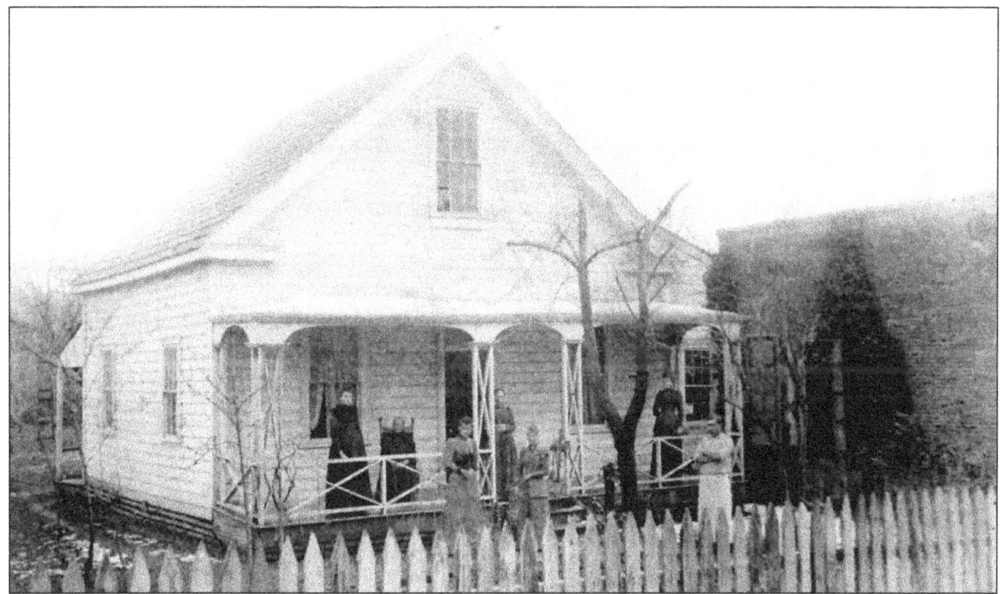

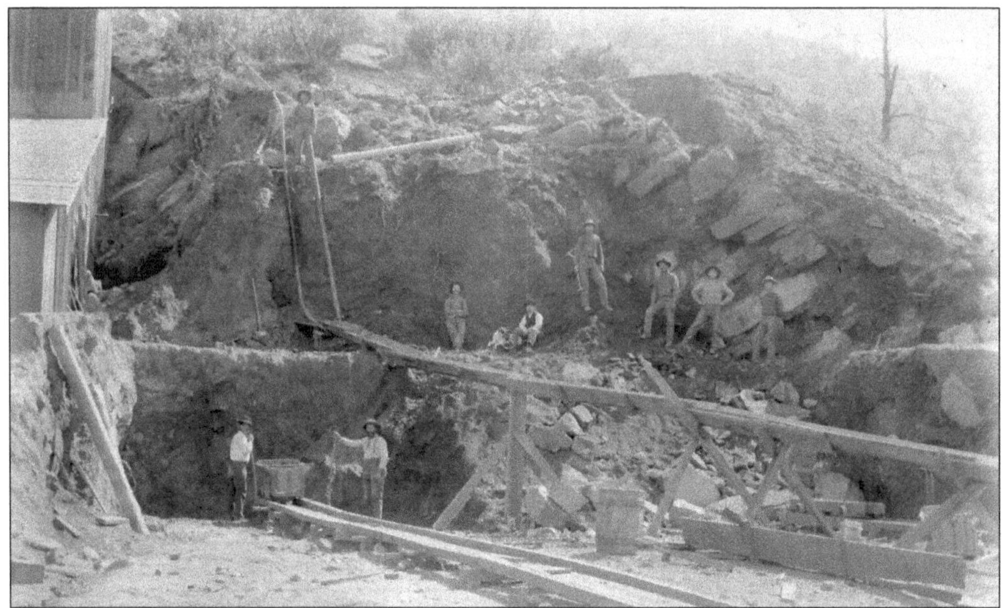

Hard rock mining was one of the major employers in the area. This image shows the Densmore Mine, about two miles north of Columbia, around 1900 to 1910. Of the men seen here only three are identified: George Williams (lower left by car), Joe McNamee (extreme right), and Henry Ebler (third from right). The recession of the early 1890s helped encourage further development of gold mines.

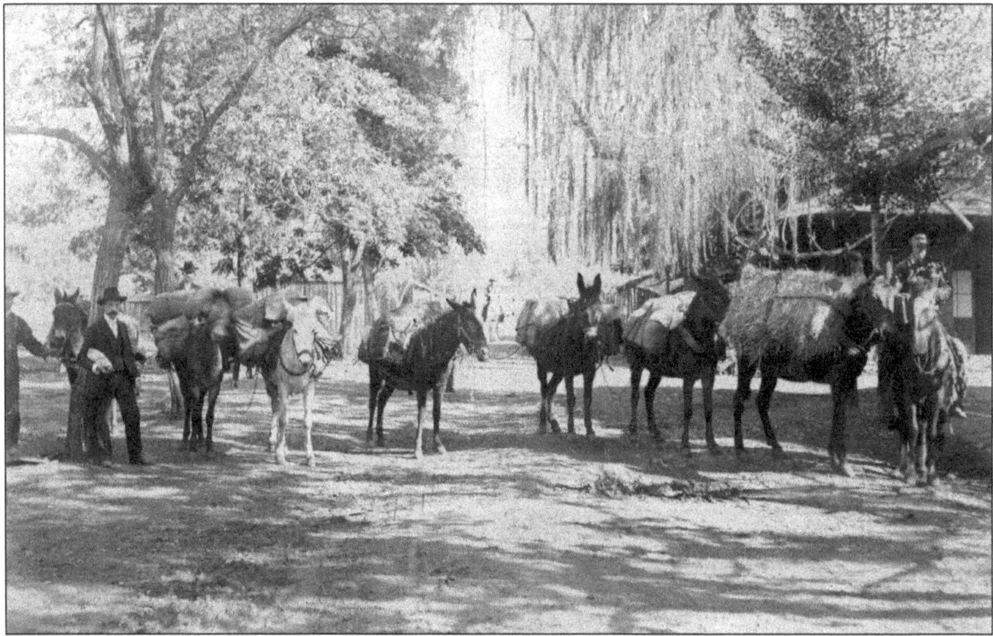

Taken in the late 1890s, this photo shows O. Frank Peterson's pack train at the intersection of Main and Jackson Streets. Peterson is on the extreme left and Bert Yuill is on the extreme right. The other men are unknown. Peterson ran pack trains to the Star, Jupiter, Mountain Lily, and other mines in the area. The brick building in the background is the Pioneer Saloon (St. Charles Saloon).

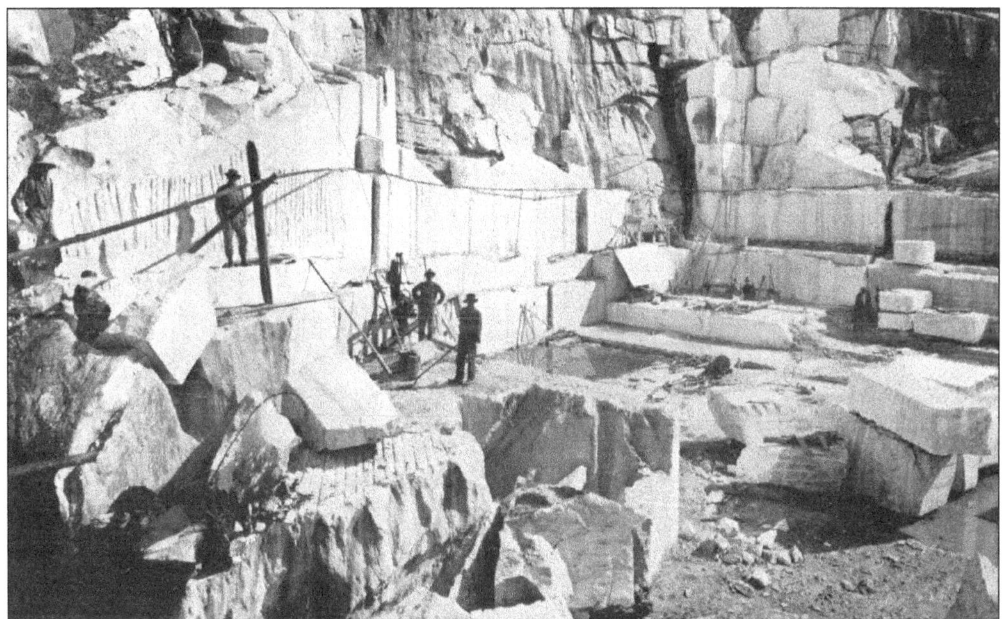

This is the working face of the Columbia Marble Company, northeast of Columbia, one of two marble quarries in Columbia. The Columbia Marble Company was in operation from the 1850s through the early 20th century. The marble was quarried and split in Columbia, then moved to Sonora where it was shipped to a finishing plant in San Francisco. The Bell Columbia Marble Company began operations in 1918 and continued into the 1930s.

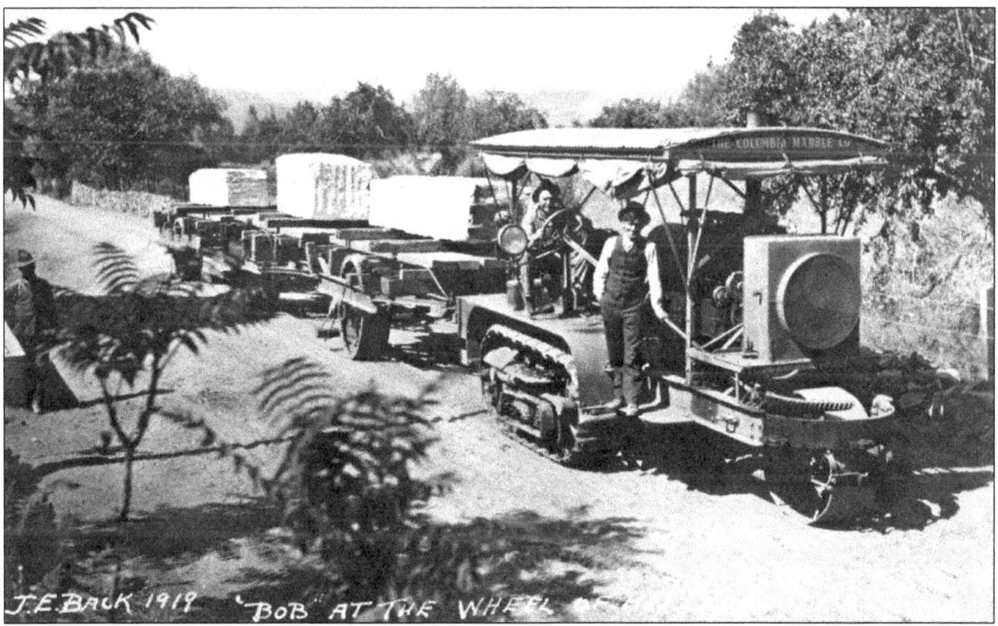

A steam traction engine moves marble from the Columbia Marble Company to the railroad in Sonora. Some of the marble produced by Columbia's marble quarries was used in buildings in San Francisco, including the Palace Hotel, the Wells Fargo Building, and the post office, as well as the Washington Monument. In Columbia, you can see marble sidewalks, steps, and stairs made of Columbia marble.

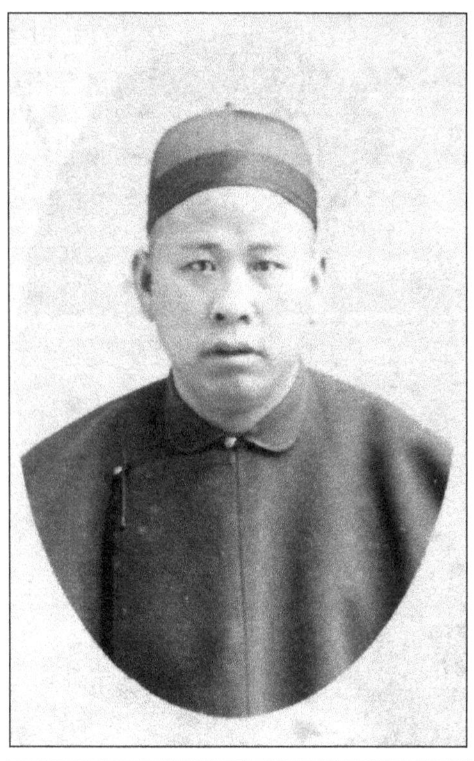

As early as 1852, records show a Chinese presence in Columbia. Although not allowed to own or work claims according to Columbia District Mining Regulations, the Chinese established businesses such as a dry goods store, restaurant, laundry, boardinghouses, and a temple. By 1870, about one-fourth of Columbia's population was Chinese, many of them families. Before the Chinese in the United States could return to China for a visit and get back into the United States, the U.S. government required a return visa. This had to be received from U.S. Customs and the application requirements included a photograph signed by an Anglo-American attesting to the accuracy of the photograph, as well as other documents guaranteeing both a certain amount of money in the bank and the applicant's good character.

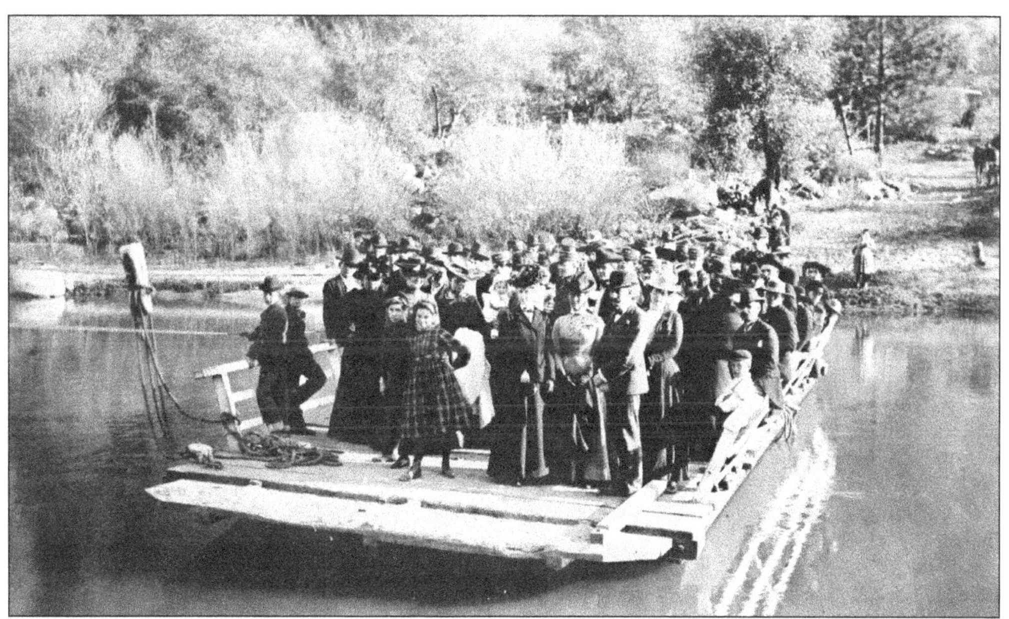

The last ferry boat makes a run across the Stanislaus River at Parrotts Ferry in 1903. Several ferries operated on the river, and Parrotts Ferry was about three miles northwest of Columbia. The ferry went through several changes of ownership before being replaced with a bridge in 1903. The photograph below shows the dedication of the first Parrotts Ferry bridge, which was wiped out by high water in 1937 and replaced with a concrete bridge in 1938. The current bridge was built in the early 1980s.

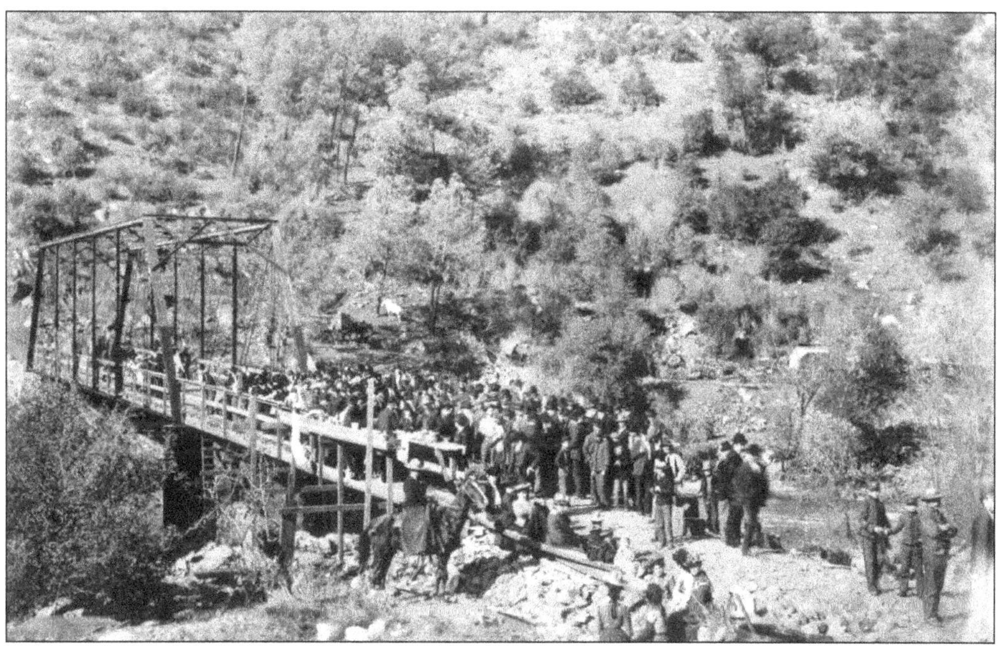

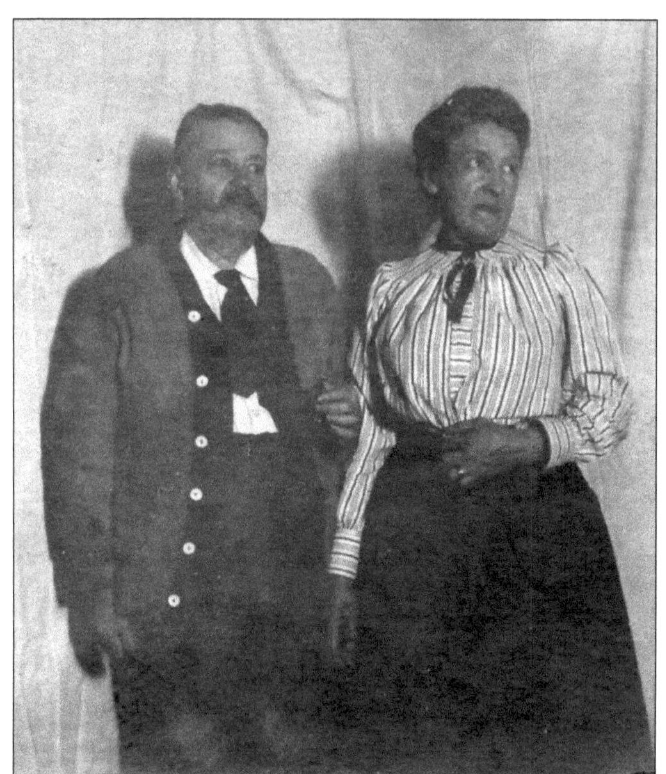

Mary and Dante Cinelli purchased the City Hotel in 1911 from Ralph Morgan, son of George Morgan who built the hotel. They repaired the brick building and added a two-story wooden frame structure at the rear housing a kitchen, pantry, and laundry, in addition to rooms for rent on the second floor. After her husband's death, Mrs. Cinelli continued operating the hotel until 1917.

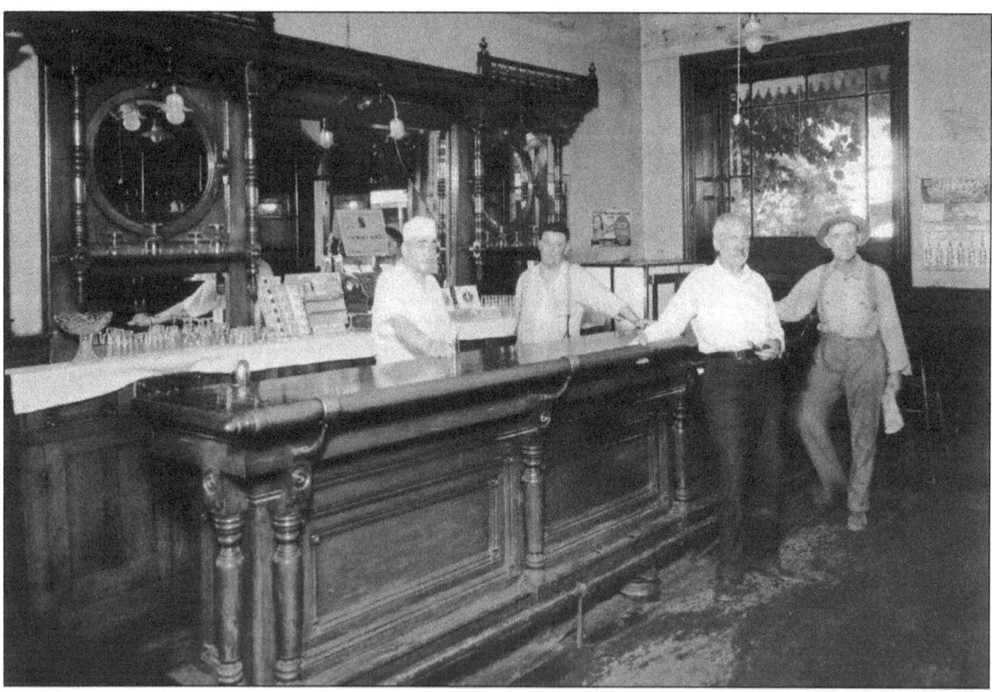

In 1930, Mr. and Mrs. Angelo Nadotti ran the hotel and bar. Board was $30 per week, which included three meals a day. This picture, taken in 1932, shows the interior of the bar, very similar to the look of today's What Cheer Saloon.

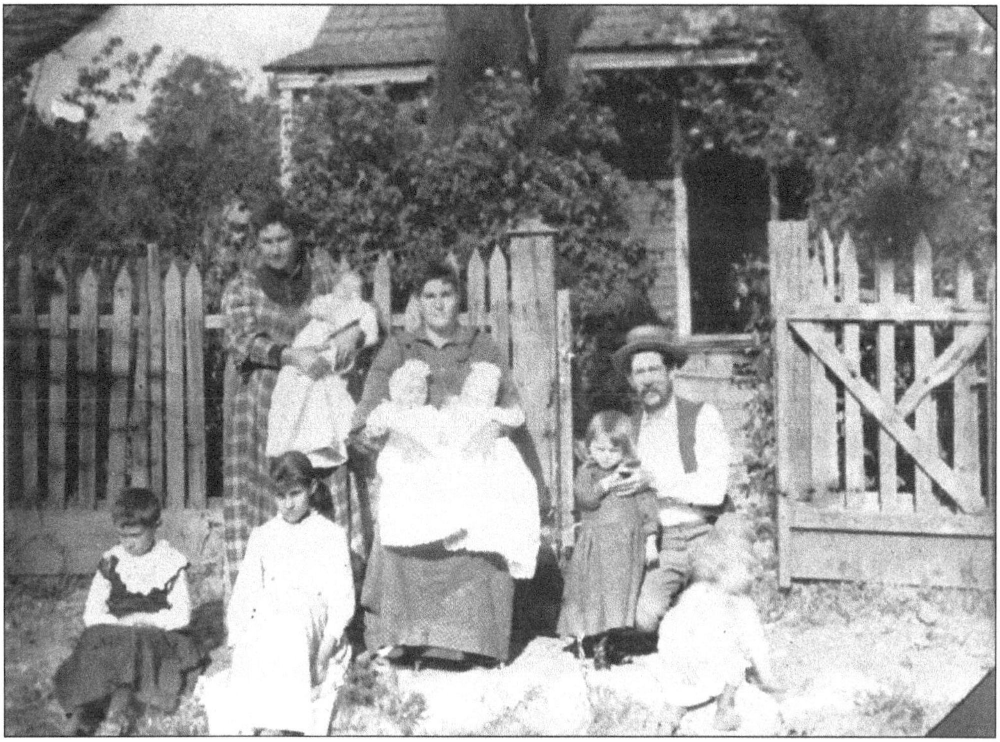

Seen here are members of the Engelke family. Sarah McGowan and her sister, both daughters of town marshal James McGowan, married two Engelke brothers. This house, on the corner of Columbia and Pacific, is still standing. The Italian cypress trees behind the family now tower above the little house.

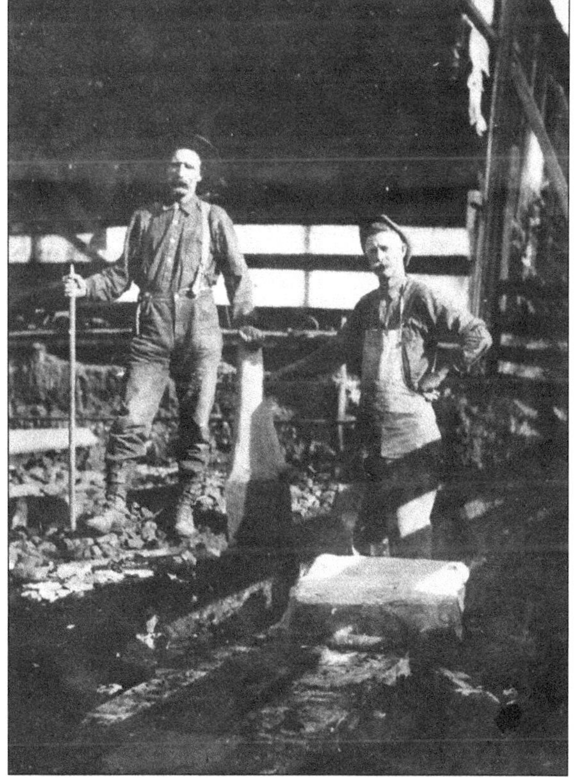

Ed Hastings (left) and Amel Nelson (right) lay the foundation for the "new" firehouse on Main Street about 1910. Tuolumne Engine Company One and Columbia Engine Company Two had united to form Columbia Engine Company One and build a new firehouse.

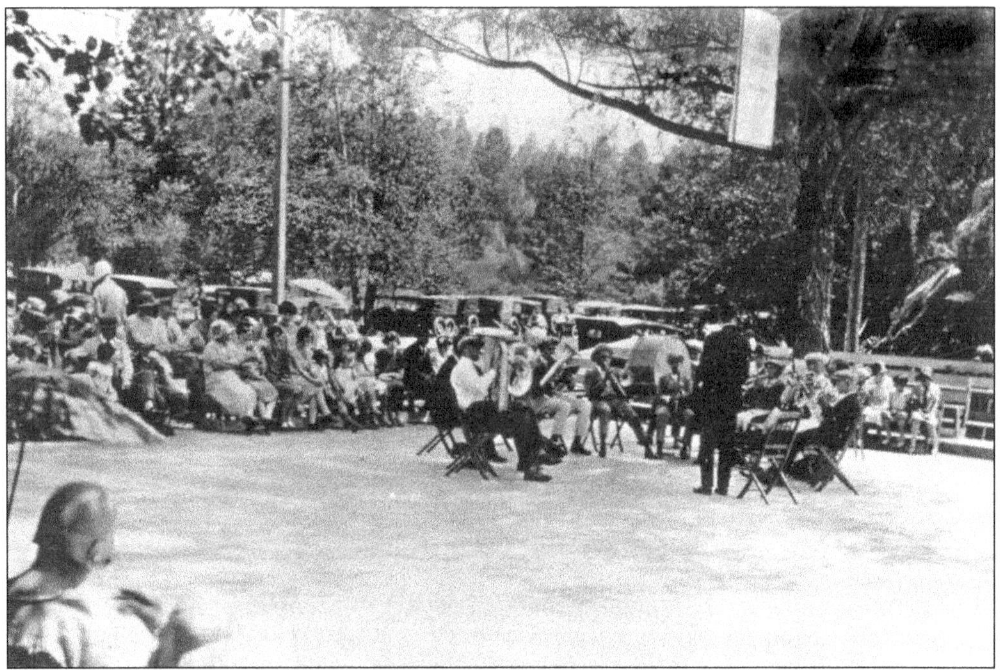

Saturday night dances and midnight suppers were very popular in the 1920s. Bands traveled from the valley to provide music for the dancers. Local women would fix midnight suppers for the participants and observers of all ages. When dances were no longer held, the wood from the dance floor was used to build a garage for Frank Hughes. The garage is still standing.

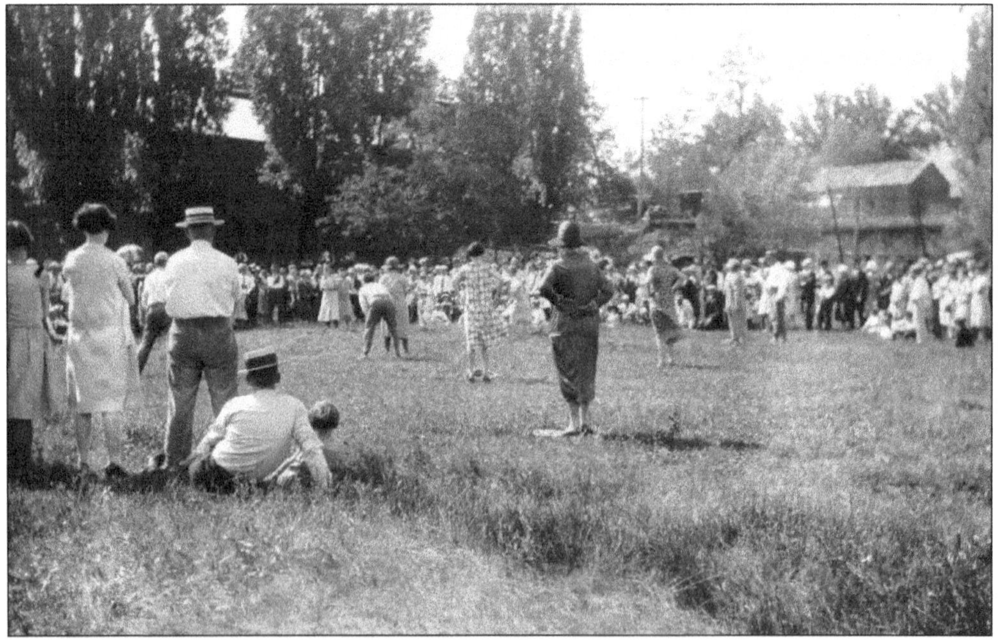

Small town entertainment included baseball games in Recreation Park, now the lower parking lot. The corner of the Fallon Theater is visible in the background. Baseball games were very popular in the 1920s and 1930s with both men and women participating.

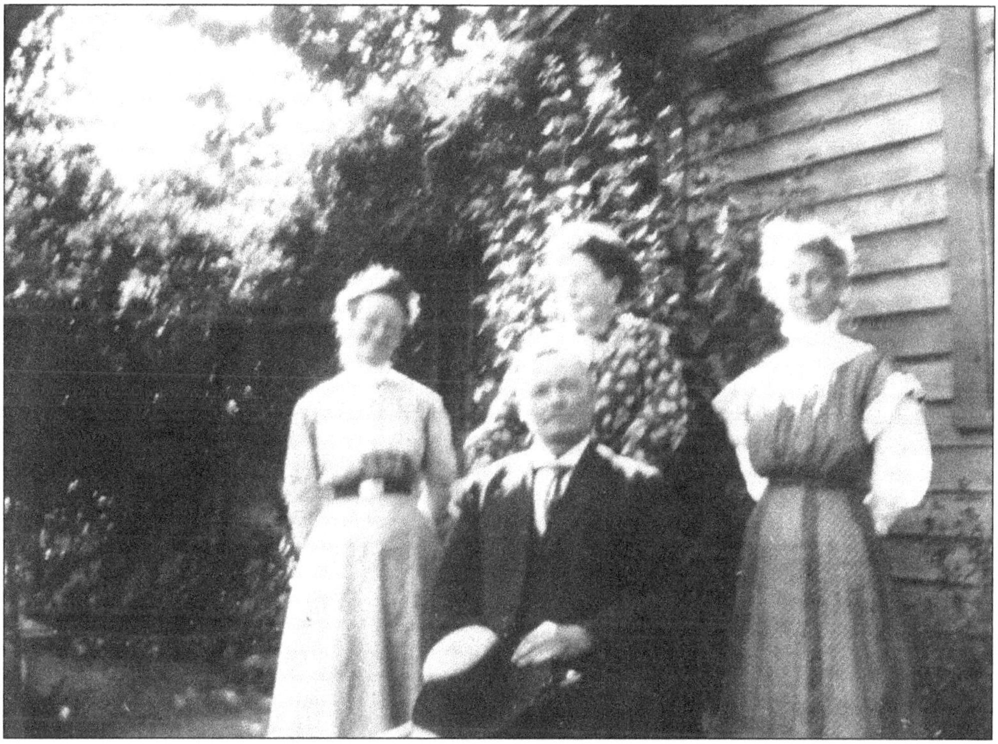

Seen here, from right to left, are Julia Conlin, Tom Conlin, unidentified, and Maggie Conlin. Tom became the third and last Wells Fargo agent in Columbia, serving from 1876 to 1914, when the agency closed. Tom and his sisters lived in the Wells Fargo building until their deaths. In the 20th century, the Conlins collected memorabilia, newspaper articles, and memories about Columbia. They also wrote newspaper articles about the town.

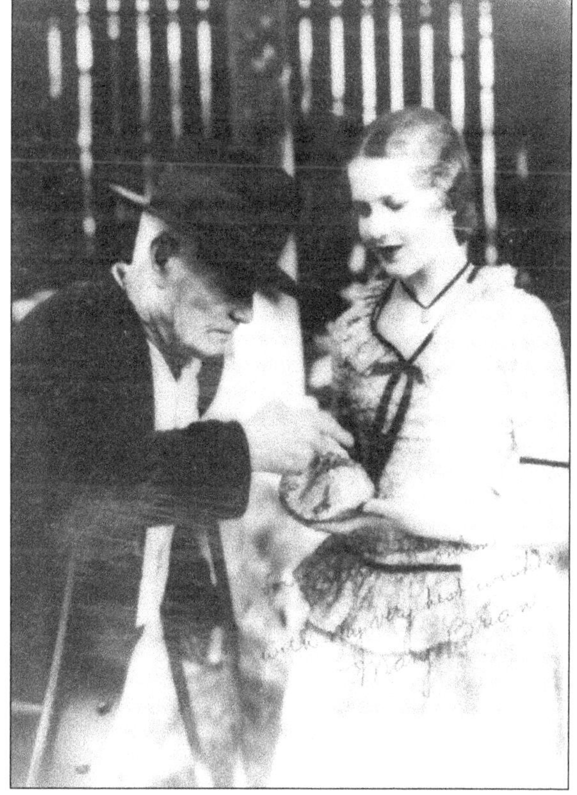

Mary Brian, one of the early movie actresses, is pictured here in Columbia giving her autograph to Tom Conlin. Movies, television shows, and commercials have been filmed in Columbia through the 20th century. Among the hundreds of films are *High Noon* with Gary Cooper and Grace Kelly, Michael Landon's *Little House on the Prairie*, *Shadow Riders* with Tom Selleck, and Clint Eastwood's *Pale Rider*.

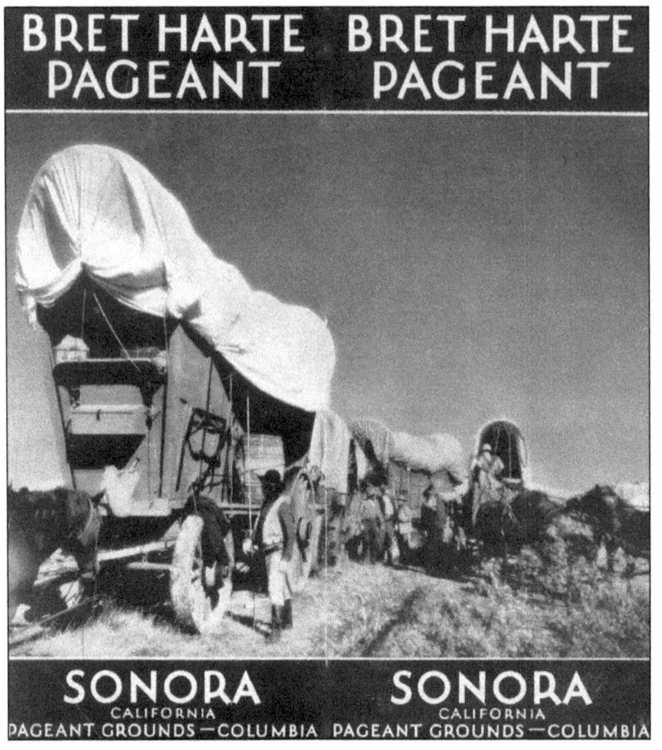

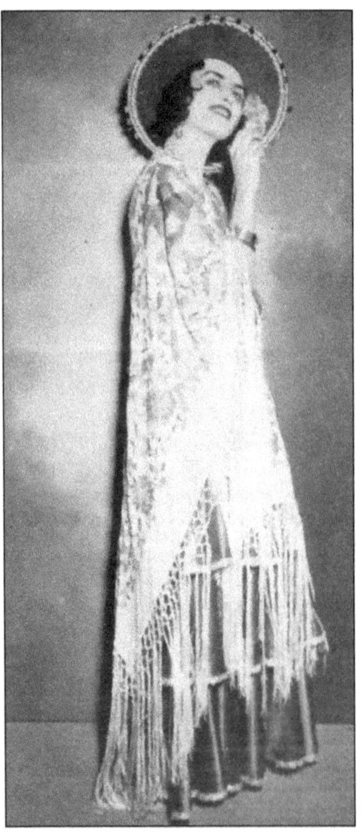

In 1932 and 1933, the Bret Harte Pageant was held about a half mile from Columbia, at the end of Gold Street. This was the culmination of years of planning for a statewide celebration called Fiesta Year. Generally based on gold rush history, the production involved dozens of local residents in the orchestra, on the stage, and constructing the sets. Marian Solari, pictured left, played the young heroine in the musical based on the dramatic production *The Golden Trail* by Charles Cadman. There were "237 characters in the play, consisting of miners, hunters, Spanish dons, Indians and their women folk."

Nine

Revival

In the late 1920s, the California Legislature commissioned Frederick Law Olmsted Jr. to travel through California seeking areas to form a state park system. Olmsted proposed that the gold rush buildings in Columbia become part of the new system, but money was not available.

In the 1930s, Otheto Weston, an artist who had lived in Columbia, launched an attempt to get people interested in saving the rundown buildings. She met Mrs. W. F. C. "Rheta" Zimmerman, who in turn was able to attract the attention of people such as George Ezra Dane, Archie Stevenot, and Gertrude Atherton, who formed the Historic Mining Towns Preservation League to "further the preservation of Columbia" and other historic mining towns. This group was able to get legislation passed to acquire buildings for a state park, but matching funds were never raised and the attempt was not successful.

In 1945, Dr. and Mrs. James McConnell, worried about the future of the town, sought help from many levels of local and state government and the Columbia Progressive Club. The consortium was able to launch a successful effort to get legislation passed and raise funds to turn the historic business core of the town into a state park. Their success was crowned when on July 15, 1945, Gov. Earl Warren came to town to sign the documents establishing the Columbia State Historic Park.

After the initial excitement, there was the long, slow process of turning the town into a park. Much controversy developed when state officials first tried to force all town residents to leave. After townspeople met with politicians and bureaucrats, a compromise was created that resulted in state government competing on the open market to buy buildings and land. Property owners were approached, buildings were purchased outright, or scenic easements were acquired on historic properties to protect the appearance of the town.

After the purchase, plans were made to protect and restore the buildings. Restoration involved research into original materials, archaeology work on the site, and mitigation to prevent such long-standing problems as water intrusion from above and below. There was no quick fix for the historic structures, and progress was slow and unsteady as state funding was unpredictable.

A few buildings that had disappeared over the years were rebuilt, and gradually the town came to present the same streetscape in the 21st century as it had in the 19th century.

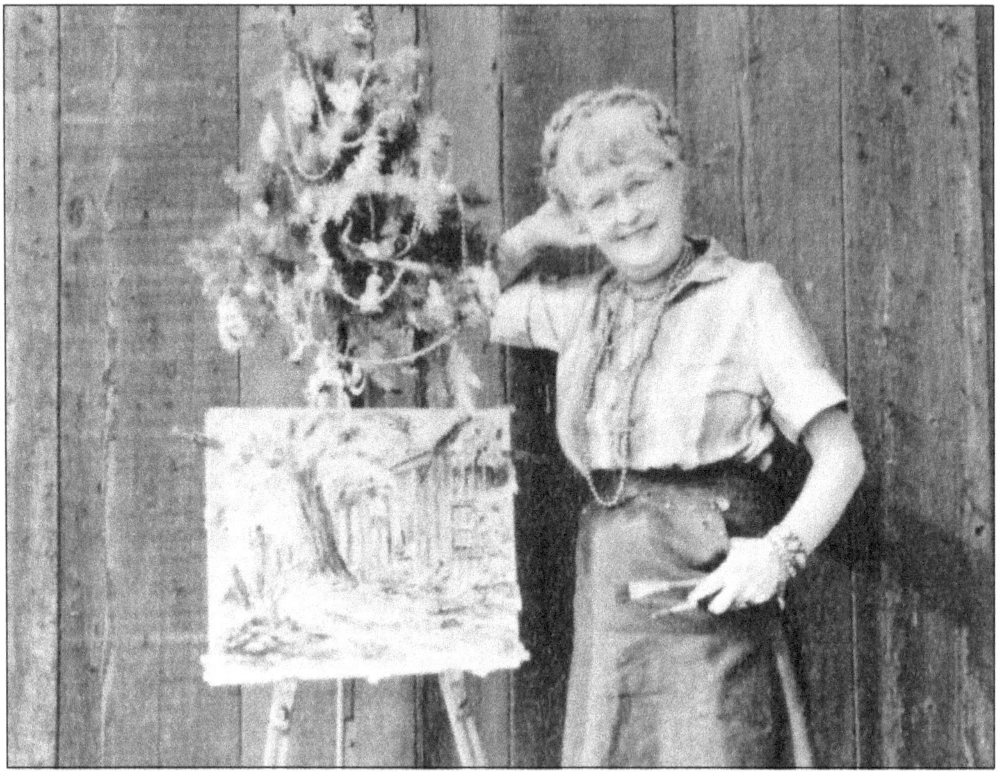

Otheto Weston, artist, writer, photographer, and historian, visited Columbia in 1922 and moved there in 1928. She became interested in the "old timers" and recorded their stories. This led to her efforts to preserve the town, including creating the "Days of Gold Fiesta" in 1934. She went on to write *The Mother Lode Album* in 1948, worked at Knott's Berry Farm, and returned to Columbia in 1956.

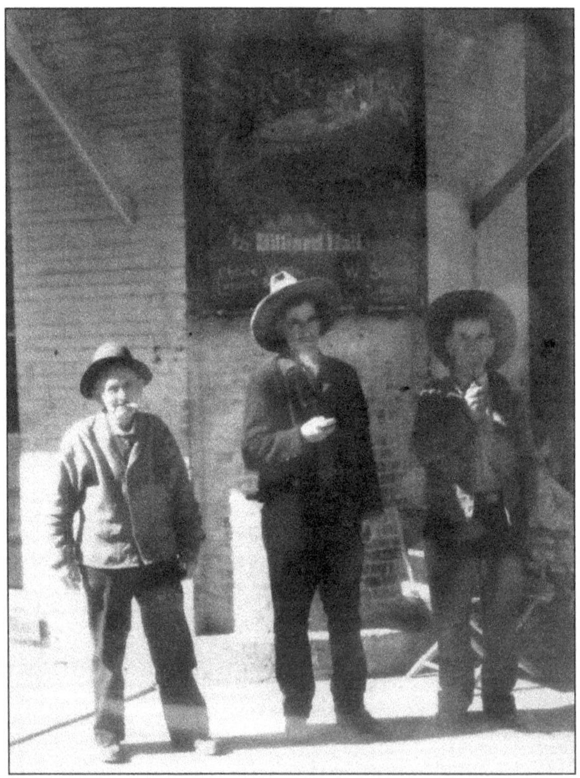

Columbia native Hubert Brady (in the middle) helped Otheto Weston restore the walls of some of the buildings in town, was a source of stories for her work, and helped with her book. Shorty Moore (on the right) was also one of the old-timers who helped Mrs. Weston, regaling her with mining stories, and singing the "Shanghai Rooster." Billy (on the left) is not further identified.

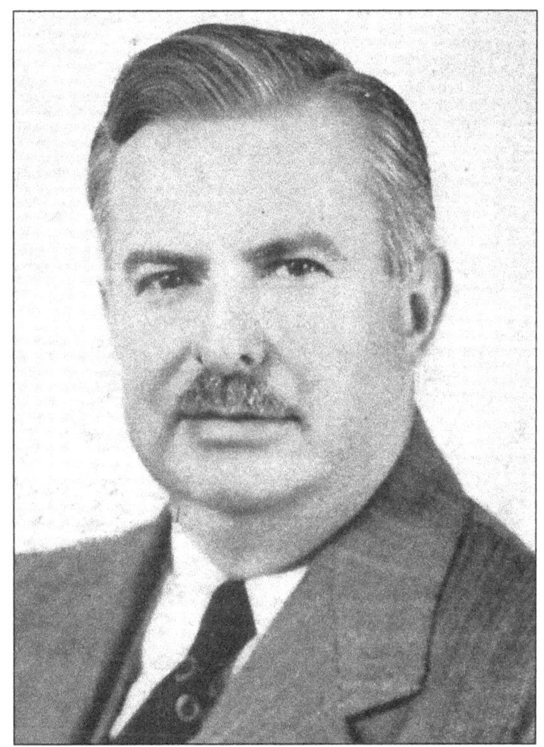

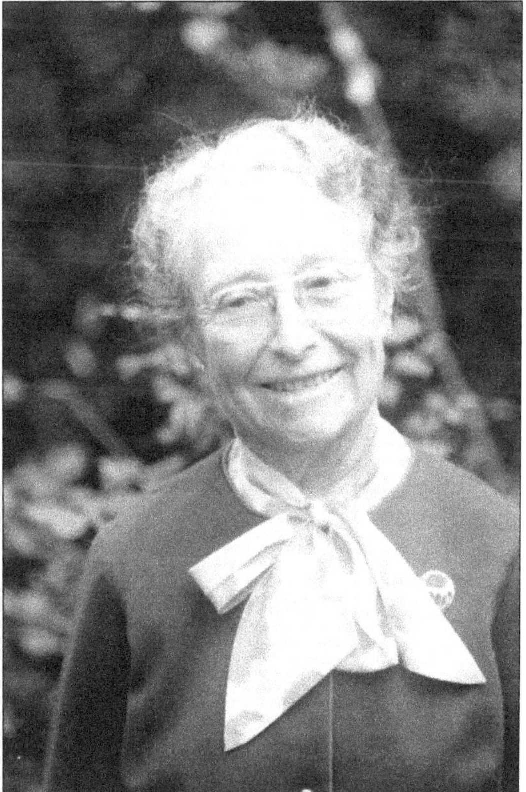

Dr. James McConnell was a dentist who moved to Columbia with his wife, Geraldine, and daughter, Margaret, in 1940, after their purchase of the Wilson House on Main Street. Becoming concerned over the plight of the historic brick structures in 1945, Dr. and Mrs. McConnell worked with the Columbia Progressive Club to interest state and local officials in turning the town into a state park. Legislation was successfully passed in March 1945, but it required raising $50,000 in matching funds to establish the park. After Dr. McConnell's death, Mrs. McConnell remained active in the park, holding a seat on the board of the City Hotel until shortly before her death.

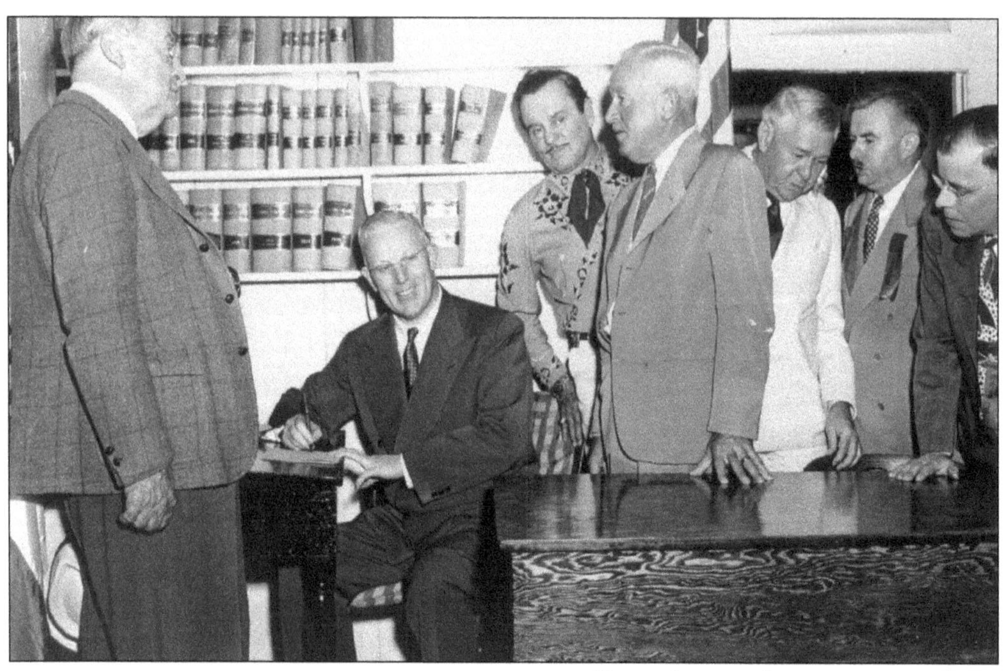

SOUVENIR PROGRAMME

Events Commemorating the Signing of the Legislative Bill by

Governor Earl Warren

. . . Creating . . .

Columbia State Park

Sunday, July 15, 1945

When Columbia was Capital of California for a Day

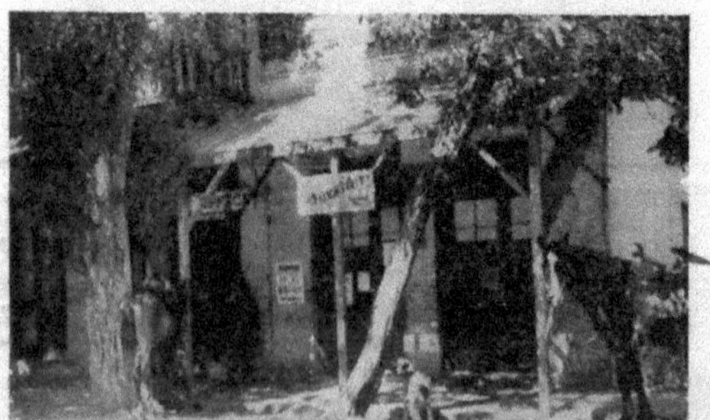

"Elias' Toy Shop". In 1854 Chas. Schneider erected the building as a "Tonsorial Parlor". Capitol of the state of California, July 15, 1945

—Photos in this folder by Pitts Studio

Price, 25c

Shown here in the justice court, from left to right, are Joseph Knowland, chairman of the Park Commission; Gov. Earl Warren; Leo Carillo, actor and member of the Park Commission; Frank Jordan, Secretary of State; William Cavalier, president of the California Historical Society; Dr. James McConnell, chairman of the Columbia State Park Committee; and state senator Jesse Mayo, sponsor of the state park bill. Governor Warren is signing the bill making Columbia a state park. The desk he is using was given to the park by Mrs. McConnell and can be seen in the City Hotel parlor. The justice court became capital for a day.

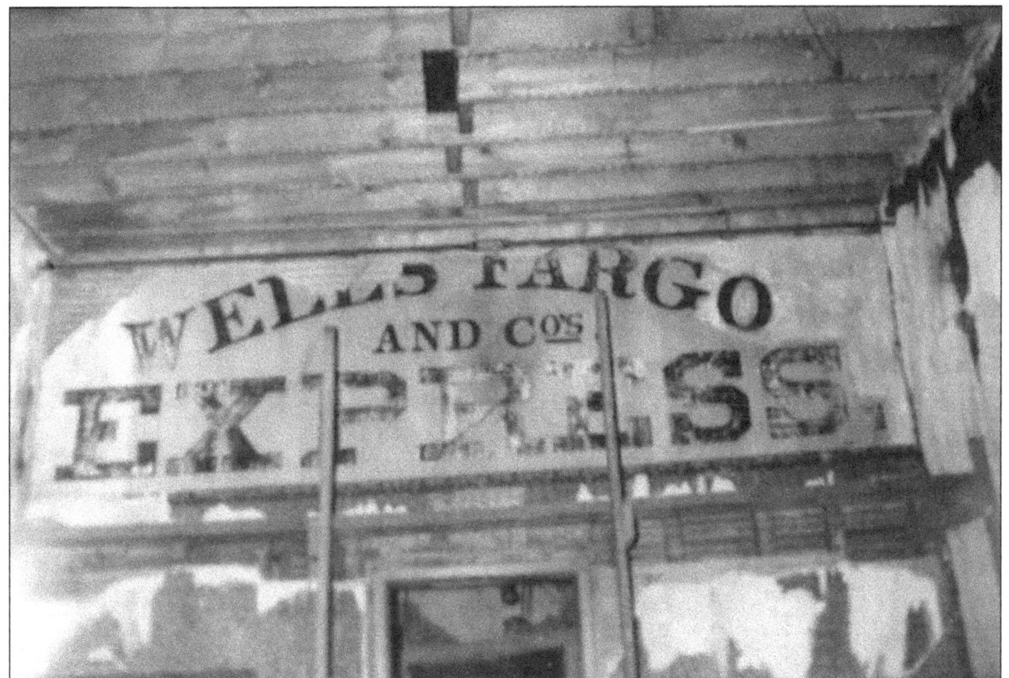

In December 1952, during the restoration of the Wells Fargo building, workers found this sign on plaster. It is believed to have been painted by Joseph Spier.

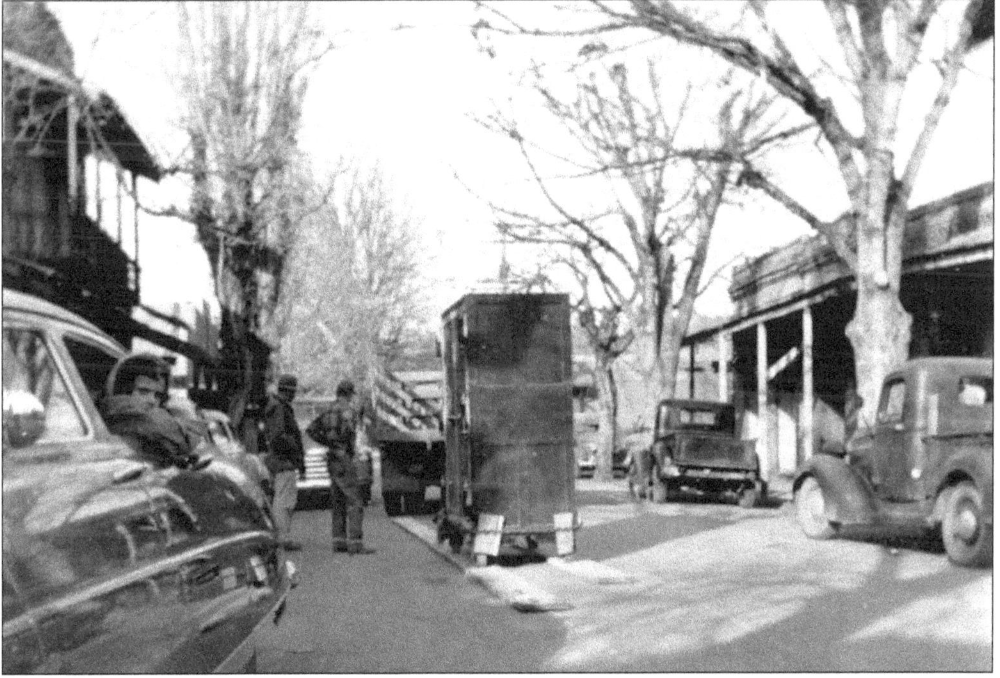
The large and very heavy safe in the Wells Fargo office had to be moved before interior work could be done in 1952. Moving the safe from the Wells Fargo building to the museum required laying track of two-inch timbers and pulling the safe with a two-ton truck. It took four hours to complete the move. The safe can still be seen in the back room of the museum.

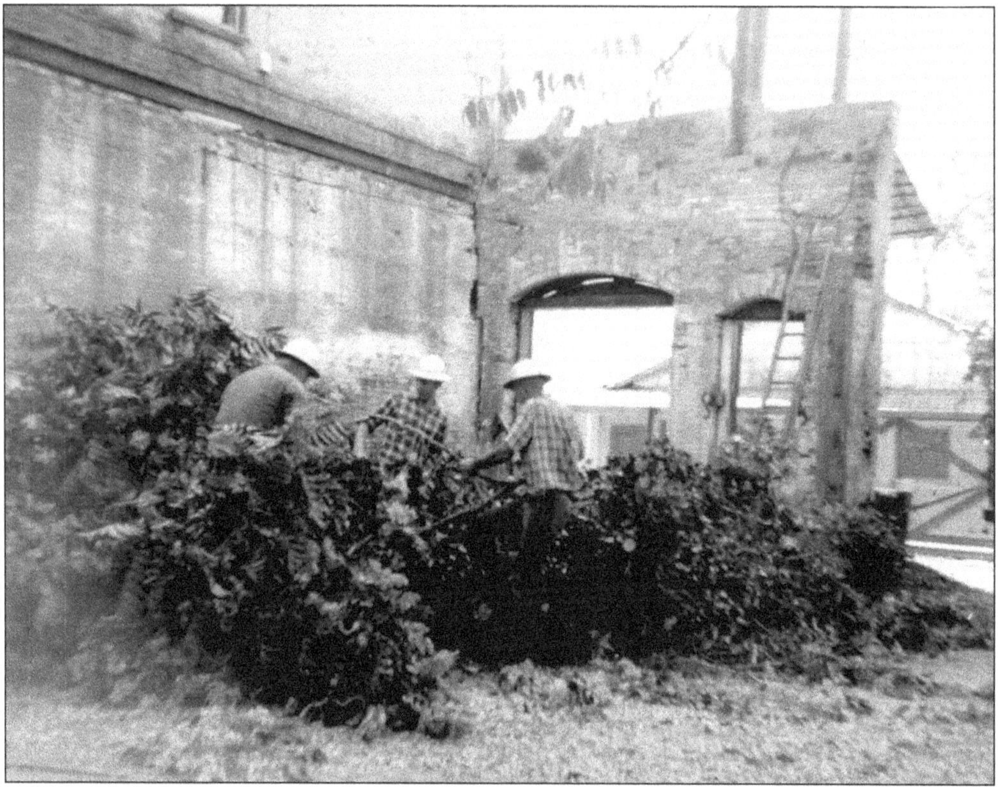

In 1958, the restoration of the firehouse and the Duchow Building on State Street began. This photograph shows the west side of the Duchow Building, and only remaining wall of the firehouse. The workers are removing a china tree (ailanthus) as it was growing against the building's foundation.

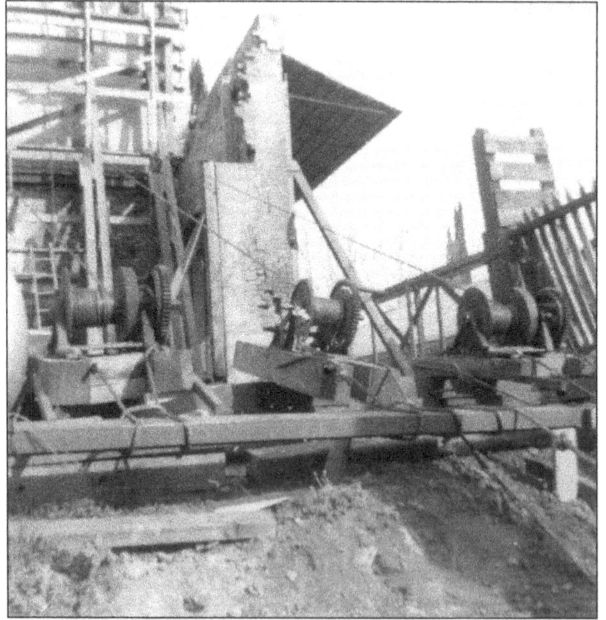

These winches, in action on the west side of the Duchow Building, were hooked to the middle of the building on the east wall with lines pulling through and over it to raise the building three-sixteenths of an inch in order to level and seal cracks. When the building lifted, iron wedges were driven under the wall and gunite was placed underneath.

The Pacific Gas and Electric Company provided the rigging that set this 500-pound bell on the new bell tower.

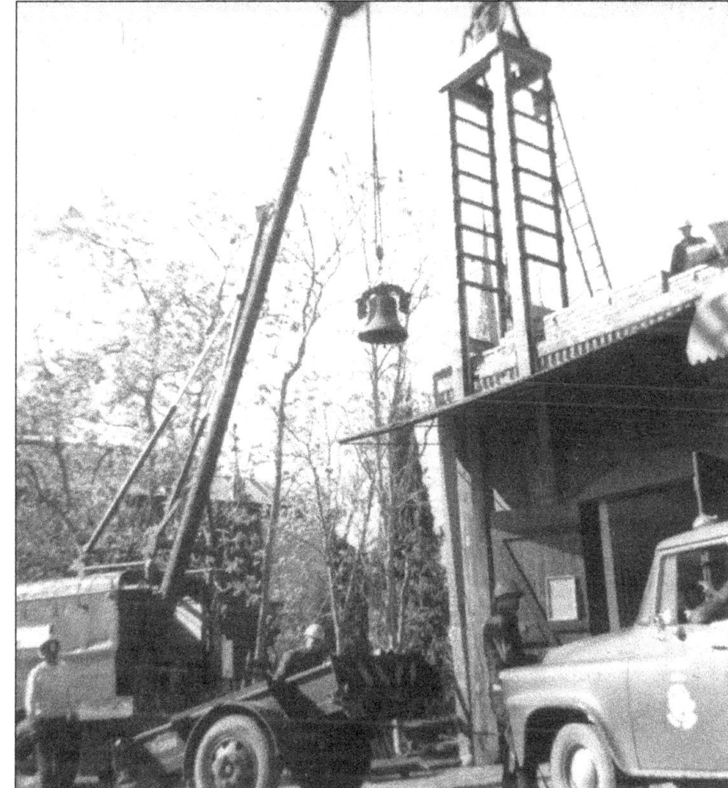

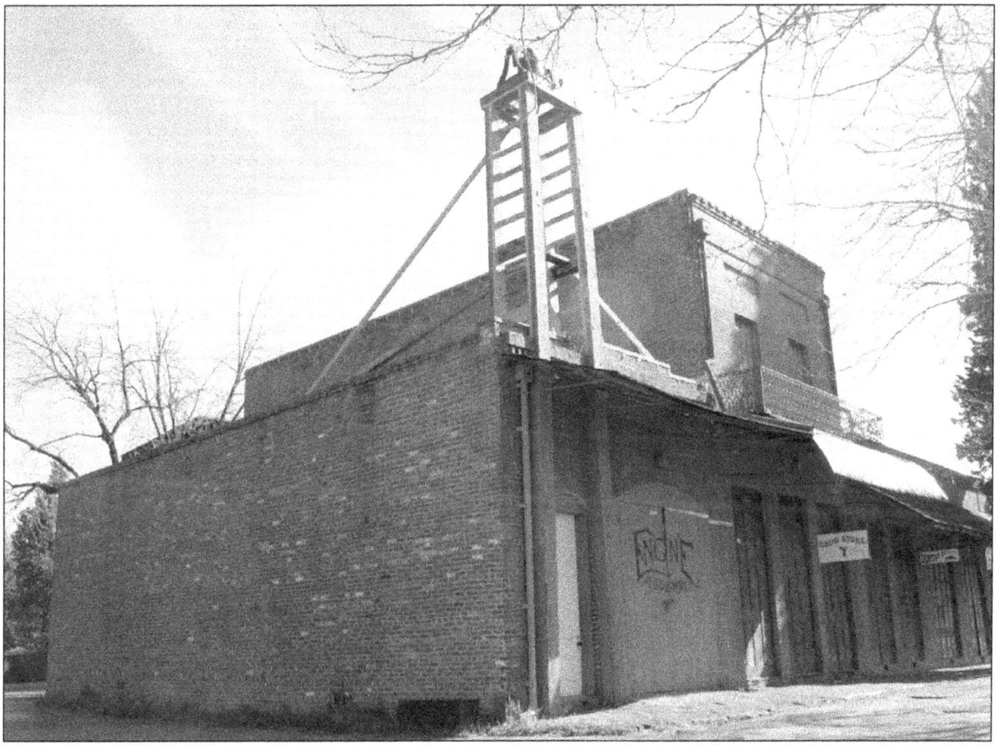

The finished buildings can be seen here along with the bracing on the bell tower. The project was completed in 1960. Local residents restored Papeete at the same time.

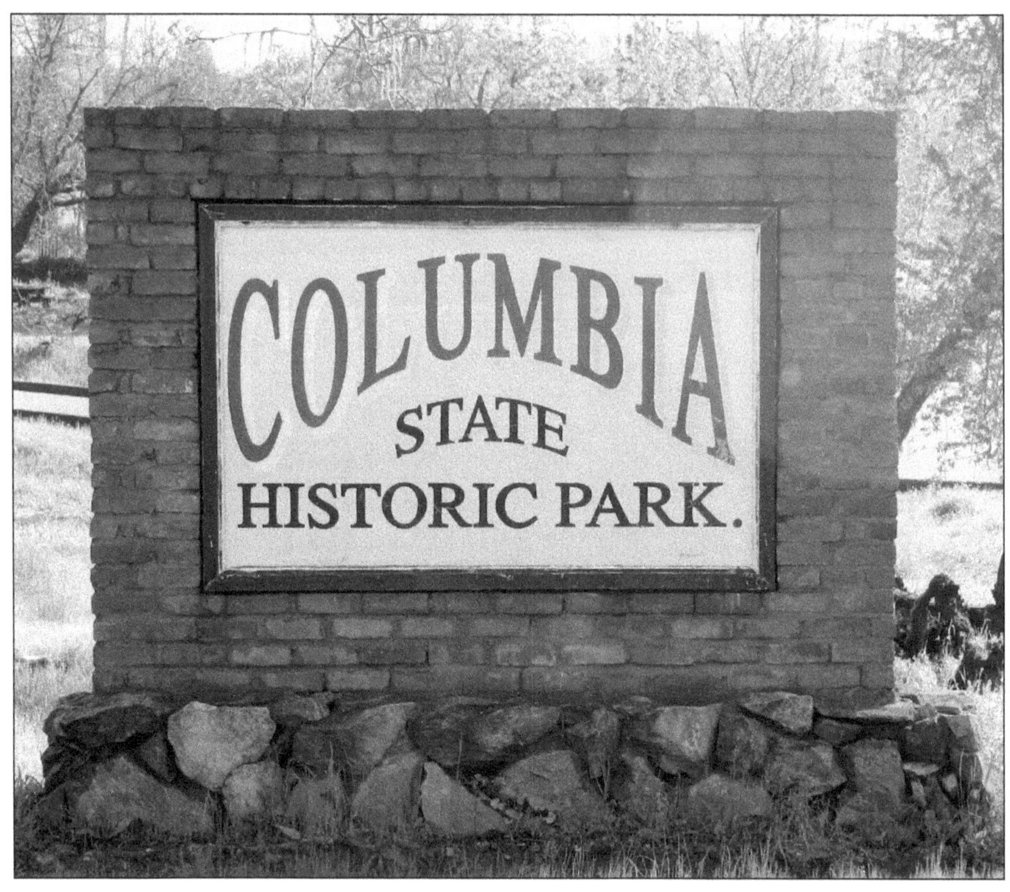

PHOTOGRAPH CREDITS

Except as noted below, all photographs are courtesy of Columbia State Parks, 2005.

page 12, bottom	Library of Congress
page 13, bottom	Library of Congress
page 14, bottom	Library of Congress
page 16, bottom	Library of Congress
page 17, top	Library of Congress
page 17, bottom	Library of Congress
page 20, bottom	Library of Congress
page 23, bottom	Grout Collection
page 47	Tuolumne County Archives
page 56, bottom	Bancroft Library, University of California, Berkeley
page 64	This item is reproduced by permission of the Huntington Library, San Marino, California.
page 80, bottom	Bancroft Library, University of California, Berkeley
page 113, top	Grout Collection
page 120, both	Grout Collection

www.ingramcontent.com/pod-product-compliance
Lightning Source LLC
LaVergne TN
LVHW060624110826
845147LV00015B/934
9780738530215